THE
OLD GUARD
AND THE
AVANT-GARDE

THE
OLD GUARD
AND THE
AVANT-GARDE

MODERNISM IN CHICAGO, 1910-1940

Edited by
SUE ANN PRINCE

ARCHIVES OF AMERICAN ART / SMITHSONIAN INSTITUTION

THE UNIVERSITY OF CHICAGO PRESS • CHICAGO AND LONDON

Sue Ann Prince (formerly Kendall), an art historian and writer who lives in the Washington, D.C. area, was formerly Midwest Regional Director for the Archives of American Art.

This book is an edited collection of the proceedings of a 1988 symposium titled "The Coming of Modernism to Chicago, 1910–1940," organized by the Archives of American Art, Smithsonian Institution, and co-sponsored by the Art Institute of Chicago.

The University of Chicago Press, Chicago 60637
The University of Chicago Press, Ltd., London
© 1990 by the Archives of American Art, Smithsonian Institution
All rights reserved. Published 1990
Printed in the United States of America

99 98 97 96 95 94 93 92 91 90   5 4 3 2 1

Library of Congress Cataloging in Publication Data

The old guard and the avant-garde : modernism in Chicago, 1910–1940 / edited by Sue Ann Prince.
    p.   cm.
   Includes bibliographical references.
   ISBN 0-226-68284-6 (alk. paper)
    1. Modernism (Art)—Illinois—Chicago. 2. Art, American—Illinois—Chicago. 3. Art, Modern—20th century—Illinois—Chicago. I. Prince, Sue Ann.
N6535 .C5043 1990
709'.773'1109041—dc20
                        90-35236
                         CIP

This book is printed on acid-free paper.

For Stephanie and Nathan

CONTENTS

ILLUSTRATIONS

Plates
(following page 40)

1. Charles Graham, *Dream City*, Manufactures and Liberal Arts Building at the 1893 World's Columbian Exposition, watercolor on paper, 1893
2. Jules Guérin, *Plan of Chicago*, watercolor and pencil on paper, 1908
3. Emil Armin, *The Open Bridge*, oil painting, 1930
4. Arthur Dove, *Nature Symbolized No. 2* (or, *Wind on a Hillside*), pastel on paper mounted on plywood, 1911–12
5. Manierre Dawson, *Lucrèce*, oil on canvas, 1911
6. Jerome Blum, *Fauvist Landscape*, oil on canvas, ca. 1910
7. Raymond Jonson, *The Trojan Women*, design for stage set, 1915
8. Raymond Jonson, *Miriam Kiper*, oil on canvas, 1919
9. Raymond Jonson, *Life*, oil on canvas, 1921
10. Stanislaus Szukalski, *Flower of Dreams*, 1917 (now destroyed), photograph, 1923
11. Rudolph Weisenborn, *Convex Space*, oil on canvas, 1930
12. Rudolph Weisenborn, *The Blue Tree*, oil on canvas, 1926
13. Ramon Shiva, *Chicago MCMXXIV* (or, *Untitled Chicago Industrial Scene*), oil on canvas, 1924
14. Anthony Angarola, *Michigan Avenue Bridge— Chicago River*, oil on canvas, n.d.

Figures

Since its founding in 1954, the Archives of American Art has been actively engaged in the pursuit of primary sources essential to the study of the visual arts in the United States. Its purpose from the beginning was to simplify the problems of the working scholar by gathering documentary materials together in one location and making them easily accessible for study. Ultimately, the goal was, and is, to encourage research in American art history.

Today the Archives holds collections numbering some ten million items. A substantial portion of the collections is microfilmed and available in research centers in Boston, New York, Washington, D.C., Detroit, San Francisco, and San Marino, California, as well as through interlibrary loan. The original documents are preserved at the Archives Processing Center in Washington.

Acquiring materials for the Archives is a fascinating business, often demanding first-rate sleuthing that can lead collectors on trails crisscrossing the continent, and even an ocean. To initiate a collecting effort, the Archives typically establishes a base in an area believed to be potentially rich in art-related source materials and begins to dig around.

The Chicago Documentation Project is just one such effort. Begun five years ago, the Project surveyed art-related archival materials in Chicago institutions and private collections, worked toward building a broader awareness of the importance of such material, and organized the collecting and microfilming processes.

In carrying out the work, the Archives was fortunate to have the dedication of Sue Ann Prince (formerly Kendall) who served as the Archives Midwest Regional Director, and who is currently on the staff of the Smithsonian's National Portrait Gallery. Betty

Blum serves as the exceptionally able Project Coordinator. The Project is located in the Ryerson and Burnham Libraries of the Art Institute of Chicago. We are exceedingly grateful to the Art Institute both for providing us a home, and for giving encouragement and support in generous measure.

Finally, the Chicago Documentation Project has generated several other programs including a guide to the art-related archival resources in Chicago institutions and collections, an African-American oral history project, and a symposium, "The Coming of Modernism to Chicago, 1910–1940," out of which this book evolved. Ms. Prince organized the symposium, gave her own paper, and is the editor of this book.

As in all complex and extended undertakings, many individuals, institutions, organizations, corporations, and foundations have been involved, and we thank them for their interest and invaluable assistance without which the work could not have been undertaken. We are proud of the accomplishments to date but know there is much that remains to be done. Our fondest hope is that more collecting, more research, and more publication will follow.

Susan Hamilton
Acting Director
Archives of American Art

ACKNOWLEDGMENTS

The idea for this book was conceived one hot August afternoon in 1984. I had just spent three days in Rockford, Illinois, sorting through crumbling letters, yellowed newspaper clippings, and other old documents that filled seemingly endless drawers and cupboards. I was in the home of the descendants of C. J. Bulliet, an early Chicago art critic whose papers contained invaluable information on Chicago's early-twentieth-century art scene.

As the new Midwest Regional Director for the Archives of American Art of the Smithsonian Institution, I had tried in vain to find recent, published information on early-twentieth-century art in Chicago. Except for a 1932 book, a few exhibition catalogs, and old newspaper articles, there was very little. It became clear that no comprehensive history of that art had ever been written. Furthermore, little material on the subject could be found in the Archives' holdings, a considerable gap in a collection that contains numerous and significant documents on the early art scene of nearly every other major American city.

My search began. In the fall of 1985 the Archives established the Chicago Documentation Project in an office in the Ryerson and Burnham Libraries of the Art Institute. Its primary purpose was to seek documents relating to Chicago art prior to World War II. For more than two years we unearthed materials that the Archives acquired and/or microfilmed—old letters, diaries, scrapbooks, sketchbooks, manuscripts, photographs, and other memorabilia. In reviewing those materials I realized that the history of Chicago art in the early twentieth century was inextricably tied to outside influences, primarily European modernism. Only by exploring the introduction of modernism into the local scene and by considering the complex interactions and struggles it created could an understanding of Chicago art be reached.

Thus emerged the subject of this volume, which was first addressed in a symposium sponsored by the Archives and the Art Institute of Chicago in March 1988. This book, an edited collection of the proceedings of the symposium, is the first major publication to explore the coming of modernism to Chicago.

Many colleagues have inspired me over the years and encouraged me during this project. Among those who deserve special mention are Martha Kingsbury, whose seminars first prompted me to take a broad, intellectual approach to art history; Richard Murray, who initially liked my symposium idea and allowed me to nurture and develop it; Neil Harris, who believed in the project's worth; Susan Hamilton, who supported me in realizing it as a book; Alan Fern, who allowed me essential time to work on it; and Garnett McCoy, whose insights always provoked further investigation.

In Chicago I am especially grateful to those colleagues who supported my efforts to establish an Archives of American Art office in their city and who encouraged me in developing the symposium, especially Katharine Lee, Franz Schulze, Richard Gray, David Sokol, John Szukalski, Don Baum, Archie Motley, and Judith Kirshner. Other Chicagoans who deserve special mention include the members of the advisory committee for the Chicago Documentation Project; chaired by Neil Harris; Jack Brown, who willingly provided office space in the Ryerson and Burnham Libraries for the Project, and Project Coordinator Betty Blum, whose skillful search for archival papers unearthed important resource materials that were used for some of the chapters in this volume.

The contributors also deserve special mention, first for sharing their research at the symposium and later for revising their papers into publishable form. Others offered essential support and cooperation in the realization of the book, especially Beth Sarantos, Maria Parisi, and Toni Reineke.

I am grateful for the support of three institutions: the Archives of American Art, the Smithsonian Institution of which it is a part, and the Art Institute of Chicago, co-sponsor of the symposium that is being preserved in the form of this book.

On a personal note, I would like to thank my children, Stephanie and Nathan, who were willing to share me with my book project, and my friend Paul, whose critical encouragement, well-chosen comments, and moral support were invaluable.

CONTRIBUTORS

Avis Berman is a freelance writer and critic and also directs the oral history program of the Archives of American Art in New York.

Richard R. Brettell, formerly Searle curator of European painting at the Art Institute of Chicago, is director of the Dallas Museum of Art.

Lloyd C. Engelbrecht is associate professor of art history at the University of Cincinnati.

Stefan Germer is assistant professor of nineteenth- and twentieth-century art at the Kunsthistorische Institut der Universität Bonn in West Germany.

Neil Harris is professor and former chairman of the history department at the University of Chicago.

Paul Kruty is assistant professor in the School of Architecture at the University of Illinois in Urbana-Champaign.

Ann Lee Morgan, who formerly taught at the University of Illinois, the School of the Art Institute of Chicago, and Columbia College, is editor of the journal *20/1 Art and Culture*.

Charlotte Moser, formerly lecturer at Northwestern University and visiting associate professor at the School of the Art Institute of Chicago, is editor of *Artweek*.

Susan Noyes Platt is associate professor of art history at the University of North Texas.

Sue Ann Prince (formerly Kendall), previously Midwest Regional Director of the Archives of American Art, Smithsonian Institution, is an art historian and writer.

Susan S. Weininger is assistant professor and director of the art division in the Department of Visual and Performing Arts at Roosevelt University.

Allen Weller is professor emeritus of art history at the University of Illinois, and director emeritus of the Krannert Art Museum.

INTRODUCTION

That visual images create unrest when they threaten an established value system is a testament to their power. The assault of modernism on Chicago was no exception: It generated a bitter struggle between an old guard and an avant-garde that endured for at least three decades.

The assimilation of modernism into the mainstream of Chicago art was similar in many ways to its integration in other American cities, and indeed it reiterates a pattern of acculturation common to any such new ideology as it inserts itself into a well-established value system. In Chicago, where individualism and entrepreneurship were highly cultivated in the business world, it is ironic that the same qualities were unappreciated in the artistic realm. But a hard-nosed business ethic fit into the prevailing worldview of the city's leaders; an individualistic art that reflected the dynamism and chaos of the contemporary world did not. It was believed that art should be an antidote to the workaday world, an expression of ideal "beauty and truth" that could be used both to enlighten the business entrepreneur and to elevate the masses of urban workers whom he employed.

What made the assimilation of modernism especially difficult in Chicago was the confounding of morality and aesthetics. Modernism not only threatened the underlying principles of nineteenth-century academic art, which were tied to aesthetic principles of ideal beauty and truth, but also it attacked notions of decency and propriety, especially with regard to the human body. These notions were based on a strict, puritanical morality widely held by Chicago's ruling cultural elite, its public, and many in its art community as well.

The term "modernism," in its international sense, usually implied something different from the more inclusive, more generic term "modern art," which was used for everything from impressionism to contemporary art (including modernism). Modernism typically referred only to progressive European art beginning with post impressionism and continuing through contemporary avant-garde manifestations, especially those works whose colors or forms deliberately challenged artistic convention and drastically distorted the visible world. Unique to Chicago, however, was an unusually francophile view of international modernism that until the mid-1930s was largely ignorant of constructivism, dadaism, and surrealism, and paid only scant attention to the various schools of German expressionism. As for local manifestations of modernism, no one particular style took root until after World War II. Unlike international modernism, which was divided into distinct stylistic groups, early Chicago modernism was defined by an attitude rather than by a style. This attitude remained strongly individualistic and idiosyncratic, such that personal visions predominated over any single stylistic influence.

Local modernism struggled with a loss of talent to New York, a situation not unlike that experienced by other cities. Yet even when an art and design school of international renown was transplanted to Chicago in 1938 as the New Bauhaus, no single style in the fine arts emerged. The school's impact on local art styles was indirect and gradual, exerting virtually no influence prior to World War II, and very little on Chicago's fine arts scene even later.

While the production of modernist art in Chicago remained doggedly individualistic, the battle it caused was waged largely by groups that transformed individual propensities into collective impulses. Indeed, Chicago was remarkable in the number of societies, clubs, and organizations that were formed to grapple with the onslaught of modernism. From design guilds to artists' clubs, avant-garde exhibition clubs to conservative amateur painting societies, no-jury exhibitions to groups promoting "aesthetic sanity," nearly every cause, both conservative and modern, was represented by at least one organization.

Chicago, like New York, was stunned by the Armory Show in 1913. But unlike its eastern rival, Chicago did not experience a burgeoning of modernist activity until the 1920s, when renewed interest gained strength from the ending of a war that had interrupted the flow of ideas from Europe to America and from the cultural and economic expansiveness of the period in general. In the thirties, there was retrenchment and suspicion about modernism caused by the Great Depression and the dual call for regionalism and social realism. In Europe, the aesthetics of modernism often conflicted with the politics of fascism. In New York, Chicago, and elsewhere in the United States, abstract modernism was frequently challenged by the tenets of social humanism, the politics of the Artists' Union, and the aims of the WPA Federal Art Project. But in Chicago, modernism still had to struggle with an entrenched self-righteous morality, propounded ever more diligently as the new art gained a stronger foothold in the city's major art institutions and among its art cognoscenti.

Antipathy to modernism in Chicago gathered strength in the thirties. A group called Sanity in Art, an unusually late manifestation of anti-modernist sentiment, distinguished itself from other 1930s political and artistic manifestations because it did not enter into the antagonism between abstraction on the one hand and the tenets of social realism and regionalism on the other, but rather railed against both. Indeed, Sanity in Art deprecated anything that was not tied to nineteenth-century ideals and Victorian morality.

Chicago's resistance to modernism has received considerable attention, as has that of other American cities. Yet many activities and events that celebrated modernism have often been overlooked. Chicago gave birth to more than one avant-garde literary magazine that championed the new art, it supported a critic whose advocacy of modernism never wavered even during the 1930s, and it spawned numerous artist protest groups and several progressive art collectors. Most remarkable were two grand exhibitions of international significance that were hosted, ironically, by the Art Institute, an institution generally regarded as a formidable bastion of conservativism (the term commonly used in opposition to modernism). On a local level the first exhibition, the Armory Show of 1913, contradicted the staid notions of the World Columbian Exposition of 1893, whose beaux-arts buildings and dream-city images influenced Chicagoans throughout the time period covered in this book. The Armory Show increased the awareness but only rarely the understanding of modernism. It was followed twenty years later in 1933, by the Century of Progress Exposition, which celebrated progress and modernity. Its blockbuster art exhibition, arranged in an innovative way that integrated modernism with the art of the past, was significant in the realm of world museums but seems to have had relatively little impact on local acceptance of modernism in art.

Each of these exhibitions, twenty years apart, made a strong statement about art to which key players and institutions in the battle for and against modernism responded. The following essays reveal how artists, literary figures, curators, critics, designers, dealers, patrons, arts administrators, and art institutions took sides on the issues only to find themselves doing battle with colleagues of the opposing viewpoint. They reveal the ambivalence, the controversy, and the occasional outright confrontation created by the collision of two different world views—one based on the hierarchical ideals of the nineteenth century, upheld by the early Chicago philanthropists, and the other on the new ideals of the iconoclastic and individualistic modernists of the twentieth century.

This volume documents the activities of many of Chicago's

art-related institutions in the early decades of the twentieth century. It also looks at the major movers and shakers of the art scene and offers insights into the work of a few local artists. It is only a beginning, however, reflecting the particular interests of the various authors rather than presenting a single, unified viewpoint.

More specifically, the works of the few local artists who are explored in depth must stand for the moment as examples of the remarkable variety of art that was produced in the city before World War II. (Chicago's early art is a subject that itself merits a book.) The impact of Chicago's jazz and blues of the 1920s on the art scene is not discussed. And architecture, whose significant history in Chicago has been widely published already, was purposely avoided in order to give attention to other, lesser known aspects of the art scene. While topics as diverse as the early avant-garde literary scene, art training at the Art Institute, and the establishment of the New Bauhaus are addressed, many other participants in the struggle for and against modernism await future unearthing and assessment, among them the Renaissance Society, the Palette and Chisel Club, the Union League Club, the Cliff Dwellers, Alice Roullier, Samuel Putnam, and numerous other individuals and institutions.

Only when more is known about the assimilation of modernism into the art scene of cities such as Chicago will we have a real understanding of the coming of modernism to America. This book begins to document Chicago's important role in the countrywide struggle to absorb and produce the new art. I hope it will serve as a benchmark for future scholarship on this role, which represents an intriguing but neglected chapter of American art history.

Sue Ann Prince

THE
OLD GUARD
AND THE
AVANT-GARDE

CHAPTER ONE

The Chicago Setting

NEIL HARRIS

For a city that is probably one of the best analyzed, most carefully described, and incessantly invoked in the western world, Chicago's art history remains a closely guarded secret. Its geography, architecture, politics, and social pathology, like its industrial and merchandising innovations and literary currents, have provoked a scholarship that is the envy of larger rivals such as New York. But little in this hubbub of celebration has been devoted to local painters, illustrators, photographers, sculptors, and graphic designers, who numbered in the thousands during the first four decades of this century. We know of Chicago schools in philosophy, criticism, poetry, architecture, sociology, journalism, and higher education; but at least before 1940, there are none to speak of in art.

Such a discrepancy seems anomalous. It also disguises the scholarly research that has gone on for decades—including work by Esther Sparks, Eugenia Whitridge, Kenneth Hey, Ethel Hammer, and many others.[1] But even when one examines the many exercises in self-celebration and local piety that Chicago has produced over the years, most discussions of visual art seem forced and artificial, commentaries with a hothouse flavor produced under pressure and without particular enthusiasm that serve only to mark civic anniversaries and expositions.

Such diffidence may soon disappear. This volume and ongoing research together may ensure that Rudolph Weisenborn and William Schwartz, Ramon Shiva and Raymond Jonson, Rifka Angel and Emil Armin, to say nothing of No-Jury, Jerome Blum, Neo-Arlimusc, and Macena Barton will return to collective memory. The prevailing scarcity in our shared knowledge of art deserves exploration. It is linked, I believe, to the larger problem of Chicago's cultural claims, which forms my present subject.

In the first third of this century Chicago was a community caught between conflicting roles and mixed identities. Inheritance and personality clashed uneasily with pretensions and expectations. Other second cities of the western world—Lyons, Hamburg, Manchester, Milan—had confronted the task of rising above their industrial and financial circumstances. They also sought to offer some cultural competition to their national capitals and to make peace with their metropolitan rivals.

But Chicago's status, as we shall see, was more painful, for almost until the end of this era, it refused to accept a subordinate position. The dreams of glory that dated from the period of rebirth in the 1880s and 1890s died hard. A lot of promises had been made, promises that could be kept only by achieving primacy. When the city finally accepted its permanent subordination (which I think it did by the end of our period) its cultural status was as powerful a symbol as any of its demographic defeat.

As we begin this long review of galleries, artists, critics, art clubs, commissions, exhibitions, patrons, and entrepreneurs, it might be useful to recollect the conventional wisdom that defined the city's cultural standing. Because the story of Chicago as an art center has been so cut off from other parts of its history, we need to begin on broad ground with some general observations that test our insights and arguments. I would like to present portions of this conventional wisdom, those assumptions about Chicago that helped to shape both secondary accounts and contemporary commentaries. Their presence is so fundamental that they continue to color our current approaches. As we move ahead we need to distinguish among them in order to determine which should survive and which be discarded, modified, or refined. My list is not complete but it represents, I hope, a start in this process of recovery.

The first presumption, which has much to do with our current state of ignorance, is that visual artists do not seem to have played a major role in interpreting Chicago for the rest of the world. When we examine Chicago—whether it is the city of the 1890s, or of the teens and twenties, or even the Depression—we find a rather startling contrast between its writers and its artists. The figures associated with Chicago literature at various moments—Theodore Dreiser, George Ade, Frank Norris, Edgar Lee Masters, Ben Hecht, Carl Sandburg, Henry Fuller, Floyd Dell, Finley Peter Dunne—not only spent time in the city, but also achieved much of their fame in writing about it. The classics of American literature that involve this city—*Sister Carrie, The Cliff-Dwellers, The Pit, With the Procession, Front Page, The Jungle, Twenty Years at Hull House, Native Son*—helped fix Chicago's image and identity for a vast public. The noise of the Loop, the splendor of the great department stores, the squalor of the stockyards, the strife and din of the wheat exchange, the corruption of politics, the misery of the slums, and the refinements of

Michigan and Prairie avenues were transmitted by poets, novelists, playwrights, journalists, and autobiographers. When they lived in Chicago they wrote about Chicago. And even when they lived elsewhere, they continued to write about it, sometimes with even greater passion.[2]

Alongside this rich tradition of urban evocation Chicago artists apparently contributed little. Our most powerful visual images of the city come not from its actual scenes but from a series of dream landscapes and imaginary constructions. Little of the urban setting penetrated the resident artist's vision. This was certainly not true in every American urban place, as texts like Peter Conrad's *Art of the City* make abundantly clear.[3]

In the 1890s, New York, for example, had already experienced several generations of artistic concern that was expressed on canvas, in photographs, and in woodcuts by both the famous and the obscure—by Winslow Homer and Joseph Byron, Jacob Riis and Edward L. Henry. New York was, moreover, on the eve of an explosion of image making by The Eight, by painters of the Ashcan School like Sloan, Henri, Glackens, Luks, and Bellows, by photographers like Stieglitz and Steichen, and by impressionists and abstractionists. A host of American artists had begun to immortalize Central Park, the Palisades, and the Brooklyn Bridge; in later years Greenwich Village, Morningside Heights, Times Square, and Coney Island obtained their artistic objectification as well. In other east-coast cities artists like Maurice Prendergast, Childe Hassam, and Thomas Eakins were rendering on canvas Copley Square, Commonwealth Avenue, Broad Street, and the Schuylkill River.

Turn-of-the-century Chicago artists, however, shied away from direct confrontation. There were lithographic vistas, paintings of fiery ordeals, and occasional street engravings—an invaluable record for urban topographers—but as a whole the actual cityscape was of limited interest. It was certainly far less evocatively presented than the boulevards and promenades of the plaster city of the Columbian Exposition, where painters, photographers, and etchers had a field day (plate 1 and fig. 1.1). The fair assumed the approved outlines of a European metropolis far more powerfully than any Chicago streets. By accepted artistic principles of the sublime and the picturesque, the White City was far more real than the grey city. It was understandable, therefore, not only that it absorbed local attention but that the most articulate art commentators on the fair were easterners like Childe Hassam, Edward Blashfield, Frank Millet, Thure de Thulstrup, or artists like Theodore Robinson who had learned elsewhere how to depict traditional urban scenes.[4]

The poor representation of Chicago artists at the Columbian Exposition itself reflected a confession of considerable weakness and a plea for critical patience, themes that would be sounded quite often by apologists for local culture. Chicago's fair was, of course, a giant promissory note, constituting a statement of

1.1 Edwin H. Blashfield, Portal of the Manufactures and Liberal Arts Building at the 1893 World's Columbian Exposition, oil on canvas, 1893. The Chicago Historical Society.

principles to guide the metropolis on its way to future glory. Serving to disguise as much as possible the economic realities which had brought growth to the city, fair planners privileged the arts and honored the artists. Since the fair's dual mission was to bring culture to Chicago and to show that Chicago was cultured, it became vital to build upon professional consensus.

Thus the exhibition in the Art Palace was conceived of as a standard-setting exercise. The seventy-four different galleries, some of them approaching five thousand square feet in size, contained more than ten thousand objects. The catalog of works listed ran to more than five hundred pages. The vast scale of the operation indicated the desperate conscientiousness of the managers to make Chicago art appear as cosmopolitan as possible. One thousand oil paintings by Americans were culled from an even larger number of entries. One-third of the artists came from New York, which was four times the number of Chicagoans represented. Thus was Chicago eager to acknowledge her artistic deficiency in the interest of this once-in-a-lifetime display.[5]

If Chicago's fair more powerfully provoked local painters and photographers than did its permanent landscape, so did some other alternative or imaginary cities. In 1900, for example, W. W. Denslow created for fellow Chicagoan L. Frank Baum his remarkable illustrations of the Emerald City for *The Wizard of Oz*. Denslow and Baum would soon move elsewhere, but these settings would enthrall generations of readers; other artists would soon rework them in books and, on an even grander scale, on the stage and screen.[6]

Shortly after came yet another landscape triumph—again imaginary but also anticipatory—for Chicagoans to examine: the extraordinary wash drawings by Jules Guérin and Ferdinand Janin for Daniel Burnham's *Plan of Chicago* (1909; plate 2). As several scholars have pointed out, the popularity of the *Plan*, both in this city and elsewhere, its success in achieving, over the next few decades, so many of its goals, rested in large part on the eloquence and grandeur of its illustrations—the dream of a park-lined lakefront, a great harbor basin, lagoons, Parisian boulevards, bedecked river fronts, all climaxed by the cathedral-like dome of a vast civic center.[7] Another excursion into the realm of the imagination had substituted itself for Chicago's reality. Local artists, unlike local writers, were apparently intent upon brighter, cleaner, and more glorious vistas than the city offered.

There were, of course, a number of painters and etchers who depicted the Lake Michigan skyline in the teens and twenties, who studied the clamor of the Loop or caught romantic nooks and crannies in different parts of the city (plate 3 and figs. 1.2 and 1.3). There were even a few who graduated to the new levels of abstraction or the simplified realism that represented the advance of modernism, like Werner Drewes, Aaron Bohrod, and Mitchell Saporin (the last two of whom depicted the city in its days of despair) (figs. 1.4 and 1.5). A number of progressive artists did feature local scenes in their rebel exhibitions. But they were not the dominant voices. If the Ashcan painters had no Chicago equivalents early in the century, Joseph Stella, John Marin, Ben Shahn, Edward Hopper, Hugh Ferriss, Charles Sheeler, and Max Weber, in their capture of New York, stood equally alone later on.

The second generalization that repeatedly attaches itself to Chicago art, beyond the indifference to the city as a place, involves the theme of exile. This motif also encompasses Chicago literature and letters. For one reason or another, Chicago found

1.2 William S. Schwartz, *A Railroad in Chicago*, lithograph, 1928. Courtesy, Hirschl & Adler Galleries, Inc., New York.

itself abandoned by its most gifted and creative children generation after generation. Given the nature of local history and geography, there is a paradox here. After the middle of the nineteenth century Chicago was a mecca for the talents of a whole continent. From New England and upstate New York, from Canada, Pennsylvania, and the border south, from the old northwest of Ohio and Indiana and the newer west of the Great Plains, enterprising young entrepreneurs arrived. Chicago's prosperity was the work of newcomers who created the great meatpacking, lumber, steel, warehouse, mail order, furniture, clothing, and printing industries among others that supported urban growth. For much of the century, the brain drain tilted in Chicago's favor.

The immigrants included poets, painters, and novelists, as well as business types. By the turn of the century Chicago's

1.3 W. S. Bagdatopoulos, *Michigan Avenue, Chicago,* painting (medium unknown), ca. 1929. Photograph from the C. J. Bulliet Papers, Archives of American Art, Smithsonian Institution.

theater, music, publishing houses, and museums were exciting the ambitions of young people across the Middle West. The city's lures were described by novelists like Willa Cather and Sherwood Anderson, among many other writers who peopled their texts with singers, composers, architects, actors, and painters who dreamed of making the trip to the metropolis of the Middle West.

But by the early twentieth century it was apparent that Chicago had become a way station rather than a terminus for many of its great talents. Having made one trip from small town to big city, they soon would make another, from big city to bigger city, and take the train east to the greater celebrity of New York or to the greater comfort of New England. It is not precisely clear just when this phenomenon began to receive extensive attention, but as early as 1897 one angry letter writer to the *Inland Printer* complained that Chicago artists seemed to be leaving the city as soon as they had attracted national attention. This writer was, to be sure, talking about commercial artists and offered a mone-

1.4 Aaron Bohrod, *Under the El, North Side of Chicago,* gouache on paper, 1933. Collection of the artist. Courtesy, Harmon-Meek Gallery, Naples, Florida.

tary explanation: Western businessmen would simply not pay the prices offered by their eastern counterparts.[8]

This explanation may or may not have been true. But by the 1890s, significant figures in Chicago's flowering had begun to depart—Will Bradley, the great illustrator, type designer, and poster maker; J. C. Leyendecker, who would go on to make the Arrow Shirt Man immortal; his brother, another influential commercial artist, F. X. Leyendecker; W. W. Denslow, who moved on to Roycroft, and Elbert Hubbard; Blanche McManus, who returned to Paris; Fred Goudy, the great Park Ridge printer and typographer, who left just a few years later for Hingham, Massachusetts; W. A. Dwiggins, an illustrator and book designer, who moved with Goudy; Will Carqueville, another great poster maker; and painters like Douglas Volk, Walter Shirlaw, Carroll Beckwith, Albert Sterner. But these were nothing to the literary and journalistic types who would soon be leaving the city behind them—Dreiser, Norris, Garland, Floyd Dell, Upton

1.5 William Jacobs, *West Side Chicago*, woodcut, 1938. Photograph from the C. J. Bulliet Papers, Archives of American Art, Smithsonian Institution.

Sinclair, Ring Lardner, Edgar Lee Masters, Sherwood Anderson, Ernest Poole, Chicago born, certified, or apprenticed, who simply did not stay. Some departed even before they were fully trained, as Harriet Monroe noted in a 1905 address to the sixty-six graduates of the School of the Art Institute, mourning the gaps left by those who had already moved to Philadelphia, New

York, and Paris.[9] Even after graduation, the ambitious made their way east decade after decade. In 1921, the painter Ralph Clarkson, writing for *Art and Archaeology*, sadly counted more than seventy artists who had left Chicago for elsewhere. Many sought New York "not to live by painting alone," Clarkson admitted, "but by some form of art practice," which normally meant illustration or commercial design.[10] On his list Clarkson could now place Orson Lowell, Neysa McMein, Dean Cornwell, Walter Goldbeck, and even a few artists who would eventually return, like Dudley Crafts Watson. By 1935 the theme of loss had become something of a joke. "We are pleased to report," wrote *The Chicagoan* that year, "a more than seasonable upturn in the net monthly total of inquiries as to the reasons why the best Chicago writers and artists go East. The question occurs at least once to every adult of standard intelligence."[11]

Despite the fact that such cultural bleeding could not be staunched, the city continued to push forward with its artistic goals. By 1929 Chicago could boast of having experienced several renaissances: first in the 1890s, next in the 1910s, then the early 1920s. But a city with more than one renaissance in its lifetime was obviously having problems of its own. The rapid shifts in mood of the city's cultural communities, as well as the alteration of their reputation elsewhere, were nothing short of startling. In 1920 H. L. Mencken proclaimed Chicago America's literary capital. "Life buzzes and corruscates on Manhattan Island, but the play of ideas is not there," Mencken wrote. It was a "shoddily cosmopolitan, second-rate European" town, dominated by a spirit of "safe mediocrity." America's masters came not from New York, nor from Boston, "dead intellectually as Alexandria," or Philadelphia, "an intellectual slum," but from the "unspeakable" Chicago, the most "thoroughly American of American cities." From the Chicago Palatinate had come the first-rate journalism of Tarkington, Herrick, Cather, Anderson, Dreiser, along with the Little Theater, a new poetry movement, sparked by Harriet Monroe and her magazine. Chicago was "a superb market for the merchants of the new," Mencken concluded.[12]

Just seven years later in Mencken's own magazine, *American Mercury*, Samuel Putnam, a local critic himself, came out with a soon to be notorious essay entitled, "Chicago: An Obituary," in which he declared that while the city came "dangerously near" on two occasions to becoming the country's literary capital, she was desolate, a cactus desert, and the "burned-out crater of a once quite lively young Vesuvius." We know, said Putnam, that with the cooperation of Cleveland, Chicago "can keep the world in false teeth. But does that mean it can still keep the world in red-blooded he-man poetry, as it came near doing for some four or five years before the war?" (fig. 1.6). Putnam reviewed the glories of the past; he examined Margaret Anderson's *The Little*

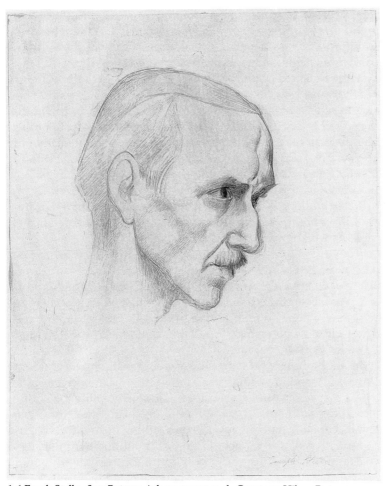

1.6 Frank Stella, *Sam Putnam*, ink on paper, n.d. Courtesy, Hilary Putnam.

Review, Maurice Browne's Little Theatre, the work of Floyd Dell, Burton Rascoe, Vachel Lindsay, Ben Hecht, Maxwell Bodenheim, Vincent Starrett, sparkplugs of the later years, and concluded that only Sandburg, Herrick, and Fuller were left, but the last two were old and used up. "Thus Chicago is now just about as thrilling, poetically, as Tucson, Ariz."[13]

Not all critics were quite as caustic as Putnam. But even before he had read the death notices, easterners were casting doubt on Chicago's cultural ambitions. When Harry Hansen's *Midwest Portraits* appeared in 1923, Stuart Sherman, Franklin P. Adams, and Allan Nevins expressed suspicion of its enthusiasms and hinted at tub-thumping.[14] Robert Morss Lovett, a long-time faculty member at the University of Chicago, wrote his essay on the city for the *New Republic* in 1927. And though he praised the city's energy, ambition, tolerance, and excitement, he too was discouraged by the alternation "of progress and regression" in its history. The great literary figures who appeared had quickly disappeared. "Except for Sandburg," Lovett concluded, "they found no continuing city."[15] Even boosters like Walter Sherwood admitted that "as soon as a Chicago artist won his spurs he packed his paint kit and took a fast train to New York."[16]

While repeated obituary notices of Chicago's creative life may have been as exaggerated as the breathless discoveries that heralded each new talent, it is hard to avoid the sense of frustration expressed by local cultural boosters about the departure of their brightest talents to far-off fields—in the case of painters not only to New York and Europe, but also to the West Coast and to the Southwest. It was fine to boast that Chicago products now shared their skills with the rest of the world, that former Art Institute students and faculty were bringing light into darkness and thus spreading news of the city's fame, but to some extent, this was whistling in the dark.

What accounted for the continuing exodus? Some critics, as I have indicated, singled out money. The financial rewards available elsewhere were greater, they argued, and Chicagoans, despite their boastings, had tight purse strings when it came to the arts. It was hard enough to live the artist's life even in a larger, richer city like New York. The odds against earning a living in Chicago were even greater.

But money alone was not the answer. Artists and writers were usually interested in something more: they wanted celebrity, attention, support, and nurturance. These were all explanations for Chicago's failings. Lovett argued again that the city's social and cultural life had always been something of a matriarchy and continued that for all its metropolitan outlook the city had "something of an inferiority complex"; it possessed "the soul of the village."[17] Hobart Chatfield-Taylor objected to the city's "puritanism" as early as the teens.[18] J. H. Oppenheim assured locals in 1937 that they had nothing to fear from still another post-fair contagion of art culture. He declared that the city had a "natural antipathy to the literary life" that would eventually "bring the local literary bacilli definitely under control."[19] Edgar Lee Masters insisted that the experience of literary men who tried to live in Chicago "shows that they were inexpressibly lonely there, and could not extract from its atmosphere enough oxygen upon which to live."[20] The exodus, as interpreted from this angle, was caused not only by a lack of money but also by inhospitality, a lack of sympathy, and an absence of critical standards.

And this brings up a third assumption about Chicago history. Whatever might be the case in the east, Chicagoans suspected the sophistication and breadth of outlook common to cosmopolitan centers. Despite the inevitable and all-encompassing enthusiasm of the big city, after all, Chicago remained a part of the Middle West. Its journalistic flagship was popularly regarded as one of the most conservative papers in the country. All was not mom and apple pie; citizens knew how to find their gin and bordellos. Moreover, war fervor was more relaxed here than in other places. But life was one thing, art another. Chicago tolerance toward human vice did not necessarily include the creative imagination. In Zenith and Gopher Prairie, Chicago might look liberal, but the view from the Atlantic coast was harsher.

Several incidents fed this reactionary reputation. First, of course, was the reception of the 1913 Armory Show (fig. 1.7). During its twenty-four-day showing the Art Institute hosted a total of 188,000 visitors and despite some initial skepticism it

International Exhibition of
Modern Art

Association of American Painters
and Sculptors, Inc.

The Art Institute of Chicago

March Twenty-fourth to April Sixteenth
Nineteen Hundred and Thirteen

1.7 Catalog cover, International Exhibition of Modern Art (Armory Show), photograph, 1913. Archives of the Art Institute of Chicago. © 1989 The Art Institute of Chicago. All Rights Reserved.

took a smug pride in the event. In its annual report the Institute noted that questions had been raised about its exhibition of work "of so extreme and radical a character." But Institute policy has "always been liberal," the report continued in a spirit of self-congratulation, and "has been willing to give hearing to strange and even heretical doctrines, relying upon the inherent ability of the truth ultimately to prevail." (fig. 1.8).[21]

This view of the museum might well have surprised some local modernists, but they would not have been shocked by the report's final observation that undercut all the honorable intentions that preceded it. Hardly anyone took the "more extreme parts of the exhibition seriously," the Art Institute concluded. The art school students, the "most susceptible" to passing influences, "appear not in the least affected."[22] Students purportedly tried to hang Matisse in effigy, after a mock trial.

This smug philistinism was precisely the problem as far as some observers were concerned. Although the Armory Show did indeed have some important effects on a whole series of artist visitors like Raymond Jonson and the young McKnight Kauffer—who was converted to cubism on the spot—the larger impact was disappointing.[23] Very little art was sold. The students were cauterized by stern lectures from Institute faculty. Local newspapers had a field day; they ferociously ridiculed the show more so than any other press.

New Yorkers professed despair. "It's a Rube Town!" Walt Kuhn wrote back from the Blackstone Hotel.[24] Fifty years later,

1.8 Gallery 52, the International Exhibition of Modern Art, photograph, 1913. Archives of the Art Institute of Chicago. © 1989 The Art Institute of Chicago. All Rights Reserved.

Neil Harris

in his definitive history of the Armory Show, Milton Brown seized on the phrase as the chapter title for the local exhibition.[25] Chicago, he noted, "was not only more provincial, but it suffered from a badly concealed sense of inferiority." The Chicago newspapermen outdid their New York colleagues "in both ignorance and outrage." And "Chicago collectors apparently preferred to make their art purchases, just as women selected their wardrobes, in New York or Paris."[26] What, after all, could be expected from a city so far from the ocean? Chicago critics, even the tolerant Harriet Monroe, in her first comments at least, raised questions about Picasso and Matisse. Moralists, preachers, critics, reformers, and legislators warned that the Art Institute was being profaned. "Why, the saloons could not hang these pictures!" declared Arthur B. Farwell of the Chicago Law and Order League.[27] And the Chicago school superintendent even considered forbidding school children from seeing the show.

There were other testaments to Chicago's provincialism and narrow-mindedness. At approximately the same time the Art Institute was hosting the Armory Show, a reproduction of Paul Chabas's painting *September Morn* was declared obscene and removed from a department store window (fig. 1.9). Chicago, cried James William Pattison, the editor of the *Fine Arts Journal*, was "disgraced in the eyes of the world." After all, he pointed out, the painting had won a Medal of Honor just a year earlier in Paris.[28] Chicago police were unimpressed. Even in the wide-open town of the twenties police descended on local exhibitions to remove the subversive and lascivious art from view.[29]

But the theme of local backwardness and repression was supplemented by one final motif during these years. This theme had particular implications for modernism. Repeatedly one finds in the literature of description and justification a reliance upon a civic organicism, touched by hints of cultural redemption. To its boosters who tended to think in terms of a life cycle, the city of Chicago remained eternally young and eternally fresh but showed signs of incipient maturity. Invariably the community seemed about to come of age and throw off the crudities of youth by nurturing the arts and the higher life.

Maturity, like prosperity, was always just around the corner. Critics, artists, and local boosters were continually scrutinizing the scene for signs. No entrails of an ancient sacrifice were examined more closely than Chicago's cultural enthusiasms. Chicago, wrote Samuel Putnam in 1931, revisiting the city just a few years after he had proclaimed its obituary, is "growing up," thanks to the Depression. If the city did not experience a new renaissance almost at once, she could expect something even better, "a steady, fructifying growth on the spiritual and aesthetic side."[30] "Pork, not Plato, has made Chicago," Price Collier had written thirty years earlier in 1897, and Chicagoans were not yet ready to change their allegiance.[31] But that day would come.

In every decade Chicago promised to make the shift. Art was valuable because it proved the city had a soul, something that skeptical visitors refused to believe. Chicago remained an "imbecile colossus," wrote Lewis Mumford in 1929, in need of civility and decorum; the most imperialist city in the world with "a stereotyped mind, an impoverished expression, indifference to intellectual issues, practical brutality and callousness."[32] Is Chicago "a metropolis"? asked Lloyd Lewis and Henry Justin Smith that same year in *Chicago: The History of Its Reputation*. Yes, they answered, "but still in adolescence." It "liked to play with blocks, and with lead soldiers . . . It was outwardly calm, well-poised, sure of itself. But it would laugh at almost nothing. It could weep hysterically. And sometimes its voice, which should have been a big bass, cracked into the treble."[33] By 1929 standards at least, these were all sure signs of puberty.

The search for civic maturity, marred during these years by the presence of Al Capone, Big Jim Colosimo, Big Bill Thompson, Bugs Moran, the Valentine Day Massacre, and other notorieties, reached its acme of interwar intensity in the 1933 Century of Progress Exposition, which, if it does not close our period, comes very close to it. Its very name suggests the way establishment Chicagoans tried to see themselves, children of a spirited past now in the avant-garde of civilization.

Chicago during the Depression seemed as unlikely a spot for a triumphal hymn to progress as the grimy industrial center of the Columbian Exposition. "This young, boisterous, and somewhat violent city has about reached the end of its road," Mauritz Hallgren commented in 1932, about the corrupt, bankrupt, and starving municipality.[34]

But it survived. If you have never been there, wrote Margaret Marshall to readers of the *Nation* in 1933, "you will be surprised to hear that it is not a heap of ruins lying beside the blue waters of Lake Michigan and filled with the smoking guns of gangsters and the dead bones of Middle Western civilization. In spite of bank panics, Insull crashes, real estate collapses, receivership scandals, five years of back taxes, toppling insurance companies, unrented office buildings, 14,000 unpaid school teachers . . . 5,000 unpaid county employees . . . Charles Dawes, Bill Thompson, the Marshall Field estate, Death Corner, repossessed cars, caught-short subdivisions, and 171,000 families on relief," in spite of all this Chicago was not dead.[35] And its fair proved it.

By 1933 the test of civic vitality had become acceptance of modernity. Ten years earlier Ben Hecht caught the shift. He wrote, "Americans [in 1913] thought that Art was men who wore long hair and talked like sissies; naked women in a garret; something J. P. Morgan was interested in; . . . any statue in a public park. In 1923 Americans think Art is something that doesn't look like a photograph; . . . anything a Russian does; turning colored lights on the orchestra in the movie palace."[36] In 1893 Chicago had shown its maturity by building neoclassical temples in a lakeside park. Forty years later and still searching for cultural respect, its tactics differed. The method now was to establish credibility by breaking with tradition—by attempting to organize an exposition on radical, modernistic grounds. Architects like Frank Lloyd Wright quickly disparaged the authenticity of the effort, particularly the superficial commercial packaging that excluded much of the modern temper.[37] The claim, nevertheless, was made in the bright colors and cubist forms of the exhibition buildings and in the two enormous art displays hosted by the Art Institute in each of the fair seasons. These were seized upon as signs of local progress in contrast with the craven spirit of academicism demonstrated in 1893. No longer did the fairgrounds need an art palace. The city had its own museum capable of hosting displays, and, except for an accent mark like Whistler's painting of his mother, all the art for the 1933 fair came from American collections.

The two Art Institute shows, especially the first, were spectacular successes.[38] "The most formidable array of paintings ever arranged for exhibition under one roof in America, for a particular occasion," crowed Dudley Crafts Watson (figs. 12.8, 12.9, and 12.10).[39] For five months after the June 1, 1933 opening more than 1.6 million people visited the museum, and 700,000 of them paid their quarters to enter the forty-one galleries that held the display. Many were turned away for the interpretive lectures in Fullerton Hall. A special police cordon handled the lines that formed on Michigan Avenue during the closing days of the show. The impact of the exhibition was so strong that the Art Institute immediately reorganized its twenty-eight painting galleries into chronological order. "There was none of the feeling of solemnity which distinguishes certain large exhibits," reported the *Literary Digest*.[40] The average visitor spent two and a half hours—far more than at any commercial display—and seemed enthralled by the modern artists burlesqued only twenty years earlier at the Armory Show. Comparing 1893 with 1933, Watson declared "there has never been in the history of the country so rapid an advance of taste in so short a time. We can begin to be proud of ourselves."[41]

For Chicago modernists, 1933 was a year for taking stock. The twenty years since the Armory Show witnessed the display of once-ridiculed foreign masters like Picasso and Matisse, as well as frequent showings by local radicals. Indeed some modernists, like C. J. Bulliet, worried about the institutionalization of protest, but the public's choice of Jules Breton's *Song of the Lark* (1884; fig. 1.10) as the most popular painting in the Art Institute must have reassured rebels that there was something still worth fighting for.[42] There was also the publication of J. Z. Jacobson's *Art of Today: Chicago, 1933*, the most impressive catalog of Chicago modern art until then, that contained statements and reproductions by more than fifty artists, including Ivan Albright, Emil

1.9 Paul Chabas, *September Morn,* oil on canvas, 1912. The Metropolitan Museum of Art, New York, purchase, Mr. and Mrs. William Coye Wright. Gift, 1957 (57.89).

1.10 Jules Breton, *Song of the Lark,* oil on canvas, 1884. The Henry Field Memorial Collection, the Art Institute of Chicago. © 1989 The Art Institute of Chicago. All Rights Reserved.

Armin, Gustaf Dalstrom, Davenport Griffen, the Biesels, the Chassaings, A. Raymond Katz, Archibald J. Motley, Frances Strain, Eve Watson Schutze, and William S. Schwartz. Jacobson's artists were the first generation of Chicago painters and sculptors who expressed "the spirit of its own time and place."[43] Jacobson disclaimed a spirit of municipal rivalry and any attempt to prove the genius of place in his declared indifference to the judgment of Chicago artists against those of New York, Paris, "or Timbuktu."[44]

But interestingly—or perhaps appropriately—enough, at the very moment of triumph, with the fair's modernism an established fact, and with modern painters enjoying publicity and exhibition space, Jacobson reflected some established local stereotypes. Where "in these paintings and pieces of sculpture is the spirit of Chicago?" he asked. Where were in these images the skyscrapers, the stockyards, the el trains, the steel mills, the factories, churches, and dance halls?[45] They were, in fact, present, but not abundant. While Jacobson defended the absence of typical Chicago subjects by declaring that artists did not have to depict familiar sites to express the city's spirit, he was concerned nevertheless. Jacobson invoked the organic metaphors commonly used by Chicago commentators. The work of these artists, he argued, was frequently rough and incomplete because "Our city is young, our city is crude; the spirit of it is not clearly and completely crystalized."[46]

And finally, although Jacobson refrained from invoking the ferocious sense of municipal competition and instead urged the art cause on its own ground, there was the inevitable mention of the exiles and departed. The only thing Jacobson omitted was talk of a future renaissance; but there were others in 1933 willing to make the promise.

Jacobson's caution was justified. In 1933, having weathered many challenges, Chicago modernists seemed on the verge of achieving victory. So many signs were favorable. Vernacular and American Scene traditions, supported by the WPA and patriotic sentiments, would soon give regional culture a new vitality. The figurative tradition, neo-primitivism, and the myth-making symbolism which were features of Chicago modernism now appeared singularly appropriate. Where other than the Middle West could the union of popular and politically conscious art be so successfully attempted?

But Chicago's version of modernism, like the design of the Century of Progress Exposition, would not become an artworld prototype. To assess what happened, and why, we must re-enter a society unsuspecting of the next generation's willed ignorance of its modernist vision. We will now survey a group of vital, self-absorbed, and productive artists, many of whom thought they had history on their side after all. That Chicago modernism was in part a false spring makes it all the more alluring.

CHAPTER TWO

"A Modest Young Man with Theories": Arthur Dove in Chicago, 1912

ANN LEE MORGAN

For a brief moment in 1912, Chicago distinguished itself with an early and surprisingly positive response to the difficult modernism of one of the country's most adventurous young painters. Arthur Dove's first exhibition opened in Chicago directly after it closed at Alfred Stieglitz's legendary 291 gallery in New York. Whereas New Yorkers had already been exposed to a breathtaking series of debut exhibitions of both European and American modernists at Stieglitz's gallery, Chicagoans had seen very little modern art. Yet they responded to Dove's show more intelligently and open-mindedly than their eastern counterparts.

The show that came to Chicago was not only Dove's first one-person appearance of any consequence but also the first exhibition anywhere of distinctly and identifiably post-representational art by an American artist. In fulfillment of early promise, Dove went on to become a major New York painter who exhibited annually at Stieglitz's subsequent galleries. The work he showed there, at The Intimate Gallery and at An American Place, demonstrated that he was arguably the most committed and inventive modernist of his generation in the United States.

Leaving New York with his paintings at the last moment, Dove arrived in Chicago only a day or two before his show opened on Thursday, March 14, 1912. He came by train at the end of an unusually severe winter which continued to dump a large amount of snow on the city during his visit. Presumably Dove was not greatly inconvenienced, for he stayed only half a block from his gallery, at the Auditorium Hotel designed by Louis Sullivan, who still had an office in the building. The major art attraction in town, the Art Institute, was only three blocks north. Dove would have found the museum looking much as it does today from its Michigan Avenue entrance. Inside, the grand staircase area had been recently finished—or rather, left permanently unfinished. (The original beaux-arts design for a dome embellished with murals was never carried farther.)

When Dove visited the Art Institute in the late winter of 1912, as we may assume he did, four special exhibitions were on display: landscapes by midwestern painters, American etchings, and individual shows of work by two popular painters—Lawton Parker, a Chicagoan who worked in Giverny, France, and Willard Metcalf, an established New York landscape artist who belonged to the progressive group known as The Ten. In addition, Dove could have heard several of the annual Scammon lectures being given that year by the well-known muralist Edwin Blashfield.

In the nearby Loop, Dove must have seen numerous examples of the now-fabled Chicago School of Architecture. These commercial buildings were emblematic of the vital metropolis that continued to expand largely as a result of its centralized location as hub of the nation's railroads and as major transit point for western agricultural products. Sometimes characterized as raw and crude, Chicago nevertheless impressed virtually everyone with its energy. Its split-the-seams growth and modern appearance seemed all the more dramatic because the physical fabric of the city had been created in only forty years following the disastrous Chicago fire of 1871. No wonder one commentator wrote, contrasting an older city with this marvel of the Middle West, "Boston is a state of mind, Chicago is a movement."[1]

But Chicago entailed more than office buildings, railroads, and meat-packing houses. In a way, it was a state of mind. Its inhabitants had in the same forty years taken intense interest in its cultural life. The Art Institute testified to that, as did Orchestra Hall with its resident symphony; Sullivan's Auditorium, the city's foremost stage for opera and other entertainment; the handsome public library with its Tiffany interiors; and the University of Chicago, which had abruptly materialized as one of the most distinguished institutions of higher education in the country. Resident writers had already made an enduring mark. They included Henry Fuller, Floyd Dell, Theodore Dreiser, Ben Hecht, Edgar Lee Masters, Hamlin Garland, William Vaughn Moody, and Robert Herrick, while Carl Sandburg and Sherwood Anderson would arrive later in 1912. At the time of Dove's visit, Chicago native Harriet Monroe was raising funds to support *Poetry* magazine, which commenced publication in the autumn of that year and almost instantaneously made Chicago the center of the English-speaking literary world. Even H. L. Mencken, who terrorized intellectual America with his sarcastic wit, called Chicago "the only genuinely civilized city in the New World." "Out in Chicago," he claimed from his perch at the New York magazine *Smart Set*, "they take the fine arts seriously and get into such frets and excitements about them as are raised nowhere else save by baseball, murder, political treachery, foreign wars, and romantic loves."[2] Mencken may have been teasing his audience, but Chicago did take the fine arts seriously. Certainly in architecture and literature, it led the nation in the development of modern expression.

Although that claim could not be made for painting or sculpture, there was nevertheless an active art community. By early 1912, about ten galleries were in business. Dove exhibited at Chicago's most progressive gallery, owned by W. Scott Thurber, who had been in business since the year Dove was born, 1880.[3] While Thurber handled a largely conservative stock of European and American paintings and prints as well as some reproductions, he always tried to interest Chicagoans in new ideas. The show that preceded Dove's consisted of Frederick J. Waugh's marine scenes done at Monhegan Island, Maine. Succeeding Dove came an exhibit of paintings by his friend Lawrence Mazzanovich, who regularly showed post-impressionist landscapes there. Other artists shown at Thurber's gallery around the same time included progressive painters such as Jerome Blum, B. J. O. Nordfeldt, Ossip Linde, and Karl Anderson, who was the brother of writer Sherwood Anderson.

Thurber's gallery may have been the most impressive modern gallery in the country at the time. Designed in 1909 by Frank Lloyd Wright, it presented a unified and elegant ensemble. Cork-covered walls gilded in a low-toned bronze surmounted a rough plaster dado, that was also gilded but in a brighter tone. Floors were finely textured white cement contrived to reflect light and were bordered in dull yellow and defined by a line of inlaid brass. Extensive fumed oak woodwork with bronze rubbed into the grain was particularly notable in a room that was divided into alcoves for the viewing of prints and small works of art. The entire glowing interior was warmly lit from above with a combination of electric lights covered by decorative glass panels and skylights.[4]

What inspired Thurber to commission an interior of such richness and distinction? He must have been impressed by Wright's previous local experience in both exhibition design and commercial interiors.[5] Wright already had planned at least two exhibitions at the Art Institute,[6] and in 1908 he had designed the interior of Browne's Bookstore located in the same building as Thurber's gallery. The proprietor of this shop, Francis Fisher Browne, was editor of *The Dial* magazine, an established and well-respected literary publication. Once Margaret Anderson started publishing her radical magazine, *The Little Review*, from the same building in 1913, *The Dial* seemed rather old-fashioned. For the moment, however, Anderson was working for Browne as a bookstore clerk.

Although the art gallery and bookstore are gone, the Fine Arts

Building, as it is called, still stands three blocks south of the Art Institute, adjacent to Sullivan's Auditorium. For the first twenty years or so of this century, it swarmed with artists, musicians, actors, writers, and craftspeople. Since then its fortunes have varied, but it remains occupied today primarily by fine arts tenants. In 1912 it was a lively center of artistic interchange.[7]

The artists and literary people in the building must have provided a ready audience for Dove's exhibition, and in turn, he could hardly have failed to be stimulated by their presence. He was, after all, rather new to this business of exhibiting his art and almost unknown in Chicago. At thirty-one years old Dove was only beginning to produce individualistic work. He had spent his childhood in Geneva, a small town in upper New York state, enrolled at Hobart College, and completed his education at Cornell University. Upon graduation in 1903 he moved to New York City, where he worked successfully as an illustrator until he departed for France in 1908. There he painted full time for about a year, absorbing the lessons of impressionism, Cézanne, and the fauves. When he returned, Dove decided to earn a living in farming, and before the end of 1909 he bought property in Westport, Connecticut.[8]

Around the same time, he met Alfred Stieglitz,[9] most likely upon the encouragement of Stieglitz's admirers in Paris, especially Alfred Maurer, who had become Dove's closest friend abroad. Within a few months, in a March 1910 group show at 291 titled "Younger American Artists," Stieglitz showed one of the last works Dove painted in France, *The Lobster* (fig 2.1). But Dove apparently never again painted anything like *The Lobster* or, for that matter, anything that resembled his earlier work. In succeeding months he produced six small oil sketches that heralded his move toward abstraction. His new ideas reached fruition in the work he exhibited in 1912 at 291 and then in Chicago. Thus, these two exhibitions of work accomplished in 1911 and early 1912 not only provided a whole new experience of public exposure for the artist, they also revealed to the public the first truly original work he had ever produced. It was a mutually startling encounter.

What works by Dove did Chicagoans see in 1912? He brought along some of his French landscapes, but the focus of the exhibition was a group of ten untitled pastels later nicknamed the "Ten Commandments." We cannot reconstruct the group today because some of them are missing, and, to complicate matters further, there exist more than ten stylistically related pastels with approximately the same dimensions.[10] Ironically, the only work that can be identified with absolute certainty has been lost. *Based on Leaf Forms and Spaces* was purchased from Thurber's gallery by Arthur Jerome Eddy, a local corporation lawyer, art collector, writer, and bon vivant.[11] We know the work only from the color illustration that Eddy published in his pioneering 1914

2.1 Arthur Dove, *The Lobster*, oil on canvas, 1908. Amon Carter Museum, Fort Worth. Acquisition in memory of Anne Burnett Tandy, Trustee, Amon Carter Museum, 1968–80.

book *Cubists and Post-Impressionism* (fig. 2.2).[12] Because the pastel later was sold, it was not acquired by the Art Institute after Eddy's death as were many other gems from his modern art collection. However, the Institute does have another of the original ten pastels, known as *Wind on a Hillside* or *Nature Symbolized No. 2* (plate 4). Yet another, *Nature Symbolized No. 3*, also found a home in Chicago, at the Terra Museum of American Art. These two are among five that have been identified as belonging to the original group on the basis of contemporary descriptions. The others are *Nature Symbolized No. 1* (fig. 2.3), *Sails*, and *Team of Horses*. A similar style, along with passing reference to its subject in a review, makes it likely that *Plant Forms* (fig. 2.4) was also among the originals. This gives us a core group of seven about which we can be fairly sure. All are characterized by simple and

2.2 Arthur Dove, *Based on Leaf Forms and Spaces* (or, *Leaf Forms*), pastel on unidentified support, 1911–12. Current location unknown; photograph taken from *Cubists and Post-Impressionism*, 2nd ed. (Chicago: A. C. McClurg, 1919). © 1989 The
Art Institute of Chicago. All Rights Reserved.

clearly defined angular or curving forms, limited color schemes, crowded and compressed space, energetic and repetitive rhythms, and forms abstracted or conventionalized from visual reality.

The other three from the original ten remain problematic. *Movement No. 1* is related in style but more abstract than any of the others, and there are no contemporary descriptions of it. Yet, among the extant candidates, this is the closest to the core group and therefore can be provisionally accepted. Another work, later titled by Dove *Circles and Squares*, has disappeared, and the tenth also may be lost. There are several other pastels of about the same size, but all of them display different stylistic characteristics, suggesting a smaller group that postdates the original Ten Commandments.[13] Thus, we know what seven or perhaps eight of the ten looked like—enough to give us a good idea of the impact they had as an ensemble.

How did Chicago react? Only Eddy responded with his wallet. The pastel illustrated in his book was the sole purchase from the show. Newspaper coverage suggests that many people saw the exhibit, and reviews in general were surprisingly sympathetic. Columnist Bert Leston Taylor of the *Chicago Tribune* made light of Dove's efforts, but his clever daily column was intended to entertain. Among his talents was a facility for versification, which he inflicted on Dove with great relish. For his column of March 25, 1912, he wrote a charming doggerel that was reprinted in the *Tribune* and elsewhere several times. Titled with mock solemnity "Lines Written After Viewing Mr. Arthur Dove's Exposition of the Simultaneousness of the Ambient," this jingle read in part as follows:

> I cannot tell you how I love
> The canvases of Mr. Dove,
> Which Saturday I went to see
> In Mr. Thurber's Gallery.
>
> At first you fancy they are built
> As patterns for a crazy quilt
> But soon you see that they express
> An ambient simultaneousness.
>
> . . . . .
>
> But Mr. Dove is much too keen
> To let a single bird be seen;
> To show the pigeons would not do
> And so he simply paints the coo.[14]

Several subsequent references to the show appear in Taylor's column where the mix of incomprehension and merriment is maintained.[15] Neither vicious nor analytical, Taylor's antics should not be taken for art criticism. More significant is the fact that Dove and his work were sufficiently newsworthy to appear repeatedly in this general-interest column.

2.3 Arthur Dove, *Nature Symbolized No. 1* (or, *Roofs*; or, *Factory Chimneys*), pastel on paper, 1911–12. The Crispo Collection.

Other Chicago journalists wrote more seriously about Dove's exhibition. In the *Chicago Examiner* and the *Record-Herald*, for example, Dove was treated with respect and interest. The *Examiner*'s review was written by its regular art columnist H. Effa Webster, who obviously had talked to the artist. He explained that Dove was after "principles in art as he sees them in nature" and then quoted him at length: "I don't like titles for these pictures, because they should tell their own story." Dove supposedly further asserted, "Yes, I could paint a cyclone. Not in the usual mode of sweeps of gray wind over the earth, trees bending and a furious sky above. I would paint the mighty folds of the wind in comprehensive colors." Apparently convinced, Webster concluded, "Indeed one of Dove's paintings represents swift and wholesome wind; we could see the refreshing folds and sturdy

2.4 Arthur Dove, *Plant Forms*, pastel on canvas, 1911–12(?). Collection of the Whitney Museum of American Art, New York. Purchase, with funds from Mr. and Mrs. Roy R. Neuberger, 51.20.

leaps into repetitions of its force—after the artist had defined the geometric forms and colors."[16]

At the *Record-Herald*, art critic Maude I. G. Oliver apparently had been primed for "the radicals of radicals," as she called the Ten Commandments, by previous exhibitions at the gallery. She wrote, "Another insurgent has found his way to Thurber's gallery." Oliver must also have had a lecture from the artist. She continued: "Now comes Arthur Dove . . . a modest young man with theories, also with an exhibition." As well, she seems to have understood that the work had to do with abstract principles and personal expression. "These present no attempt at representation of form but of the abstract idea of form . . . or of some . . . sensation or emotion. They delineate, in other words, a series of symbols." The writer doubted that such works would ever supplant representation, but she admitted, "Certainly they are original. As decorative motifs they are exceedingly interesting."[17] A week later, reporting that attendance at the Dove exhibition had been good, she noted, "Chicago people, if not altogether convincible, are at least sufficiently progressive to be curious."[18]

Indeed, even the *Chicago Evening Post*'s cautious critic—later known as the local voice of reactionary conservatism—was won over by the young artist who, in her words, "does not preach his art." Lena McCauley devoted more than half of her column to the Dove show two days after it opened. Commenting that it was "the collection of the week that will provoke the most discussion," she went on to emphasize at several points its experimental nature, which she realized was allied to international developments. Revealing her source, she told her readers, "Mr. Dove's works become intelligible when the artist talks of them in the galleries." From Dove's remarks, she was able to grasp that these works were designs based on nature yet independent of imitation, and she understood they harbored potentially symbolic or expressive content.[19]

In addition to Bert Leston Taylor's playful commentaries, the *Tribune* presented reviews of Dove's show by its music and art critics. The first, Glenn Dillard Gunn, was a pianist whose regular columns reveal his sympathy for difficult contemporary music. He too seems to have grasped Dove's underlying motives. Gunn described the pastels as experiments made "to discover direct reflexes of emotion and sensibilities in line and color that are not concerned with the reproduction of anything in nature." The viewer, he thought, "will surely carry away with him an impression that puzzles and fascinates."[20]

The *Tribune's* regular art critic, who commented in the same Sunday edition, was none other than Harriet Monroe. She, too, had evidently been talking to Dove and understood his message. Perhaps at the artist's prompting, she likened his interest in mathematical laws, rhythm, and harmony to modern music. Proceeding a step further, she explained, "Modern minds, he thinks, are reaching out toward an art of pure color and form dissociated from 'representation.' " But Monroe, who knew firsthand of recent developments in Paris, tried to place Dove within that context. "Mr. Dove brings to Chicago the message of the autumn salon," she told her readers. "To those of us who are out of range of the volcano, these manifestations of its activity will seem somewhat startling, but the true Parisian will find Mr. Dove's crescents and polygons a rather smooth and academic version of the movement. They seem to me studies of decorative pattern, some of which might be effectively used in some art nouveau mansion innocent of motives from classic, Gothic, renaissance, Chinese, Ethiopian, or any other of art's historic styles."[21]

If Harriet Monroe was the most perceptive and informed Chicago critic, the most enthusiastic was novelist and playwright

George Cram Cook, whose thoughts appeared in the *Friday Literary Review*, the *Chicago Evening Post*'s supplemental weekly section edited by the socialist Floyd Dell.[22] Three years later, Cook, who was Dell's older friend and editorial assistant, and his wife, the writer Susan Glaspell, departed for the bohemia of Greenwich Village and Cape Cod, where they were the moving spirits behind the formation of the legendary Provincetown Players.[23] But for the moment, Dove's abstractions inspired Cook to produce a lengthy rhapsody to liberation. Goaded by Taylor's poem in the *Tribune*, Cook sarcastically commented, "Someone in every group quotes, 'He paints the coo.' How grateful they must be to B. L. T., being relieved by the phrase of the necessity of thinking." Connecting Dove to international modernism, Cook told his readers that Dove's "groping," as he called it, was "what les fauves are doing in Paris, in London, in America. And their work is the point of the wedge that is being driven into the future. This is the real creative art impulse of our century." Unlike most other journalists in town, Cook gave no evidence of having talked to the artist, but he understood that the work's abstract tendency could be justified in terms of its parallels with music and that the images were intentionally suggestive. Speaking of the pastel that evokes the forms of roofs and chimneys, Cook pointed out, "It is the cutting, vertical lines of the chimneys— their cuttingness, their verticalness, their parallelness that interested the artist, not their chimneyness. He leaves chimneyness to photography and those who imitate photography in painting." Returning to his own agenda later in the review, Cook declared, "Escape from lifelong habit is just the liberation offered by art. That's why new art is necessary when old art has become fixed in habit." The old art, he said, was exhausted. As for Dove's work, "Anyone with eyes can see the new energy working here—breaking a way into the untried, experimenting, taking new hold of visual elements."[24]

It is worth considering for a moment the collective significance of Dove's Chicago reviews. As a group, they are better than those that appeared in the New York art press. To be sure, New York reviewers were intrigued by Dove's work, but their columns were superficially descriptive and much less perceptive. They saw pleasing patterns in Dove's pastels, but they offered no insights into his aims or meanings.[25] In contrast, Chicago reviewers seem generally to have understood Dove's basic intentions: his desire to create works of art that did not reproduce the visible world, his attachment to nature and the principles that could be extracted from it, and his interest in subjective expression. The fact that most Chicago journalists were able to talk to Dove probably aided their understanding. (Parenthetically, we might wonder why the New York reviewers had no contact with the artist. Did Dove have more time on his hands in Chicago? Or did Stieglitz do all the talking?)

It is also worth noting that Harriet Monroe and George Cram Cook, who wrote the most perceptive reviews published in either city, represented different intellectual constituencies. Although Monroe's name is historically linked with the avant-garde magazine *Poetry*, in 1912 she was no flaming young radical. At age fifty-two, she was an established, somewhat genteel poet and a well-connected habitué of the Chicago literary scene. Her contacts with old money were at least as important as her sympathy for new literature in making *Poetry* a reality. Since 1909, her well-informed art columns had appeared in the *Tribune*, where she educated Chicagoans about traditional as well as progressive art.[26] On the other hand, George Cram Cook, a newcomer to the city, represented the upstart generation in revolt against the good taste that informed Monroe's aesthetic. Thus, Chicagoans of varied points of view had critical access to Dove's work. Newspaper responses suggest that the show attracted a wider public in Chicago than it had at Stieglitz's elite gallery in New York. In addition, though it was not much, Eddy's acquisition of a pastel was one more sale than Dove had made in New York.

Is there any way to account for Chicago's relatively tolerant, even perceptive reaction to Dove's work? He was not well received because of Chicago's understanding of recent avant-garde art from Paris and New York, for that was not the case. On the other hand, by the time of Dove's visit, commercial galleries were providing a healthy array of exhibits, and an expanding national art press kept Chicagoans in touch with developments elsewhere. Moreover, local art enthusiasts had been extremely well-informed for a generation about recent tendencies in contemporary American art and to a lesser extent those in European art. In the 1870s and 1880s annual Interstate Industrial exhibitions had included surveys of contemporary painting.[27] These exhibitions developed into the most comprehensive and distinguished regular group shows in America.[28] Subsequently, the annual American and local vicinity shows at the Art Institute provided nationally recognized forums; the American shows were unique in the country in that they always included a large group of paintings by Americans living abroad. The Institute also had an active program of smaller shows and one-person exhibitions that supplemented the large salons, as they were sometimes known. In addition, it had a small but relatively good collection of recent and contemporary American art, including the largest collection anywhere of paintings by George Inness.[29] Evidence of the museum's enlightened collecting practices may be seen in just some of the American paintings it acquired in the two years prior to Dove's visit: J. A. M. Whistler's *Artist in the Studio*, Mary Cassatt's *The Bath*, Childe Hassam's *Against the Light*, Frank Benson's *Rainy Day*, Arthur B. Davies's *Maya, Mirror of Illusions*, Daniel Garber's *Towering Trees*, and John Francis

Murphy's *Hill Top*. Moreover, the museum had an active program of lectures, and the school attracted major artists as visiting teachers.

Thus, Chicagoans were entirely familiar with progressive art and the ideas behind it. This art characteristically stressed form and color as bearers of the aesthetic experience, alluded to nature but did not precisely reproduce it, and, above all, emphasized the artist's personal, inner response.[30] As the reviews suggest—especially those based on Dove's own explanations—it was precisely by exaggerating these commonplace aspects of a well-established but non-academic aesthetic that Dove arrived at his own form of highly original expression. Chicagoans, especially those reviewers who were able to talk to the artist, made the connection.

Equally significant for Chicagoans' sensitivity to the visual qualities of Dove's Ten Commandments was the fact that the city was a major center of the late nineteenth- and early twentieth-century decorative arts movement in the United States,[31] second only perhaps to Boston. Chicago produced a great quantity of stained glass, jewelry, furniture, metalwork, ceramics, glassware, and other finely designed items. The city also was home to one of the major theorists and champions of the Arts and Crafts movement, Oscar Lovell Triggs, who taught English at the University of Chicago.[32] In addition, the renown and personal connections of Hull-House founder Jane Addams drew attention to the important role of Arts and Crafts at the settlement house.[33] The Fine Arts Building, where Thurber's gallery was located, was the local hotbed of Arts and Crafts activity.[34]

Crafts did not interest Dove, who never produced a decorative object in his life. However, the Ten Commandments are, by the artist's own admission, designs extracted from natural forms. This approach was at the heart of the anti-historicist Arts and Crafts design purpose and method. Arts and Crafts practitioners, as well as related theorists such as Boston's Denman Ross, produced dozens of design books and hundreds of articles that drew attention to principles of beauty and order in nature.[35] Given his professed interest in the same goal, Dove may have been stimulated by such writings.[36]

In fact, Dove, Stieglitz, and others in their circle surely were more aware of the decorative art movement than historians have recognized. For instance, telling evidence of the interconnectedness of avant-gardism with Arts and Crafts can be found in *The Craftsman*, a monthly journal published by Gustave Stickley. This journal, where interest in design reform was accompanied by regular reports on social questions, literature, and the arts, published a great deal of information about 291, Stieglitz, and the avant-garde environment in general.

To some extent, decorative arts enthusiasts and nascent modernists formed overlapping communities during the first decade of the twentieth century. Sharing similar extra-aesthetic motivations, both groups were attentive to the relation of art to life, concerned about the place of art in the reform of society, and attracted to the virtues of simplicity and sincerity. Thus, just as Stieglitz and 291 were known to readers of *The Craftsman*, Arts and Crafts work, attitudes, and methodology must have been familiar to radical modernists, including Dove. In fact, his decision to abandon a comfortable life as an illustrator to become a farmer can perhaps be understood in relation to the Simple Life movement[37] that was closely allied to Arts and Crafts ideology. This movement advocated an agrarian, self-sufficient lifestyle as an alternative to the decadence, corruption, and strife of industrialized urbanism. *The Craftsman* itself encouraged small, independent farming as a morally superior, economically feasible way of life. Interpreted in this light, Dove's decision carries cultural weight and loses its mysterious romanticism.

Similarly, seen in the context of the design goals of the Arts and Crafts movement, Dove's breakthrough to abstraction seems a logical step. But perhaps Dove moved independently toward organic abstraction. Although it cannot be proven that Dove was aware of the Arts and Crafts movement and its literature, abundant evidence demonstrates that educated Chicagoans were. In this context Dove's pastels must have made sense to them, as they did to Harriet Monroe when she noted that the educated eye would find "Mr. Dove's crescents and polygons a rather smooth and academic version" of the modern movement and that his "studies of decorative patterns" might be "effectively used in some art nouveau mansion." Perhaps she thought of interior design because architects in Chicago were particularly involved with the Arts and Crafts community.[38] Among others, both Wright and Sullivan had strong personal and professional connections. Wright's path toward abstract design was guided by an Arts and Crafts aesthetic. And Chicagoans who noted the vigorous abstractions of organic form on the facade of Sullivan's Carson, Pirie, Scott department store building on the main commercial thoroughfare had some preparation for Dove's pastels.

In summary, Dove's positive critical reception in Chicago was colored by three factors. First, there existed a vital, cultured society that already had experienced early modernism in some areas of artistic expression, notably literature and architecture. Second, the art community had a long-standing, sophisticated familiarity with the period's major forms of painting (aside from radical modernism). Third, there was an unusually strong awareness of the decorative and expressive potential of non-historical design based on organic motifs.

Finally, a brief epilogue. What happened to Dove, and to Chicago, after his show? On March 30 Bert Leston Taylor bid him good-bye in the *Tribune*: "Arthur Dove, the rising young post-futurist, is going back to Westport, Conn., today, his picture show being over. Come again, Art. We may get you in time."[39] But Dove never returned, and Chicago became more perplexed by modern art. When the Armory Show arrived at the Art Institute about a year later, an uproar ensued. The reaction to this exhibition, with its bewildering array of advanced "isms"—in contrast to the rather benign reception of Dove's abstractions—underlines the relative accessibility of Dove's work to the Chicago audience. His memory inspired another Taylor poem, "The Brooding Dove":

> Arthur Dove is raising chickens.
> He has put his paints away:
> Tell me, Chronos, where the dickens
> Are the Cubes of yesterday!
>
> Dove was real, Dove was earnest,
> But his efforts came to nix.
> Bowing to decree the sternest
> He has gone to raising chicks.[40]

Indeed, Dove was literally raising chicks. He did not participate in the Armory Show, and his artistic productivity fell off precipitously. Not until 1925, thirteen years after his Chicago show, did he have new work to exhibit. During this extraordinarily long hiatus, Dove must have experienced an artistic crisis, the nature of which lies beyond the scope of this book. He nevertheless always remembered Chicago fondly. More than thirty years later he reminisced in a letter, "It is a very enthusiastic place."[41]

CHAPTER THREE

Lorado Taft, the Ferguson Fund, and the Advent of Modernism

ALLEN WELLER

From the time of the 1893 World's Columbian Exposition until his death in 1936 Lorado Taft was the most distinguished artist in Chicago. Yet he, like many of his colleagues, never espoused modernism. He had a national reputation which led to important commissions throughout the country, was the author of a pioneering book which remained the standard source of information in its field for over sixty years, and played an important role at the School of the Art Institute as a teacher for twenty-five years and as a charismatic lecturer for many more. It was only in middle age that a catastrophic event, the 1913 Armory Exhibition, showed him that the ideas and the ideals which had formed him and his style had been totally rejected by a radical younger generation.

Taft is an example of an artist who was never able to adjust to new cultural conditions. He is one of many securely established as dominant and significant figures in Chicago who found themselves rejected and largely ignored by their younger contemporaries. He represents the entrenched art establishment that the proponents of modernism confronted when they emerged in the Windy City.

Taft, born in central Illinois in 1860, educated at the Ecole des Beaux-Arts in Paris in the 1880s, established himself in a studio on State Street in 1886 when he started teaching sculpture at the School of the Art Institute. Like all artists who emerged from the tradition-bound atmosphere of the Beaux-Arts, he was primarily a clay modeler whose works were fluent and detailed, with lofty ideas and content based on a kind of literary symbolism. Abstract ideas were expressed by ideal human figures. The principal opportunities for a young sculptor in the 1890s were Civil War monuments, grave memorials, and portrait busts. Taft did them all and did them well.

His decorative work for the Horticulture Building at the 1893 World's Fair established him firmly as the pre-eminent local sculptor. Almost all of his biggest sculptural ideas were conceived by the time of the 1913 Armory Show, though many of them were not realized until many years later. By 1901 he had designed and exhibited his *Solitude of the Soul*, but it was not to be carved in marble until 1913. In 1903 his finest Civil War monument, *The Defense of the Flag*, was erected in Jackson, Michigan, though it had been designed many years earlier. His book, *The History of American Sculpture,* was published in the same year. The great group of *The Blind*, inspired by a symbolist drama by Maurice Maeterlinck, was first exhibited in 1908, though it was not to be cast in bronze for another eighty years. His *Eternal Silence* was placed in Graceland Cemetery in 1908. The colossal *Blackhawk* in Oregon, Illinois, was dedicated in 1911. His characteristically beaux-arts *Columbus Monument* was erected in Washington, D.C., in 1912. The *Fountain of the Great Lakes*, which had first been conceived as a classroom project ten years before, was finally completed and dedicated as the first of the Ferguson Fund monuments in 1913. By 1909–10 Taft had already conceived the monumental designs for the *Fountain of Time* and the *Fountain of Creation* for the Midway in Chicago, though the first of these was not completed until the 1920s and the second remained unfinished at the time of his death. During the 1920s Taft continued to produce major works in the traditional style which was the basis of his work such as the *Lincoln* and the *Alma Mater* in Urbana, Illinois (1927, 1928) and the *Pioneers* in Elmwood, Illinois (1928). Throughout all of these years he produced many portrait busts and reliefs, of which the Hamlin Garland and the Israel Zangwill are outstanding examples. Taft was unusual among the sculptors of his generation who created major public monuments in that most of his works were not commissions but were made because he wanted to make them. The ideas behind them were his own, not those of individuals or institutions who commissioned him to embody them.

Taft himself was completely specific about his role as an artist when in 1899 he declared: "The goal of every great artist's ambition is the rendering of the human body. . . . The body is to him the fairest thing in nature."[1] Art was to convey a noble message, to teach, to uplift. These ideals which seemed hopelessly old-fashioned and unacceptable to the artists whose works astonished Chicago in 1913 were considered progressive and even revolutionary by Taft and his contemporaries. It is no small wonder that they were confused and outraged by the modern art they saw.

In the years just before 1910, two important events that took place in Chicago had a positive and an exciting effect on plans for municipal art during the remaining years of the early twentieth century. One was the establishment of the Ferguson Fund

Plate 1. Charles Graham, *Dream City*, Manufactures and Liberal Arts Building at
the 1893 World's Columbian Exposition, watercolor on paper, 1893. The Chicago Historical Society.

Plate 2. Jules Guérin, *Plan of Chicago*, view looking west of the proposed civic center plaza,
watercolor and pencil on paper, 1908. © 1989 The Art Institute of Chicago. All Rights Reserved.

Plate 3. Emil Armin, *The Open Bridge,* oil painting, 1930. Collection of Illinois
State Museum, Gift in memory of Irma Thormann Morgenthau.

Plate 4. Arthur Dove, *Nature Symbolized No. 2* (or *Wind on a Hillside*), pastel on paper mounted on plywood, 1911–12. Alfred Stieglitz Collection, the Art Institute of Chicago. © 1989 The Art Institute of Chicago. All Rights Reserved.

Plate 5. Manierre Dawson, *Lucrèce*, oil on canvas, 1911. The John and Mable
Ringling Museum of Art, Sarasota, Florida.

Plate 6. Jerome Blum, *Fauvist Landscape*, oil on canvas, ca. 1910. Private Collection. Courtesy, David David Gallery, Philadelphia.

Plate 7. Raymond Jonson, *The Trojan Women,* design for stage set, 1915. Collection of the Jonson Gallery of the University Art Museum, University of New Mexico, Albuquerque.

Plate 8. Raymond Jonson, *Miriam Kiper,* oil on canvas, 1919. Collection of the Jonson Gallery of the University Art Museum University of New Mexico, Albuquerque.

Plate 9. Raymond Jonson, *Life*, oil on canvas, 1921. Collection of the Jonson Gallery of the University Art Museum, University of New Mexico, Albuquerque.

Plate 10. Stanislaus Szukalski, *Flower of Dreams*, 1917 (destroyed). Photograph taken from Stanislaus Szukalski, *The Work of Szukalski* (Chicago: Covici-McGee, 1923). © 1989 The Art Institute of Chicago. All Rights Reserved.

Plate 11. Rudolph Weisenborn, *Convex Space,* oil on canvas, 1930. Courtesy, Gilman/Gruen Galleries, Chicago.

Plate 12. Rudolph Weisenborn, *The Blue Tree,* oil on canvas, 1926. Courtesy, Gilman/Gruen Galleries, Chicago.

Plate 13. Ramon Shiva, *Chicago MCMXXIV* (or *Untitled Chicago Industrial Scene*), oil on canvas, 1924. Courtesy, Thomas McCormick and Melissa Williams, Kansas City, Missouri.

Plate 14. (*above right*) Anthony Angarola, *Michigan Avenue Bridge—Chicago River*, oil on canvas, n. d. Courtesy, ACA Galleries, New York.

Plate 15. (*below right*) Anthony Angarola, *German Picnic*, oil on canvas, 1926. Courtesy, ACA Galleries, New York.

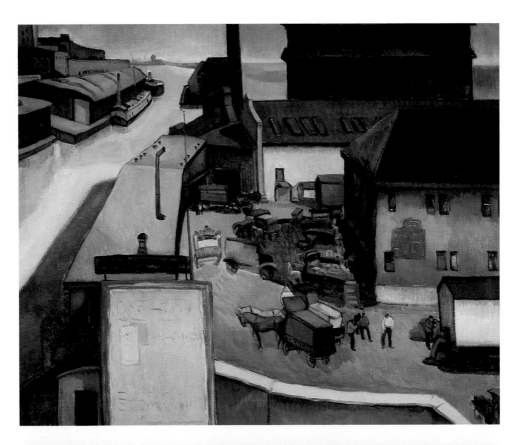

Plate 16. Anthony Angarola, *Christ Healing the Sick,* oil on canvas, 1921. Courtesy, ACA Galleries, New York.

Plate 17. Macena Barton, *Clarence J. Bulliet*, oil on canvas, ca. 1933. Collection of James and Ruth Romano, Chicago.

Plate 18. B. J. O. Nordfeldt, *Floyd Dell*, oil on canvas, 1913. Collection of the
Newberry Library, Chicago.

Plate 19. Will Barnet, *Homage to Léger with Katharine Kuh,* photograph, 1982. A portrait of Katharine Kuh painted at the same time her oral history was conducted. Collection of the artist.

Plate 20. Lee Atwood, *The Kuh Gallery,* watercolor, ink, and pencil sketch on paper, ca. 1938. Courtesy, Katharine Kuh.

in 1905; the other was the publication of Daniel Burnham's *Plan of Chicago* in 1909.[2] Both of these events were of particular importance to Taft.

Burnham's far-reaching plan for the development of Chicago was the outgrowth of the 1893 World's Columbian Exposition, for which he was chief of construction. Here a harmonious collaboration of architects, sculptors, and landscape designers was exploited with spectacular success. He envisioned a great development of the lakefront with extensive arterial boulevards, monumental bridges over the river, a ring of parks and forest preserves within and surrounding the city, and, west of the river, a tremendous civic center, dominated by an enormous building with a vast dome. All of these were sumptuously published in architectural drawings and illustrations by Jules Guérin that reveal architectural forms in an elaborate beaux-arts style. Taft must have seen the Burnham plan as a setting for monumental public sculpture, providing sites on the great projected boulevards and at the astonishing proposed civic center, where sculpture of the beaux-arts, Renaissance-inspired style so lavishly provided at the 1893 fair would have been appropriate. It is significant that the only work of sculpture reproduced in Burnham's book is a small illustration of Taft's *Fountain of the Great Lakes*, at that time only to be seen in a small preliminary sketch model.

Even before the publication of Burnham's grandiose plan, the establishment of the Ferguson Fund in 1905 had created a great deal of excitement among all who envisaged a greater and more beautiful Chicago. Benjamin Franklin Ferguson was a wealthy lumberman who had accumulated a fortune and left a remarkable will.[3] Aside from a number of small personal bequests, his entire estate was to remain intact until it reached the proportions of one million dollars after which time the annual income was to be "entirely and exclusively used and expended by [the Art Institute] under the direction of its Board of Trustees, in the erection and maintenance of enduring statuary and monuments, in the whole or in part of stone, granite, or bronze, in the parks, along the boulevards, or in other public places within the City of Chicago, Illinois, commemorating worthy men or women of America or important events in American history."

Ferguson had never been identified as an art collector, and apparently this imaginative plan was the result of suggestions which came to him from Burnham himself. The Fund was not left to the Art Institute but was to be administered by its trustees, who had complete control over choice of subjects, artists, and location of works. Charles Hutchinson, then president of the Art Institute, assured the public that only the very finest sculptors would be selected and that "the Trustees of the Art Institute feel honored by the confidence placed in them by Mr. Ferguson and appreciate the responsibility of so great a trust. I feel sure that the people of Chicago will have no just cause for complaint of the manner in which the trust will be administered." Taft, in an enthusiastic article about this unexpected and generous gift, was delighted that the Ferguson will had said it was to be used to "commemorate" rather than to "represent" worthy men or women, for he was anxious that only works which were ideal and symbolic would be commissioned rather than portrait statues of individuals. The *Chicago Tribune* declared: "The bequest would in another generation make Chicago the richest city in the world in sculpture and the mecca of artists."

The future was bright, and prospects seemed unlimited. When Burnham returned from a visit to Paris in 1910 he declared that the French capital was worried and feared that it would lose its reputation as the world's most beautiful city. In an article in the *Chicago Daily News* headlined "Jealous Paris Fears Chicago Beauty Plan," Burnham declared: "The day will come when the people will realize that they can have whatever they want if they will only get together. . . . The children must grow up dreaming of a beautiful city."[4] At the same time Taft, in an ecstatic mood, wrote: "Lo! a wonderful thing is happening among us, the beautiful art of the Greeks, transplanted to these welcoming shores, is taking sturdy root and promises a new revelation to the world. It is America's turn next."[5]

The first work to be commissioned by the Ferguson Fund was Taft's *Fountain of the Great Lakes*, a concept which had started out as a classroom project in 1903. It was dedicated with appropriate ceremonies in 1913 as a memorial to Mr. Ferguson himself, creating a precedent that such memorials could be symbolic rather than literal in theme. In the eighteen years that followed, twelve works (including Taft's own *Fountain of Time*) were commissioned and installed. The last two were Ivan Mestrovic's *Indians* on Michigan Avenue and Carl Milles' *Triton Fountain* in the Art Institute.

Then a strange thing happened. For the next thirty-eight years no other works of sculpture were commissioned by the Trustees of the Art Institute. Mr. Hutchinson had said, at the time the bequest was announced, that "the provisions of the will are so direct and clear that only works in marble, granite, or bronze of the highest type may be purchased." But two years after the last Ferguson work had been unveiled the Trustees filed a complaint to the Circuit Court of Cook County asking that the word "monument" in Mr. Ferguson's will might be construed to include a "building." This legal action was accomplished without any publicity and was approved in two minutes without discussion by the Court.

During the long ensuing period, the income from the Fund was accumulated and used to construct a major office wing of the Art Institute building, which was given the official name of the Ferguson Memorial (though Ferguson, of course, had already been memorialized in the *Fountain of the Great Lakes*). It was only gradually that the general public realized that the income from the Fund was being used for purposes which had certainly not been in Mr. Ferguson's mind. The National Sculpture Society, the Chicago Chapter of Artist's Equity, the Chicago Heritage Committee, and other public bodies as well as many private individuals submitted petitions and statements, but without results. A lengthy article by a distinguished lawyer appeared in a learned legal publication; it called the action a "case of the clear abuse of a charitable trust." As a result the state legislature eventually passed the Charitable Trust Act of 1961, which, however, has no proper safeguards. Once the Ferguson Wing had been built and paid for (by 1958) the Fund again became active in the erection of public sculptural monuments. We can only speculate as to what other works might be in existence had the Fund continued in its original purpose throughout these years.[6]

Into the complacency (some might call it the inertia or apathy) of the Chicago art world burst the bombshell of the Armory Show.[7] This famous exhibition held in the 69th Street Regiment Armory in New York in February and March 1913 gave the American public its first comprehensive view of pre-World War I European art. The initial public reaction was ridicule, but the impact was enormous. The New York showing included about 1,300 works; the American section included young and somewhat radical artists, but it was the comprehensive European section which aroused shock and indignation. Almost immediately plans were made to bring substantial portions of the exhibition to Chicago, though the director of the Art Institute, William M. R. French, evidently anticipated problems and diplomatically arranged to be on vacation when the show opened on March 24. The Chicago showing consisted of 634 works, including most of the more controversial pieces from the New York venue.

The Chicago reaction was intense. The Armory Show, more than any other single event, aroused interest in the new movements of twentieth-century art. It also created a new breed of collectors (more in New York than in Chicago) who laid the foundations of many of the great collections of early twentieth-century art.

It would be fascinating if we could see with Taft's eyes the paintings of Gauguin, Van Gogh, Kandinsky, Picabia, Picasso, Léger, Braque, and Duchamp, all of whom were included in the Armory Show, and many of which he must have been seeing for the first time. Even more important would be his reaction to the sculpture included in the exhibition by such artists as Matisse, Brancusi, Epstein, Lehmbruck, Picasso, and Archipenko. Taft was a voluminous and facile writer and published an enormous amount of newspaper and periodical criticism, but no specific discussion of the Armory Show has been found among his papers. In his Scammon lectures, however, delivered at the Art Institute in 1917, there are a number of remarks which must reflect specific reactions to some of the novel forms which he encountered there.

It was difficult for artists whose minds and spirits and technical processes had been formed in the late nineteenth century to accept or understand a later generation which rejected all of the standards in which they believed. As a student in Paris Taft considered the greatest contemporary sculptors to be Dubois, Falguière, and Mercié. He greatly admired two earlier sculptors, Rude and Carpeaux, and he eventually recognized the unique importance of Rodin, though he could not admire the more extreme examples of Rodin's style. But what was he to do with the postimpressionists, the cubists, and the futurists—the generation which in the years just before World War I in Paris turned away from all of the long-accepted standards? What was his view of modernism?

To Taft, the work he saw in Paris in the years before the war and in the 1913 Armory Show was the product of incompetent charletans. In his 1917 lectures he dismissed it and poked fun at it.[8] He even suggested that some of it may be the work of respectable artists who were exhibiting under assumed names some of the undisciplined aberrations which may be thoughtlessly created in the studio. He did not take it seriously and he could not believe that it was anything but hypocrisy on the part of the artists who produced it. When he showed his audience a reproduction of a recent statue by Matisse he remarked, "You can imagine the emotions of a wistful artist returning to the scene of these early loves to find them replaced by strange new gods like this foolish caricature of a woman. It is the work of the notorious painter Matisse. You see he is quite as good a sculptor as he is painter!"

Taft was particularly savage in his denunciation of the ill-fated Gaudier-Brzeska. He characterized him as a "deluded youth . . . who for mischief or through sheer imbecility . . . turned to this form of prostitution." Taft referred to his "infantile productions" and dismissed the far-famed *Mlle. Pogany* and a companion piece as "The Mislaid Egg." After quoting the fervid remarks of a contemporary enthusiast, he concluded: "In the presence of such mysteries of thought and diction we can but bow and reverently withdraw."

Lehmbruck's *Kneeling Woman* puzzled Taft because he could not deny its technical competence. "Another example of the lengths to which the up-to-date sculptors go is shown in a figure by Lehmbruck. It is not lacking in a certain kind of grace suggestive of Gothic decoration—but it is difficult to treat such work seriously even when it reveals, as here, the skill of a trained sculptor. Indeed such perversion of ability makes the crime unpardonable."

Taft was pleased to note that few Americans seemed to be influenced by the young Europeans who confused him. He said, "The excremental school makes no appeal to the average American." He suggested that it was perhaps the American sense of humor which lead them to reject it. He saw in American art "a dependable sanity most gratifying to meet amid the eccentricities and vagaries of current endeavor. . . . We do not expect to find a Carpeaux nor a Meštrović among us, but neither shall we add to the world's art horrors the misguided activity of a Matisse or an Archipenko. . . . Thus in place of a self-respecting art worthy of its ancient lineage, the Paris of yesterday—that is the Paris of immediately before the war—offered her visitors the puerile effronteries of these harlequins, delighting through their very ineptitude a public avid of new sensations. Unbridled realism and cleverness had run their course, and the jaded critics found refreshment in pretense of naïveté and in willful bungling."

He noted that it was possible that some of the new work might eventually be accepted by the public yet added, "But some of the old fogies are hoping to be dead before that day!" When he found himself unable to devise an adequate comment on another work he concluded, "Why attempt to characterize what obviously one does not understand?"

I myself heard him conclude one of his lectures by saying that after standing in front of a particularly puzzling work he backed away in order to get a more distant perspective of it. He kept backing away farther and farther until he found himself at the front door of the Institute—"and I just turned around and went home!"

The single most important event in the dissemination of modernism during Taft's later years was the 1933 Century of Progress Exposition. This was mounted for two summers during the depths of the Depression, which hit Chicago with devastating violence. Employment in the city's industries was cut in half, pay rolls declined almost seventy-five percent. Over 163 banks closed their doors. It is amazing that a great exposition which glorified the future and exploited in every possible way the uses of new materials and new techniques was successfully launched—and that it also was a remarkable triumph. Though the Depression continued, over thirty-nine million people visited the fair, and many of them must have been exposed for the first time to new architectural and decorative forms. The fair was a financial success and even ended up with a cash surplus.[9]

The basic physical character of the Century of Progress was achieved by a theater designer, Joseph Urban, who was called a "color engineer." The buildings used new materials such as processed concrete, asbestos board, and sheet metal, and they exploited color as never before. The Travel and Transport Building had walls of sheet metal that were bolted and clipped together. Its great dome, larger than that of St. Peter's, was suspended from a series of cables like those used in suspension bridges rather than being supported by walls or piers as all earlier domes had been. The chairman of the architectural commission stated: "The Fair stands as a symbol of the architecture of the future, the icons of the past cast aside, the ingenuity of the designers of the present thrown on their own resources to meet the problems of the day—strengthened only by the background of scientific engineering and inventive genius." How did painters and sculptors deal with the new forms with which they were faced?

Scant attention has been paid to the art of the 1933 fair. In contrast to the enormous bibliography that covers almost every possible aspect of the 1893 World's Columbian Exposition, there has been very little analysis of the stylistic accomplishments of the 1933 fair. I should like to call attention particularly to the use it made of sculpture.[10] Lee Lawrie was appointed director of sculpture and, in addition to his own work, major pieces were created by Ulric Ellerhusen, Leo Friedlander, Alfonso Iannelli, Raoul Josset, Gaston Lachaise, John Storrs, Louise Lentz Woodruff, and Lorado Taft. Taft was by far the oldest artist of this group, and the only sculptor of his generation who was given a major commission. Three of the sculptors mentioned had been his students.

Unlike the "White City," which was the 1893 World's Fair, the Century of Progress was a riot of color. By 1933 the availability of new materials and new techniques had created a new style which came to be known as Art Deco and which had perhaps first begun to define itself in the Exposition of Decorative Arts in Paris in 1925. Strong horizontal and vertical accents with sweeping streamlined curves determined most of the simplified decorative forms. The emphasis was linear, with a kind of machine-look about everything: geometric shapes; symmetry and repetition; sunburst patterns; flat surfaces with decoration an integral part of the wall surface; glittering, brash colors; and a deliberately impersonal quality which excluded the personal touch of the designer. Small utilitarian objects and major large-scale creations were sustained by a similar aesthetic. No clear distinction was made between the fine arts and industrial design.

The beaux-arts-inspired sculpture which Taft and his contemporaries had provided so successfully for the 1893 fair had been three-dimensional, full of movement, brilliant, aggressive, highly detailed, and individualistic, often almost overwhelming the architectural forms which supported and exhibited it. Sometimes it seemed to break away from the wall surfaces to claim an almost independent existence. All of these characteristics were avoided in 1933. Reliefs clung closely to the wall, indeed in some cases they appeared to have been excavated into the surface itself. Individual figures emerged organically from architectural elements. A new kind of architectural sculpture, defined by Lee Lawrie in his work for the Nebraska State Capitol in 1925, was obviously very much in mind as artists went to work for the 1933 buildings.[11]

The Electrical Building made extensive use of sculpture. Two enormous panels, both forty feet high, were on either side of the main entrance in the circular court. These were the work of Ulric Ellerhusen, who had been Taft's student at the School of the Art Institute. *Stellar Energy* was a soaring female figure surrounded by astronomical symbols. *Atomic Energy* was a huge male figure who forces his way through highly stylized earth forms (fig. 3.1). A kind of negative relief made these works an integral part of the wall surface. Long and imposing inscriptions were provided by Hartley Alexander, a philosopher who had published widely on mythology and symbolism. The two reliefs were green and therefore contrasted with the vermillion and black walls.

To the left is Lee Lawrie's *Water Gate*—two extraordinary pylons with a complicated symbolic program, yellow figures against a red background (fig. 3.2). One figure is dedicated to Light, the other to Sound. A huge sphynx (The Unknowable) at the base is surmounted by a stylized serpent (Wisdom) with three figures above it. On the side of Light are the sun, moon, and man-made light; on the side of Sound are thunder, music, and the telephone. On a higher level are abstract, angular figures of the two elements hurtling through space. A contemporary critic characterized them as "modern but [with] an Aztec leaning." Certainly no academic work of an earlier generation could have been more explicit in content, and it was characteristic of fair decorations as a whole that they convey understandably and appropriately symbolic meaning.

The entrance wall of Communications Hall in the electrical group was decorated with an enormous relief by Gaston Lachaise titled *The Conquest of Time and Space*. Its elaborate program had also been created by Hartley Alexander. At the base a crowded humanity marched toward positive and negative poles. In the huge space above were a generator, a searchlight, a telescope, a telegraph, and telephone wires, and finally the gigantic figure of Human Genius with outstretched arms. Narrow reliefs on either side depict Science revealing itself to Man and the Course of Time through the Ages.

Three very different sculptural silhouettes by Raoul Josset adorned the Agriculture Building, but they are equally explicit in content. They depict three aspects of agriculture: primitive manual labor, the use of animal power, and the mechanization of agricultural labor.

At the end of the Avenue of Flags, that is to say at the main

ENERGY
THE SUBSTANCE OF ALL THING
THE CYCLES OF THE ATOMS THE PLAY OF THE ELEMENTS ARE ITS FORM
AS BY A MIGHTY HAND TO BECOME THE WORLD'S FOUNDATION

3.1 Ulrich Ellerhusen, *Atomic Energy,* sculpture (medium unknown) 1933, Century of Progress, Electrical Building. Photograph taken from Jewett E. Ricker, ed., *Sculpture at A Century of Progress, 1933, 1934,* p. 14.

3.2 Lee Lawrie, *The Water Gate,* sculpture (medium unknown), 1933, Century of Progress, Electrical Building. Photograph taken from Jewett E. Ricker, ed., *Sculpture at A Century of Progress 1933, 1934,* p. 17.

entrance of the fair, was John Storrs's *Knowledge Combatting Igno-rance* (fig. 3.3). Storrs was born in Chicago and had been a student of Taft's. He had lived for many years in Europe and was fully aware of the newest Parisian art movements. In the 1920s he was the first American artist to make completely nonobjective forms. The two huge white figures against a brilliant blue background suggested a neo-archiac Heracles and the Hydra. The repeated vertical panels and the scalloped border were characteristic Art Deco patterns.

The crowning figures on the large fountain in front of the Hall of Science represented *Science Advancing Mankind* and were the work of Louise Lentz Woodruff, who had also worked with Taft. This extraordinary composition depicted two somewhat naturalistic figures, one male and one female, overshadowed and controlled by a gigantic robot. Symbolism in 1933 was nothing if not obvious! This is one of the few Century of Progress works which still exists. At the conclusion of the fair it was presented by the sculptor to Joliet Township High School, where it can still be seen. The robot was named "Steelman" by the students.[12]

The Social Science Building contained two different decorative elements. Alfonso Iannelli, a decorative jack-of-all-trades, produced a series of panels illuminated with blue neon tubes which combined with the jet blacks, silvers, and blues of the panels themselves to bring out the essential qualities of radio. The broad central panel presented classical music on one side, jazz on the other. The narrower panels to left and right presented X-ray, television, the dissemination of intelligence, and the SOS signal. The horizontal panels represented electromagnetic waves. The north bridge entrance of the building was dominated by four soaring pylons, each sixty feet high, which surmounted groups of four figures by Leo Friedlander. These were also loaded with appropriate symbolic references. To the left was the God of Fire, followed by the God of Light, then a female who symbolized the solar system, and finally the God of Storm. Though they were rendered in relief, the figures appeared more three-dimensional than most of the sculpture of the fair.

The United States Government building had three pylons supporting a dome; they symbolized the three branches of government. The building's sculptural decoration consisted of three twenty-foot-high figures which seem to emerge organically out of the architecture. These figures were executed by three different sculptors but in such a similar style that the artists must have collaborated in the overall composition. The Executive Branch figure was designed by Raoul Josset. A severe, archaic-looking figure was given the physiognomy of George Washington. The figure's highly simplified drapery resembles a column. The Legislative Branch was designed by John Storrs. It represented an equally austere figure who holds a tablet in one hand and rests the other hand on a vertical architectural element. The Judicial Branch was the work of Lorado Taft. A female figure

3.3 John Storrs, *Knowledge Combatting Ignorance*, sculpture (medium unknown), 1933, Century of Progress, Avenue of Flags. Photograph taken from Jewett E. Ricker, ed., *Sculpture at A Century of Progress, 1933, 1934*, p. 14.

holds the scales of justice and is supported by the classical fasces. It would be interesting to know how these three sculptors managed to remove any trace of individual style so as to achieve a common, almost anonymous quality. It also would be interesting to know how Taft adjusted to new situations. He was a full generation older than all the other World's Fair sculptors. In his work here, he discarded not only every trace of his beaux-arts background, but also the broad fluency of his own style.

There are at least four other works by Taft from his final years, which exhibit the same rather unexpected rejection of the beaux-arts manner upon which his personal style had been founded. Two years before the Century of Progress Fair Taft's black granite figure entitled *The Crusader* was erected in Graceland Cemetery in Chicago on the grave of Victor Lawson, the editor of the *Daily News* (fig. 3.4). The vision of an armored medieval knight with a prominent shield and sword had haunted Taft for years. He used it in a number of compositions—some achieved final form, others never reached beyond the study stage. Here a new emphasis was placed on sheer mass, which was not apparent in his earlier works, in which the fluency resulted from the modeling of the clay. Of course, the original was modeled in clay, but Taft scrupulously avoided any trace of the artist's personal handling so that a uniformly smooth surface resulted. Realistic details were omitted in order to allow the essential stone mass to speak for itself. At seventy-two, Taft had entered his final artistic phase, which understandably showed considerable changes from his earlier work.

In the years just before the 1933 fair, Taft was working on what was to be his last big public monument, the new state capitol in Baton Rouge, Louisiana. Taft, along with Lee Lawrie, Ulric Ellerhusen, and Adolph Weinman, was commissioned to work on this project, which was carried out in a modified classical style. Taft's work consisted of two large groups of figures on each side of the main entrance, the *Pioneers* on one side, the *Patriots* on the other. In each, a colossal central figure towers above a group of smaller figures. The theme of a medieval knight in armor appears in the *Patriot* group. The works were created with great difficulty and can hardly be considered successful. Taft was working under great pressure and was hospitalized for several weeks during a crucial stage in the preparation of the models. The carving was done hastily and with less than adequate skill. Moreover, the compositions were simply reworked from a number of earlier projects, and the sculptor's enthusiasm seems to have waned. Taft himself was disappointed with the final results.

Another piece by Taft for the 1933 fair has been almost completely forgotten. It is a large relief, fourteen feet high, made for the Hall of Religions. Entitled *Come Unto Me,* the composition was in no way Taft's own (fig. 3.5). He was commissioned to

3.4 Lorado Taft, *The Crusader*, black granite sculpture, 1931, Graceland Cemetery, Chicago. Photograph from the Lorado Taft Papers, Record Series 26/20/16, University of Illinois Archives.

3.5 Lorado Taft, *Come Unto Me*, sculpture (plaster with ivory finish), 1933, North Shore Baptist Church, Chicago. Photograph taken from undated pamphlet published by the North Shore Baptist Church, Chicago.

make a sculptural copy of a little-known painting in Copenhagen by the nineteenth-century Danish artist, Karl Heinrich Bloch. Taft's earliest full-scale figure in the 1880s had also been a copy after the work of another artist. It was only now in old age and for probably purely financial reasons that he agreed to translate the composition of a painting into low relief. Photographs of Bloch's painting suggest that Taft's copy is far more interesting than the original. In very low relief, the plaster is finished with an ivory-like surface with a gold background. Few people would recognize it as Taft's work; it has never been properly cited and remains almost unknown. At the conclusion of the 1933 fair the relief was purchased for the North Shore Baptist Church where it is impressively installed and dramatically illuminated in the chancel. It has the same kind of uniform, simplified surface as the grave monument *The Crusader*.[13]

A public monument of another kind was proposed but never realized in the 1930s. Taft was asked to prepare studies for a series of decorative reliefs to be used on the Hoover Dam, the vast engineering structure being built on the Colorado River. He made studies for two of a projected series of panels which introduced the official coats of arms of the states involved with or affected by the great dam. In one, a stylized American eagle surmounts two shield-like emblems. These were to be executed in a style very much like that of the decorative sculpture at the fair with smooth surfaces and simplified details.

The most interesting of the late Taft works also was never realized in permanent form. In 1930 the Society of Medalists began commissioning and distributing a series of medals twice a year. Almost all of the more conservative American sculptors eventually were asked to create a medal for this purpose. In 1935 Taft was asked to design such a medal, the subject to be chosen by the artist but approved by an advisory committee. Taft chose the subject of peace but treated it in a powerful, unconventional fashion. On the obverse side, a monumental seated figure in voluminous, ecclesiastical-looking garments holds laurel wreaths over the heads of two young helmeted soldiers who have almost identical faces. The central figure has a death's head and is decorated with a large cross on its chest. The two young men each hold pistols against each other's heads, while two aged men behind them urge them on. Above this troubling group an inscription reads "On Earth Peace Good Will Toward Men," while at the base the inscription says "Dulce et decorum est pro patria mori." A powerful composition on the reverse side shows the back of a spectral, hooded figure who stands silently and gazes out over unending rows of graves marked with crosses; the whole medal inscribed "Christianity in the Twentieth Century of our Lord" (figs. 3.6 and 3.7).

This Peace Medal presented problems to the Society of Medalists. Certainly it represents the greatest possible contrast to the conventional Civil War monuments which Taft had produced in the 1890s, to glorify warfare as the ultimate expression of patriotism. Perhaps it is the use of the cross on the death's-head figure which disturbed the Society most. Taft preserved among his papers a lengthy exchange of correspondence with the Society,

3.6 Lorado Taft, *Peace Medal I*, obverse, plaster model (designed for bronze but never cast), 1935. Lorado Taft Papers, Record Series 26/20/16, University of Illinois Archives.

3.7 Lorado Taft, *Peace Medal II*, reverse, plaster model (designed for bronze but never cast), 1935. Lorado Taft Papers, Record Series 26/20/16, University of Illinois Archives.

which revealed that it found his unexpectedly grim piece controversial. The Society requested that he submit an alternative design. Taft reluctantly did so. He submitted another medal which simply reproduced in reduced scale the composition of the *Great Lakes*, with an idealized head of one of the graceful figures on its reverse. Taft's peace medal was never cast and exists now only in photographic form.[14]

The last work which Taft completed was the Lincoln-Douglas Debate relief for the city of Quincy, Illinois. The sculptor attended the dedication of the relief—which was erected on the spot where the actual debate took place—just two weeks before his own death. It is a competent but rather pedestrian production that evidences many of the conventional and conservative qualities of the beaux-arts tradition.

When he died in 1936 at age seventy-six, Taft had already completed the small-scale model of a monument to George Washington with his contemporaries Robert Morris and Haym Solomon, two wealthy businessmen who in part financed the Revolutionary War. After Taft's death, three of his pupils and associates, Nellie Walker, Mary Webster, and Leonard Crunelle, modeled the full-scale figures and supervised their fabrication. The monument was dedicated in 1941 on Wacker Drive. It represents a return to realistic historicism but is handled broadly with appropriate dignity. Taft had always been able to fill large public places impressively.

Taft presents an interesting case of an artist who during the greater part of his career considered himself and was generally considered to be in the mainstream of contemporary art in Chicago. He suddenly found himself unsympathetic to new artistic movements, while he also discovered that his work was being rejected by his younger contemporaries. Almost in spite of himself, he was influenced—at least briefly in the 1930s—by some of the new movements championed by those contemporaries. Indeed he was a bridge, though an unwilling one, between the full flower of the beaux-arts tradition of the 1893 World's Columbian Exposition and the new and very different art world of the 1930s.

CHAPTER FOUR

Modernism and Chicago Art: 1910–1940

SUSAN S. WEININGER

In 1932, J. Z. Jacobson, who must have assumed that one can never be too avant-garde, published a compendium of important contemporary artists, *Art of Today: Chicago, 1933.* It is a collection of over fifty artists' statements and biographies that includes "all but a very few of the modern artists of consequence who are at present living and working in Chicago."[1] Ranging from the familiar and well-known Ivan Albright to the long-forgotten Murvin Willis Gilbert and Romolo Roberti, the book covers as wide a range of stylistic approaches as it does artists. Attempting to understand what Jacobson meant by "modern art" offers us a clue as to what this term referred to in the second, third, and fourth decades of twentieth-century Chicago.

According to Jacobson, "any artist who is genuinely alive, sincere and competent will of inner necessity produce modern art."[2] In 1912, the Russian-born artist Wassily Kandinsky had explained the formal diversity of art work in the *Blue Rider Almanac (Der Blaue Reiter Almanach)* in a similar way: "The most important thing in the question of form is whether or not the form has grown out of inner necessity."[3] To both Kandinsky and Jacobson any art form emerging from an "authentic" internal experience was valid.

Many of the beliefs of Kandinsky and Franz Marc, co-editor of the *Almanac*, were shared by artists working in Chicago in the early twentieth century. In the subscription prospectus to the *Almanac*, Marc described the interconnectedness of the book's contents, which included examples of modern French, German, and Russian painting, Gothic and primitive art, African and Asian art, folk and children's art, recent musical movements in Europe, and new ideas in theater.[4] In the minds of the editors, all of this work was free from the perceived superficiality and crass materialism of post-Renaissance western civilization. This freedom is what allowed artists to tap into authentic experience—what we might describe as their getting in touch with their feelings—and to use that experience as the basis for their creations. In the same way that the *Blue Rider Almanac* recognized the value and expressiveness of various non-western or pre-Renaissance traditions, early modernist artists in Chicago regarded the traditions of the American Indians or of their own ethnic roots as suitable catalysts for artistic creation.

Another important attitude shared by artists in Chicago was a vision of modern America as something unique and positive. Americanism, like modernism, placed a value on individualism and freedom, and the American experience was beginning to be seen as different from, and independent of, European models. Thus, the kind of authentic experience important to Kandinsky and Marc could also be found in the new American city, viewed either as a melting pot of individual ethnic groups or an infinitely hopeful creation of the modern machine. Unlike the bourgeois European city of the past, the American city provided a release from drudgery and material needs and thus offered an opportunity to realize spiritual freedom. Chicago artists also believed that the modern artist was a savior of the world—another parallel to the ideas of Kandinsky and Marc. The artist was often seen in the guise of a prophet, a martyr, or a god; art was understood as a means to spiritual reawakening and salvation.

All these ideas and attitudes, shared by Chicago artists with their European counterparts, account for Jacobson's legitimation of the "various tendencies within the wide province of modern art."[5] In Chicago, this included late-nineteenth-century derivations, amalgams of numerous early-twentieth-century European movements, and pure abstraction.[6]

It should come as no surprise that the exemplars of modernism in the second decade of the twentieth century in Chicago were few and isolated. The brief career of Manierre Dawson, born in Chicago in 1887, evidences the difficulties faced by a truly innovative artist working in a completely modern manner in the early part of the century. Despite an early and abiding interest in the visual arts, Dawson first studied civil engineering at Armour Institute of Technology (now Illinois Institute of Technology) in deference to his parents; he earned his degree in 1909. He began painting as early as 1903–4 and taught himself all the mechanics. By 1908 he had begun "blocking things out without rhyme or reason other than to make the pictures look *right*."[7] He already articulated an attitude that was wholly modernist and manifested it in his *Still Life* of 1910. Later the same year, a six-month sojourn in Europe allowed him to experience the architecture, sculpture, and painting of the past, which inspired modernist works like *Lucrèce* of 1911 (plate 5), a bold transformation of Corregio's *Danaë* as Mary Gedo has shown.[8]

In Paris Dawson visited Gertrude Stein who purchased the first work he ever sold. He also visited Vollard's gallery where he saw the work of Cézanne. No matter what modern art Dawson saw in Paris, however, he was already developing a non-objective style independent of European models.

Arthur Davies asked Dawson to contribute to the Armory Show. While he was unable to exhibit in the New York venue, he did manage to show one work in the exhibition when it came to Chicago. He felt buoyed and encouraged by the other artists working in a manner similar to the one he developed in isolation. He wrote in his journal on March 27, 1913: "I am feeling elated. I had thought of myself as an anomaly and had to defend myself, many times, as not crazy; and here at the Art Institute many artists are presented showing these very fanciful departures from the academies."[9] Perhaps reassurance from the outside world gave him the courage to quit his job with the architectural firm of Holabird and Roche to devote himself to his painting. He exhibited several times in 1914, the year he decided to become a fruit farmer on family property in Ludington, Michigan. He hoped the move would offer a regular income as well as time to paint. The increasing demands of a family and a farm made it more and more difficult for him to produce paintings. He continued to paint until his death in 1969 but had a considerably smaller output than when he lived in Chicago; he did not exhibit often and ultimately had little permanent effect on the city's modernists. Dawson's ideas, however, were shared by other early Chicago artists. In the catalog for an *Exhibition of Painting and Sculpture in "The Modern Spirit"* held in Milwaukee in 1914, Dawson explained that

> to reach the emotions most completely through the eyes one must present the aesthetic optics of a thought or appearance rather than its mere physical form . . . the greatest mystery to humanity is itself, and the greatest interest in humanity is itself. So it is that [the] painting which most accurately translates something of the human spirit is the painting which will tell most.[10]

Dawson, like many Chicago artists to come, was interested in communicating spiritual truths directly through pure visual form.

While Chicagoans were being introduced to visual examples of European and European-derived modernism, the theoretical underpinnings of the movement were beginning to appear. Arthur Jerome Eddy's *Cubists and Post-Impressionism* was published in Chicago in 1914, asserting that "the keynote of the modern movement in art is *expression of self;* . . . that is, the expression of one's inner self as distinguished from the representation of the outer world."[11] A great admirer of Kandinsky, Eddy also discussed *Über das Geistige in der Kunst (Concerning the Spiritual in Art)* before its English translation appeared in America. Literary magazines of great importance to all the arts because of their modernist positions emerged in Chicago. Harriet Monroe's *Poetry—A Magazine of Verse* was published for the first time in 1912 but elicited only laughter from the eastern establishment. Assuming that a down-to-earth meat-packing capital could not generate or support such refined activity, for example, an editorial in a Philadelphia newspaper dubbed Monroe's venture "Poetry in Porkopolis."[12] Margaret Anderson's *The Little Review* commenced publication in Chicago in 1914, taking a position in favor of freedom of expression, spontaneity, and the value of the individual.[13] Architect Louis Sullivan was expressing similar ideas about freedom and the importance of individual expression, particularly in a democracy.[14]

The post-war period was a time of worldwide optimism. Many intellectuals were certain that a renaissance was coming, particularly in the United States, which emerged strong and prosperous after the war. In 1920, critic H. L. Mencken predicted that the rebirth of literature would begin in Chicago.[15]

The literary renaissance that did begin in Chicago in the second decade of the twentieth century was part of a more general cultural ferment. The support for it came from an alliance of visual artists and creative artists in other fields who shared an attitude toward artistic creation whether it be in poetry or stage design. The interaction of artists, writers, and performers was important in the cross-fertilization and support of the arts in Chicago. Harriet Monroe, who wrote art criticism for the *Chicago Daily Tribune,* treated modernism in art with as much fairness as possible. She supported the work of Jerome Blum, shown at the Thurber Gallery in 1912 (plate 6). Also, prior to the opening of the Armory Show in Chicago, she tried to prepare Chicago audiences by introducing them to European theories of modernism, like those of Clive Bell.[16] Although she admitted to Manierre Dawson that nothing she saw at the Armory Show impressed her, she supported freedom of expression, respecting the rights of each individual.[17] B. J. O. Nordfeldt, whose early modernist work in Chicago has been discussed thoroughly by Paul Kruty,[18] was connected with the literary and theatrical community, many of whom he memorialized in portraits, like those of artist Katherine Dudley and actress Elaine Hyman. He designed sets for the Little Theatre, a modernist dramatic group that paralleled *The Little Review,* as did his student Raymond Jonson, who devised stunning stage designs for their productions from 1913 until the Theatre's demise in 1918.[19]

Jonson arrived in Chicago in 1910 after an itinerent midwestern childhood which culminated in training at the Portland, Oregon, Art Museum School, where he probably became familiar with Arthur Wesley Dow's theories of abstract pictorial design.

When he came to Chicago, he enrolled in classes at the Academy of Art and the School of the Art Institute. His experience with modernist art in Chicago, which included his friendship with Nordfeldt and the opportunity to design for the Theatre (plate 7), supported his desire to "create the spirit of emotion that is felt."[20] Although his early Chicago paintings, like *Field Museum* of 1912, are reminiscent of impressionism, he developed a style characterized by flat, decorative color areas and attention to light as an expressive device. Jonson's portraits of *Miriam Kiper* (1919; plate 8), and of his wife Vera (in a 1918 painting called *Violet Light*), both of whom were actresses in the Little Theatre, or that of Miriam Marmein in her dance, "Evil," indicate his connection with those involved in other kinds of artistic endeavors.

In 1921, Jonson first exhibited his painting *Life* (plate 9) at the "Salon des Refusés," which he helped organize that year. Before Jonson completed the painting, he read Kandinsky's *The Art of Spiritual Harmony* (the British translation of what would be known in America as *Concerning the Spiritual in Art*). Jonson considered it "the greatest book concerning art I have ever read" and believed "we must sooner or later know him to be right, at least in theory—and that is the point, theory."[21] He described *Life* in his diary as a picture of "good and evil emerging from the same source—the earth, typified by the pool of blood," but he qualified that "good is always threatened by evil." More importantly, he wrote:

> The evil things stands [*sic*] as a barrier to vision. The great joy, the mystery, that which makes life possible, the dark mass, seeping through in a glorious shaft of color and radiance. It is the complement of life. . . . The idea of life, the great thoughts, and hopes, and faiths being forever mocked at, abused and handicapped and finally poisoned by the materialistic, the darkness, the first tempter on earth—the serpent.[22]

A later entry explained that he had "tried to build a composition that gives the sense of movement, struggle, light and therefore, life, not by the objects used so much as by the arrangement and range of forms and colors."[23] The Symbolist style and the literary explanation of the work belie to some extent Jonson's assertions regarding direct communication through formal configuration. But life as a struggle of spirit over matter was a constant and recurring theme in this period; the artist was seen variously as the prophet who heralds the coming of a spiritual rebirth, the God who creates it, or the martyr to the materialism which is the natural enemy of Jonson's "great thoughts, and hopes, and faiths." Like Jerome Blum, Nordfeldt, Dawson, and many other artists, Jonson left Chicago for good. In 1924, he moved to New Mexico, a place he felt would be more hospitable and perhaps more inspiring to him as an artist.

In 1913 an eighteen-year-old Polish immigrant arrived in Chicago and galvanized the city's art world. Stanislaus Szukalski, "painter, sculptor, architect, [and] philosopher,"[24] took Chicago by storm. During the ten years he spent in Chicago, he expressed in words and actions as well as images the concepts that enabled modernism to take root and grow in the city. Contemporary reports described Szukalski as a character whose life embodied many of the ideas expressed in *The Work of Szukalski*, a 1923 publication of his parables along with illustrations of his work.[25] Despite his desire for honesty, sincerity, freshness, and innocence as well as his disdain for posturing, he was the ultimate *poseur*, "who wore his thick black hair bobbed like a girl's, crowned . . . with a left-bankish tam."[26] He was noticed almost immediately after his arrival at the School of the Art Institute and was honored in 1916 and again in 1917 with one-man shows at the Art Institute.[27] In 1917, Szukalski tore his works from the walls after his drawing *Man and His Brother* (fig. 4.1), was barred because of its anti-English political sentiment. One newspaper account described him standing in the debris of his work announcing "either they shall show all my drawings or none."[28] One year earlier, he publicly destroyed an honorable mention awarded to him at the Annual Exhibition of American Painting and Sculpture, "because he did not regard the trustees of the Institute capable of judging his work sufficiently to give awards."[29]

These well-publicized events give us a picture of Szukalski that he himself created. They also convey the idea of the primacy of the individual over the institution. Proclaiming himself his own teacher, he described his four years in the Kracow Academy of Art as an experience of "obedien[ce] only to my insistent nonconformity, suspicious of advice of authority . . . work[ing] from my imagination."[30] He dropped out of the School of the Art Institute because "they had nothing to teach him."[31] In Szukalski's view, training was actually destructive to the artist. The content of his work was idiosyncratic but highly literary. His precise and elegant draughtsmanship must be credited to the academic training he received, though he would have denied this claim emphatically. According to Szukalski, discovering what was true within oneself was the key to becoming an artist; a student should not be shown "the masterpieces of the past until he himself is able to create his own primitives, and you will oblige him to invent a new, worthy, native art."[32]

The conviction that technique was far less important than honest and sincere expression was the same attitude that Jacobson expressed in 1932. The concomitant idea that primitive, non-European, or pre-Renaissance European art was sincere and authentic, because it was unencumbered by the academic restrictions which stifled spontaneity and individuality were again similar to those expressed by Kandinsky.[33] Looking to childlike or naive perceptions as the source for creation was im-

Susan S. Weininger

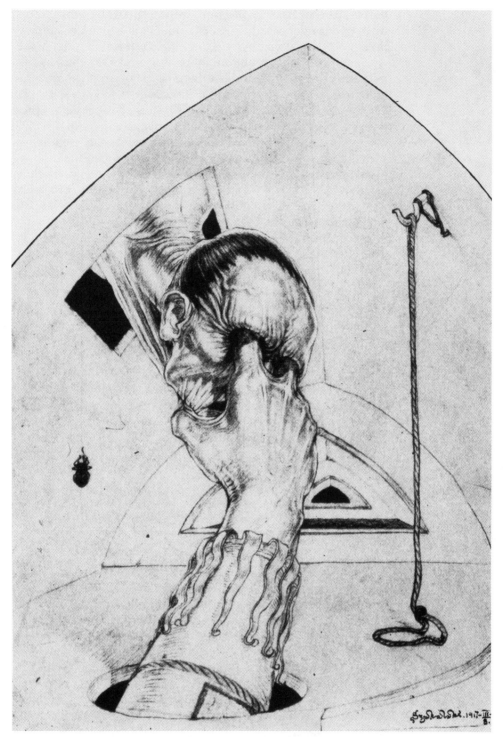

4.1 Stanislaus Szukalski, *Man and His Brother,* drawing (medium unknown), n.d. (destroyed). Photograph taken from *The Work of Szukalski* (Chicago: Covici-McGee 1923). © 1989 The Art Institute of Chicago. All Rights Reserved.

portant to Szukalski. In addition, he proclaimed his ethnic roots with great pride, asserting that "I am a Pole—that fact summarizes most of my 'biography.'"[34] In an interview published in the Art Institute student publication in 1916, Szukalski emphasized in broken English the simple origins of his desire to become an artist: "In [sic] the age of eight I carved out of soft stone images of animals, birds and figures. Those things I gave to girls. From the very beginning I like girls; that explains why I am a sculptor."[35] The deliberate naïveté of such statements seemed to ensure the sincerity of his art. Finding one's own spirituality connected one to the primitive soul of the world, and gave one the wisdom to create art, whether it was poetry, painting, or music. That art, no matter what its form, would then communicate directly with the audience.

In Szukalski's second book, *Projects in Design*, published in Chicago in 1929, he articulated his ideas about the relationship of art and society:

> When the arts are virile and creative, they aid materially in the making of a new civilization—a new culture, but when the institutions of this civilization find it necessary to be loyal to traditions only, and foreign traditions at that, then hardening of the arteries begins.[36]

The ideal sought by the traditionalists and their commercial supporters carried seeds of its own destruction, as the 1917 print *Flower of Dreams* (plate 10), accompanied by Szukalski's lengthy and turgid commentary, made clear:

> An idealist in his loneliness puts his head into the vise which holds him in place, while the roots of his flower ideal enter his brain and devour his blood. . . . The stem of this curious flower anxiously gives out its bloom. This is the laboratory of the idealist. The bubble of blood in the blossom is a transbirth of this hapless love.[37]

The idealist and all adherents to doctrine, as his works *Prisoner of Conviction* and *Man and his Conscience* indicate, were doomed to turn in on themselves in their backward-looking idealism. For Szukalski, idealism was the search for perfection based on tradition and rules that were characteristic of the academic attitudes of cultural institutions like the Art Institute.

Szukalski's impact was profound. While his artistic style did not influence anyone, his personality gave others support for their rebelliousness. His codification and elaboration of ideas, some of which were already in the air, acted as a powerful catalyst in Chicago's art world. The idea that the artist has the power to create a new civilization by following no authority, but instead relying only on himself with the guidance of the authentic expressions found in primitive art, enjoyed great currency in this period.

In 1919, Szukalski made a drawing of his artist friend Rudolph Weisenborn (fig. 4.2). Despite Szukalski's vehement insistence on originality, the penetrating characterization of Weisenborn, enhanced by the bold asymmetrical placement of the head, is characteristic of the sitter's own highly individualistic style as evidenced in a drawing of *Clarence Darrow* (fig. 4.3) exhibited in the 1923 Chicago No-Jury Society of Artists show.[38] Weisenborn is represented by Szukalski as a monk, the spiritual ascetic of his era, and a missionary who ultimately spreads Szukalski's ideas. Religious imagery in art became popular in the twenties as a way of declaring the parallel between the artist and the Christian martyr, both guardians and prosyletizers of spiritual truth. Art could act in the way religion did to affirm life and offer salvation from the corrupt, material world.

Weisenborn, who was orphaned at nine, lived in various midwestern locations before settling in Colorado where he eventually enrolled in the Students' School of Art and paid his tuition with money earned working as a janitor. He learned to paint in an academic manner, which is evidenced in his self-portrait of 1903; we know he was very proud that this work suggested Rembrandt's style. He arrived in Chicago in 1913 wearing six-shooters and a Stetson hat.[39] Weisenborn became a central figure in a movement which resulted in the organization of a series of artists' groups in Chicago that were characterized by their anti-institutional attitude. A statement in the catalog of the 1921 "Salon des Refusés" exhibition undoubtedly expresses Weisenborn's point of view about the function of art in its assertion that "the 'radicals' of art [the participants in the show] . . . are . . . stimulating to a development in art that will rival the scientific and commercial strides made by our country."[40] This statement is explicit about the role of the artist and the function of art in postwar America. Art, like science and commerce, is an expression of the modern world, the world of today rather than some yearned-for ideal of an imaginary past. Like technology and industry, art could lift the country out of the devastation of war into a new era. The transformative power of art, its emphasis on the spiritual values which struggle to emerge in a material world, make it even more important than other signifiers of progress.

It is in the work of Weisenborn, an artist who spent the majority of his adult life in Chicago, that we see the emergence of a true Chicago modernism. Although an unfortunate fire in his studio in 1922 destroyed much of his early work, he continued to produce large-scale portrait heads like that of Clarence Darrow in the early twenties. His portraits of poet Mark Turbyfill and Annie Glick (subtitled *Structural Steel*) manifest the variant on cubism that evolved in his work.[41] While lacking the intellectual rigor of the European style, they have a forceful, dynamic vigor that conveys a tense and unyielding energy resonating with the life of the modern city.

4.2 Stanislaus Szukalski, *Rudolph Weisenborn*, charcoal on paper, 1919. Courtesy, Michael Lowe Gallery, Cincinnati.

4.3 Rudolph Weisenborn, *Portrait of Clarence Darrow,* charcoal on paper, 1923. Courtesy, Gilman/Gruen Galleries, Chicago.

The 1930 painting *Convex Space* (plate 11) combines a series of muscular nudes expressionistically depicted in an angular, faceted style characteristic of his portraits and a view of highrise buildings, a truck on a highway, and factory chimneys in the distance. Precisionists, like Charles Sheeler, were representing the American city and industrial development in a cubist-derived mode; Weisenborn's work, however, combined references (not appropriations) to cubism, expressionism, and even fauvism, and represented a unique marriage of the modernist formal vocabulary with a contemporary Chicago subject. In *The Blue Tree* of 1926 (plate 12), Weisenborn depicts a landscape dominated by a tree that, in the words of his wife, "is rigid and tense, a tree that you react to as you would a steel bridge, a figure that gives you a feeling of a steel monument, Steel Modernism. We are howling for the expression of steel thru [sic] the artist."[42] Even nature is transformed by the artist into an element of the great vitality of the new age.

Weisenborn was described as a visionary by Sam Putnam, a contemporary critic who championed modernism.[43] This is consistent with the image such artists had of themselves. Weisenborn took it one step further when he made the analogy between the non-objective artist and "a God that is compelled to create a new world in each creation [work of art]."[44] The Chicago No-Jury Society of Artists, formed in 1922 under the leadership of Weisenborn, Raymond Jonson, Carl Hoeckner, and Ramon Shiva, made it possible for any artist who paid the small membership fee to exhibit publicly. A statement in the catalog of the second annual show in 1923 expresses the motivational idea behind the group, that "freedom from juries gives the artist liberty to develop individual ideas."[45] The cover of the catalog, with its flat, decorative design featuring a "primitive" figure, was designed by Emil Armin (see fig. 5.3); the figure was used for the first time in the second exhibition catalog and became the No-Jury emblem.

Armin, a Rumanian Jew who immigrated to the United States in 1905, took evening classes at the Art Institute while working at various menial jobs to finance his education; he finally graduated in 1920 at the age of thirty-seven.[46] An artist who consciously tried to forget the training he had so dearly paid for, Armin sought the sincere expression of "what [was] in him"[47] through a conscious return to simplified, childlike forms. He made the first of numerous trips to New Mexico, the destination of many American artists seeking connection with native American roots, in 1928. This locale and its people inspired many of Armin's works, like *Mountain Farm, Santa Fe* (1928) (fig. 4.4) and *Indian Corn Dance* (ca. 1929). Armin drew upon these experiences, as well as his Jewish upbringing (*Seder Night*) and Rumanian peasant origins, as a source for the rich variety of sincere and honest images he was to create. This naïveté did not preclude images of the city, however, which were executed in the same energetic and directly expressive style as images with more primitive subject matter.

Perhaps the most original images of the city produced in Chicago were done by Ramon Shiva, a fascinating and accomplished artist who is better known as the developer and manufacturer of Shiva Artists Oil Colors. Shiva, born in Santander, Spain, in 1893, claimed he had lived in France, Italy, Austria, Greece, Turkey, the West Indies, and Panama before settling in Chicago in about 1912.[48] Trained as a chemist, he worked for the Edwards and Deutsch Lithograph Company, gradually developing the formula for his own oil colors. His painting was done in the evening and on weekends. Although he spent three years at the School of the Art Institute, he never graduated. He was actively associated with some of Chicago's independent artists' groups like the No-Jury Society, Cor Ardens, and The Ten.[49]

Shiva's *Chicago MCMXXIV* (1924; plate 13) was exhibited in the third Chicago No-Jury Society of Artists exhibition. It is an industrial scene dominated by brilliant shades of pink, purple, and deep blue and embodies the sensitivity to color that was Shiva's main interest. What is remarkable about Shiva's presentation of the midwestern industrial landscape—with its low fac-

4.4 Emil Armin, *Mountain Farm, Santa Fe*, woodcut, 1928. Gift of Joseph R. Shapiro, 1956.578. © 1989 The Art Institute of Chicago. All Rights Reserved.

tory buildings set against a background of huge chimneys, storage towers, and tanks, and all linked by a pattern of swirling smoke—is its combination of power, energy, and sheer sensual beauty. The rich, dense application of paint and the sumptuous color elevate the industrial landscape to the equivalent of the nineteenth-century Romantic landscapes of Constable and Turner. Shiva shows us the infinite possibility and beauty of a new America rooted in the midwest. His work marries the pristine precisionist industrial landscape with expressive color to create a unique expression of not only the potent energy of America but also its spiritual possibility.

Shiva shared the attitudes of other Chicago modernists. He described himself as a rebel and viewed art as something that derived from the inner being of the artist:

> No, I do not believe in art museums, and I certainly
> do not believe in art schools, though I have studied in

them. I do not believe there should be any art schools. Teach art? How silly! Art does not come from without but from within, from the inside of the artist. How, then, are you going to "teach" art? How are you going to put something on the inside of a painter when there is nothing there to begin with?[50]

Like his fellow artists, Shiva believed that art schools were unnecessary if not actually detrimental. Who the artist was rather than what he knew was the most important determinant of good art.

The range of style in the No-Jury exhibitions was enormous but all of the artists who participated were considered modernist. For example, a regular contributor to these exhibitions was Anthony Angarola, referred to by critic C. J. Bulliet as one of Chicago's "radicals" in a biographical sketch published in 1936.[51] Largely forgotten because of his premature death in 1929 at the age of thirty-six, Angarola is another modernist whose life and work are crucial to our understanding of Chicago modernism.

Born in Chicago in 1893, Angarola graduated from the School of the Art Institute in 1917, having already won a student prize for six paintings displayed in the Art Students League Exhibition the previous year.[52] His family refused to support his aspiration to become an artist so he worked during the day to finance his evening classes at the Art Institute; it took him nine years to finish his education. Like most of the artists whose work we have looked at, art was a struggle; Angarola was poor for most of his life and sold few paintings. While associated with the "radicals" from the beginning of his career, exhibiting with the Introspectives, in the "Salon des Refusés" of 1921, and in numerous No-Jury shows, "such was the good nature of this soft-tongued, rather timid grandson of Italy," according to Bulliet, "that he escaped the brunt of the broils."[53]

The work of Arthur Davies, which Angarola saw at the Art Institute in 1917, impressed him profoundly. He related his feelings to his fianceé Marie Ambrosius in a letter dated July 11, 1917:

His work is of the modern *but* it is not that new color school or that sensational or cubistic school. I stop [*sic*] and looked in Amazement [*sic*]. I thought and thought more and more of the wonderful simplicity in which he carried out his scheme . . . his subjects are of the deep, underneath stuff.

He found encouragement in Davies's work which was "quite alike in arrangement" to his own. He also described the difference between academic art and the new art, suggesting the way real art should function:

Other painting like the Peyraud [a popular academic artist] or the clever brush men, you stop and look and remark, My, but that [sic] a clever piece of work look at that brushwork, that [sic] all you have to say but when you look at real *Art* you stop and think you are amazed you want to cry out your [sic] joyous it makes you happy.

Despite the fact that he was not as outspoken a radical as Weisenborn, Angarola attempted to "pictur[e] ideas and spirit" in his work, noting that a painter "sees not only the surface, but he sees inside . . . and what a painter sees, he paints. . . . A good painter is an honest painter."[54] In this sense, he approached painting as a modernist.

Although, as Bulliet pointed out, Angarola managed to avoid confrontation, he was committed to the anti-institutional ideas of education characteristic of the members of Chicago's modernist movement. Of Angarola's plan to open an art school in Chicago in 1925, a *Chicago Evening Post* writer says, "Mr. Angarola expects to conduct his school so that his students may have absolute freedom of thoughts and moods. . . . He will try to encourage each student to express his inner artistic being."[55] Angarola was reputedly an excellent teacher and held positions at the Layton School in Milwaukee, the School of the Art Institute of Chicago, and the Kansas City Art Institute School, among others. A number of his students won prestigious scholarships and prizes, and their training was praised by other teachers. In 1927, a colleague from the Kansas City Art Institute School wrote him with the flattering news that two of Angarola's former students, studying now with Ernest Lawson in Colorado, had been told by Lawson that "he [was] sorry he did not have an instructor as good as they had, it would [have] save[d] lots of his canvases from the wastebasket."[56] Angarola was irritated with students who copied his style after he encouraged them to pursue their individuality.

Critic Eleanor Jewett found an "amusing similarity" between Angarola's work and "a group of drawings, made by 8th grade pupils" because they share "the same bulky sincerity." She went on to comment:

> It is a compliment to both children and Angarola that this should be so. Simplicity is often lost with practice, and sincerity overlaid by vain teachings. To depict the truth as the truth appears to you is a great achievement.[57]

One is reminded of Kandinsky's pronouncement that "in each child's drawing the inner sound of the subject is revealed automatically."[58] Even to this conservative critic, Angarola's work was better because it had a child's untutored quality and authenticity of vision. It may have been his moderate personality as well as his relatively moderate style, visible in *Kansas City Workmen* and *Winding Road*, that made his work so acceptable. Like that of his friend Raymond Jonson, his work had similarities to late-nineteenth-century art.[59]

Angarola, like so many of his modernist contemporaries, sought to go back to his roots to get in touch with his inner consciousness. In 1928, he was awarded a Guggenheim Fellowship to study in Italy. His application stresses his interest in wanting to study the Italian primitives; this is parallel to the emphasis Szukalski and Armin placed on their peasant origins; it is similar also to Jonson's move and Armin's repeated trips to the southwest.

Landscape painting was one of Angarola's special interests. He loved to paint out of doors and often would take his classes to favorite spots. In a typescript of a WMAQ radio talk entitled "Chicago for the Artist," Angarola emphasized the abstract potential of the colors and shapes in the urban landscape that offered material to the artist. In his description of the old Halsted Street Bridge, the importance of the content as well as the form was conveyed: "It appeals to me because of straight majestic lines, and watching it go up one can get a thrill. As it soars above the old boats moving below, the background of the bridge serves splendidly . . . Stella I believe could do it justice." Angarola's *Michigan Avenue Bridge—Chicago River* (plate 14) does not have the mechanical energy of Stella's *Brooklyn Bridge* (1917) nor the tense vitality of Weisenborn's work. Rather, this "radical" used the modern city as a vehicle for the depiction of an ideal, simple, primitive existence unencumbered by the rush and dynamism of modern life. Using the strong colors and flat patterns of the modernist vocabulary to depict modern Chicago and small-town America, Angarola's work expresses a different, but no less valid, vision of modern America.[60] Seeking to show the success of the "melting pot," Angarola often painted ethnic areas of the city. Works like *German Picnic* (plate 15), *Ghetto Dwelling*, and *Bohemian Flats* are attempts to integrate all of America into one unified whole.

In *Christ Driving the Money Changers from the Temple* and *Christ Healing the Sick* (plate 16), Angarola uses Christian themes to convey the power of art in the modern world. The simple forms and bold, bright colors communicate clearly the hope, still strong in Angarola and his contemporaries, for a world in which the spirit can liberate itself from material corruption and ensure us lives of health and joy.

Despite certain disadvantages—conservative training at the School of the Art Institute, patrons who bought elsewhere, and critics who treated the indigenous Chicago tradition as second-rate—Chicago artists lived in a city that exemplified in many ways the unique potential of America and was particularly suited to the development of a modern American idiom. To some extent, the potential was unrealized since numerous artists settled in Chicago only to leave after a short time. Yet there

Susan S. Weininger

were many artists such as those we have considered here who produced works that represented Chicago to the nation and the world as an energetic and thriving center of commerce and industry, the essence of the American ideal. In their works are qualities that developed out of both the particular artistic experience they shared in the midwest's largest city[61] and the philosophical position on the nature of art articulated by Jacobson in his *Art of Today: Chicago, 1933.*

In conclusion, those qualities common to the works of most modern artists working in Chicago between 1910 and 1930 continued to prevail in the thirties and forties in the works of such artists as Gertrude Abercrombie, Julia Thecla, Macena Barton, and many others. The attitudes implicit in their works, along with the belief in the dynamic potential of the American city, predominated well into the second half of the century in Chicago. Ed Paschke, a contemporary Chicago artist who has achieved international reknown, was speaking not only for those of his own generation but also for those who lived seventy-five years ago when he said, "To me Chicago is the most American city. To me New York is like a European city. Chicago is the essence of an American city."[62] The artists discussed here, who lived in the "most American city," developed their own midwestern vernacular and with the authenticity of their expression they became, in Kandinsky's words, "enviable co-worker[s] on the spiritual pyramid which will reach to heaven."[63]

CHAPTER FIVE

Declarations of Independents:
Chicago's Alternative Art Groups of the 1920s

PAUL KRUTY

In the 1920s Chicago supported a number of independent art groups dedicated to exhibiting progressive contemporary art, frequently in jury-free exhibitions. At the beginning of the decade, the concept of jury-free shows was radical and controversial; by its end, it had become a success to such an extent that the system of jurying contemporary art at the Art Institute had been changed and the jury-free shows outside the Institute had themselves begun to grow stale, even outdated.

The sources of Chicago's independent art movement go back to the first jury-free exhibition in Europe in the nineteenth century—the Salon des Refusés, created in 1863 by Emperor Napoleon III in France in response to the outcry that followed the rejection of seventy percent of the artists who had submitted entries to the official government-sponsored salon. The significance of Napoleon's Salon des Refusés was immense; indeed, it has been said that "The Salon des Refusés may very well represent the most decisive institutional development in the progress of modern art."[1] It served as the model for the first exhibition in 1874 of the impressionists.[2] A decade later in 1884, the Belgian group Les XX ("The Twenty") was formed.[3] It guaranteed artists that all paintings would be shown at eye-level, their placement determined by lottery.

That same year, 1884, the idea of the Salon des Refusés, in effect, became institutionalized in the Societé des Artistes Indépendants—the "Paris Independents."[4] This group, which lasted until the first World War, became the model for the independent movement in America, beginning in 1898 with a protest against the National Academy of Design by a group of American impressionists called "The Ten," and continuing in 1908 with a protest among the so-called Ashcan school artists.[5] More significant was the 1910 New York show called the "Exhibition of Independent Artists," which was open to every artist who cared to exhibit.[6] Despite critical acclaim and public interest, Robert Henri, one of the organizers, was opposed to the show becoming permanent and explained, "the thing that interests me is . . . the idea of encouragement of independence and individuality,"[7] rather than the formation of a society to do so.

The first successful jury-free organization in America debuted in April 1917 with the exhibition of the Society of Independent Artists.[8] John Sloan, the Society's second president, became instrumental in spreading the gospel of independent exhibitions to other American cities, including Chicago.

In the early twentieth century, opportunities to show controversial art in Chicago were very limited, depending entirely on the taste of W. Scott Thurber, Albert Roullier, and J. W. Young, three progressive dealers who offered early shows by Arthur Dove, Jerome Blum, and B. J. O. Nordfeldt.[9] Significantly, in 1916, a year ahead of the New York organization, a group of Chicago artists formed the "Independent Society of Artists" and succeeded in holding one show. Yet the number of paintings was small and the exhibition had little lasting effect.[10] Also in 1916 the Arts Club opened its doors. When it was reorganized two years later and came under the control of Rue Winterbotham Carpenter and Alice Roullier (see fig. 12.5), the Arts Club became the leading voice for modern art in the city.[11] Yet at the end of the teens, there was a growing sense of frustration among Chicago artists that the city was too tied to tradition and too limited in exhibition possibilities. The time for a jury-free organization run by the artists themselves was at hand.

However, the painters who eventually became the core of the no-jury movement in Chicago were first brought together not by the inspiration of the New York organization but by the arrival in Chicago of several members of a New York art group called the introspectives. Four artists united by a common interest in imaginary symbolist painting founded the group: Benjamin Kopman, Abraham Harriton, Jennings Tofel, and Claude Buck. At their first show at the Whitney Studio Gallery in March 1917, they were joined by Felix Russmann and, shortly afterward, by Marguerite and William Zorach.[12]

One impressed visitor to these New York shows was the Chicago gallery dealer J. W. Young, who bought five paintings by Claude Buck. The ready market Young found in the midwest for all five paintings encouraged him to give Buck a Chicago show in March 1918. Young also began exhibiting the work of Buck's fellow introspective, Kopman, and his friend Russmann. This active interest on the part of a Chicago dealer convinced Buck to move to Chicago early in 1919; he was soon followed by both Kopman and Russmann. In April 1920, W. Scott Thurber's gallery gave Buck a major one-man show.[13]

The arrival of this New York art movement, the introspectives, with its catchy name, caused much excitement among Chicago's emerging radical artists. In May 1921 the Arts Club held a large exhibition of the introspectives which included not only the transplanted Chicago members, Buck and Kopman, but also the other two painters of the original New York group, Harriton and Tofel.[14] Showing with the four Introspectives were several Chicago artists who were soon to make a mark on the local scene: Emil Armin, Raymond Jonson, Rudolph Weisenborn, Fred Biesel, and Frances Strain.[15]

Although this first Chicago exhibition also turned out to be the introspectives' last, the idea of an alternative art group with its own credo that would hold exhibitions made a lasting impression. By summer's end, 1921, a new group had formed around the Chicago radicals, the Cor Ardens, with Raymond Jonson as president and Rudolph Weisenborn as vice-president.[16] The guiding force behind the group was their secretary, Carl Hoeckner, who served as president during the second and third years.[17] The constitution, primarily the work of Hoeckner, announced that Cor Ardens, or "Ardent Hearts," was to be "a concrete move to bring together, at least in spirit, sympathetic isolated individuals." As is evident from their honorary membership list, these purportedly "isolated individuals" included the Belgian playwright Maurice Maeterlinck and the Finnish painter Axel Gallen-Kallela.[18] The Cor Ardens declared that "We must walk the rising road to grandeur, enthusiasms and achievement with all the powers of our spirit."

Perhaps having undertaken too complicated a venture, the Cor Ardens failed to arrange an exhibition until late the next year, 1922. What turned out to be their only major Chicago show was held from November 16 to 29 at the Arts Club. The catalog lists thirty-five paintings and three sculptures. In a letter to its members, the exhibition committee warned artists about what they were undertaking: "It is extremely important that each member carefully judge his entry, since there is no jury acting upon the Cor Ardens exhibits. . . . Not only our work is on trial, but our very method and system."[19] The Cor Ardens were thus even less bound by stylistic similarities than their predecessors, the introspectives. The group's functions already included those of a no-jury society; but its unrealistic, if idealistic, stance ultimately doomed it to failure.

The gap in time from the founding of the Cor Ardens in August 1921 to its first exhibition in November 1922 witnessed the arrival of an extremely successful independent show in Chicago, the Salon des Refusés. The title was not only a reference to the 1863 Paris Salon des Refusés, but to the actual reasons for the show. Of the 1,100 paintings submitted to the fall exhibition of American Artists at the Art Institute, all but two hundred were rejected, among them the work submitted by nearly every member of the Cor Ardens group. Rallying around Jonson, as well as Weisenborn, Hoeckner, and Buck, they had convinced the owners of Rothschild's department store to spend $50,000 on installation and advertising. In November 1921, almost three hundred works were exhibited at Rothschild's on State Street. As the group announced to Chicago newspapers:

> We do not believe in juries and this show is being hung not by a jury but by the artists themselves. We want the people to see *our* works, and those that the *institute* has accepted . . . and decide whether or not we, the "radicals" of art, are not more stimulating to a development in art that will rival the scientific and the commercial strides made by our country."[20]

The affair drew huge crowds but few sales. As the art critic C. J. Bulliet noted, at least Rothschild's did "a land office business in suspenders, shoe laces, [and] corsets . . . [that] the visitors . . . saw . . . in the aisles leading to the 'Salon des Refusés' "[21]

The year 1922 proved to be even more stimulating for Chicago's artists than 1921 had been. In September the Art Institute exhibited sixty-seven works from the collection of the late Arthur J. Eddy that revived the controversy of the Armory Show.[22] At the same time the painter Albert Bloch joined the faculty of the city's progressive art school, the Chicago Academy of Fine Arts. Bloch had been the only American member of the Blue Rider group in Munich. Because several members of the Cor Ardens and the Salon des Refusés committee taught at the Academy, including Jonson and Buck, Bloch's experience with a radical exhibition society must have been particularly enlightening to these Chicago artists.[23]

The success of the Salon des Refusés, or the "Refuses" as it came to be called, led those involved to wish that something permanent could be established in Chicago. Thus, while Carl Hoeckner was still trying to organize the first Cor Ardens show, a much more lasting organization—one directly modeled after the Society of Independent Artists in New York—was in the making. In August 1922 the *Chicago Evening Post* reported that the "Chicago No-Jury Society of Artists" had been formed and would hold its first exhibition in October.[24] The society's first president, quite naturally, was Rudolph Weisenborn (figs. 4.2, 5.1). Its secretary was Charles Biesel, a New England painter and member of the New York Independents. The treasurer was Biesel's future daughter-in-law, Frances Strain, who had also shown with the New York group and had studied with John Sloan, the driving force behind that group.

Like the Refuses, the No-Jury board arranged for one of the large department stores on State Street, now Marshall Field's, to host the exhibition.[25] An entrance fee of four dollars would allow an artist to exhibit two works. For another four dollars and

5.1 Rudolph Weisenborn painting a portrait of an unidentified woman, painting in background, photograph, n.d. Rudolph Weisenborn Papers, Archives of American Art, Smithsonian Institution.

a photograph, any painting would also be reproduced in the catalog. All works would be hung alphabetically by artist's name. And, last, the Society boldly promised that "all works must remain as originally placed; and no work may be removed." The catalog explained that "considering the fact that the very men who were makers of our Art History have, almost without exception, been rejected by the exhibition juries, we can only conclude that this system is a failure and that any new system which allows the free development of creative ability [must] be encouraged."[26] To the charge that jury-free exhibitions were often chaotic, the introduction countered, "To create beautiful walls in exhibitions by selecting and hanging works which are harmonious and of equal merit is of no importance. From a work of art, we demand individual conception and style." The first No-Jury show was, if anything, more successful than the Refuses of a year earlier. Critic Lena McCauley noted that "the 200 men and women represented are able to fill eight galleries, in all half a street block long, on the second floor of Marshall Field and Co."[27] Among the works on display was Emil Armin's whimsical "late entry" to the Chicago Tribune Building competition.

The classicizing cover to the catalog suggested that the exhibition was primarily an attempt at artistic freedom, not a radical style or a complete break with tradition (fig. 5.2). Indeed, at the 27th Chicago and Vicinity Exhibition held two months later at the Art Institute, all of the major activists in the No-Jury Society exhibited: Armin, Buck, Hoeckner, Jonson, Weisenborn, Strain, Charles Biesel and his son Fred, and Ramon Shiva.[28] However, an important change came over these painters the next year. After the second No-Jury show, held in October 1923, none of these artists exhibited at the Art Institute's spring show, and they continued this policy of boycotting the Institute for several years. The new posture was immediately evident in the second catalog. In place of the Greek god languishing over an easel while holding the flame of Truth, a wild Polynesian in a grass skirt wields the flame defiantly upward, while brandishing a fistful of rushes that could be arrows (fig. 5.3). This image, designed by Emil Armin, soon became the symbol of the No-Jury Society.

The artists' move toward independence was fostered by the arrival in Chicago of two critics of major importance, C. J. Bulliet (plate 17) and Sam Putnam (fig. 1.6).[29] Both men were primarily literary critics, yet each was passionately interested in modern art and felt that the Chicago art scene was worth defending. Both became strong supporters of the No-Jury Society. Putnam had attended the University of Chicago, pursued a career in journalism, and was working as literary critic for the *Chicago Evening Post* by the early 1920s. In 1925 Putnam presented his case for the complete withdrawal by Chicago's serious artists from any exhibitions at the Art Institute. To a crowd assembled, ironically, at the Institute, he declared:

> I am and always have been an uncompromising believer in the Independent or No-Jury principle. . . . To me, a No-Juryite today is an artist who, like John Sloan or Ramon Shiva, refuses, under any conditions, to submit his work to a jury. Otherwise, what are you? You are simply the Outs, those who . . . for one reason or another are unable to get into the institute. . . . Either be a No-Jury artist or an Institute candidate. You can't send canvases to a juried show and still be an Independent.[30]

Bulliet later explained that, although the new group had been "patterned after the New York Independents," it chose the confrontational if slightly awkward name "No-Jury Society," rather than the neutral "Chicago Independents," "as expressive of the determination to have done with the Art Institute methods."[31]

Also during the second season, Rudolph Weisenborn, realizing that the society needed more publicity and a source of income, decided that a costume ball would solve both problems. Taking its cue from the New York Independents, which had produced a "prismatic" costume ball the previous year, the Chicago group decided to host a "cubist" dance at the new Trianon Ballroom. For this affair, held in October 1923, each member was to dress as a work of modern art. Weisenborn had high hopes that the event would generate enough revenue to allow his dream for a new exhibition space, a "Gallery of Living Artists," to become a reality. He expressed these aspirations in a drawing that depicted a Chicago artist, paintings under arm, approaching the sacred gallery (fig. 5.4). For many of the artists themselves, the event promised an evening of light-hearted entertainment rather than any real possibility of making money, as is evident in the advertisement published in the *Chicago Literary Times* (fig. 5.5). The second and third cubist balls were held at the Midway Gardens, which had been designed in 1913–14 by Frank Lloyd Wright but had since fallen on hard times.[32]

Although not enough money was raised by the cubist balls to build Weisenborn's dream gallery, the No-Jury shows, with their three hundred to five hundred works, became a regular feature of Chicago's art year.[33] Marshall Field's hosted the first six shows, where it was reported that on one day 4,500 persons passed through the galleries. In his catalog introduction to the third show of 1924, Sam Putnam reiterated that "the one thing the No-Jury artist holds closest to heart is *freedom*." By the eighth show of 1930, although he often criticized the actual work, Bulliet observed in that year's catalog introduction that "it is in the interest of the individual artist, eager to reveal his work to the world, that No-Jury can continue to play" an important part in the city's life.

The Chicago group kept close ties to the New York Independents largely through the efforts of Fred Biesel and Frances Strain (fig. 5.6). Biesel served as midwest representative for the New York group, and in turn invited New Yorkers to show in Chicago. For example, John Sloan exhibited at the No-Jury Society five times between 1924 and 1928. Sloan assisted Weisenborn in the hanging of several shows (fig. 5.7). With a major contingent of New Yorkers, the Chicagoans were inspired to show some of their best work. And the public responded accordingly: the 1926 exhibition, held in February, was one of the most popular. Bulliet noted approvingly that, by "co-operating with the New York Independents, and inviting artists from the Atlantic to the Pacific to participate, the show takes on something of the aspect of an 'All-American.' "[34] Fred Biesel designed the catalog cover, employing repetitions of Armin's skirted figure, and

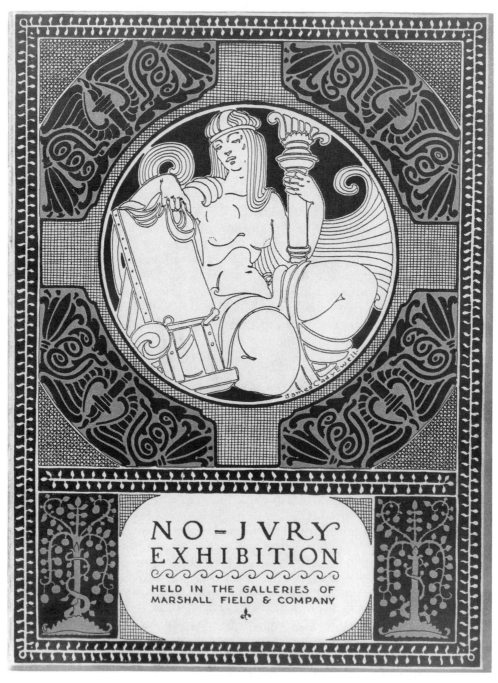

5.2 Cover of the first No-Jury Exhibition Catalog, 1922. C. J. Bulliet Papers, Archives of American Art, Smithsonian Institution.

5.3 Cover of the second No-Jury Exhibition Catalog, 1923, designed by Emil Armin. Emil Armin Papers, Archives of American Art, Smithsonian Institution.

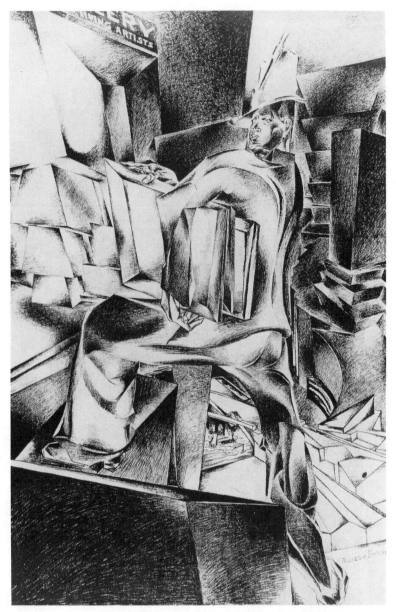

5.4 Rudolph Weisenborn, *Artist Approaching the Gallery of Living Artists*, drawing (medium unknown), n.d. Rudolph Weisenborn Papers, Archives of American Art, Smithsonian Institution.

showed several nudes. In Frances Strain's *Cabaret* (fig. 5.8), Bulliet found that the artist had "looked into a Chicago dance hall . . . with bold, comprehending eyes"; Bulliet further praised works by Felix Russmann and sculptor Tennessee Mitchell Anderson.[35] At this show, Archibald Motley joined the ranks of the No-Jury artists.[36]

In mid-1926, the dynamics of the No-Jury Society and its sup-

5.5 Emil Armin, cartoon, "The Parade of the Chicago Artists to the No-Jury Artists Cubist Ball," advertisement in *Chicago Literary Times*, October 1923. Emil Armin Papers, Archives of American Art, Smithsonian Institution.

5.6 Emil Armin, *My Neighbors*, oil on canvas, 1929. Double portrait of Fred Biesel and Frances Strain in their 57th Street Studio. National Museum of American Art, Smithsonian Institution. Gift of Hilda D. Armin.

porting critics changed. In the fall, Sam Putnam sailed for France with his wife and young child, where they remained until 1933. Although he continued to send essays and commentaries on modern art to Chicago, Putnam was no longer able (nor especially willing) to keep abreast of the progress of art in Chicago.[37] Also in the fall, as the No-Jury group was planning its fifth exhibition, Weisenborn became embroiled in an argument over both the annual dance and the exhibition. Weisenborn had served as president of the No-Jury Society during its first four years. He was so determined to build the Gallery of Living Artists that he endlessly pushed for fundraising events. Despite their appeal, the cubist balls had never been financial successes,[38] and many people wanted them stopped. Weisenborn suddenly resigned from the No-Jury Society in a huff. Gustav Dahlstrom became president and a number of artists less didactic than the intransigent Weisenborn joined the Board of Directors, including Tennessee Anderson and Felix Russmann.

Within a few days Weisenborn announced the formation of a

5.7 John Sloan and Rudolph Weisenborn looking at art works, probably for a Chicago No-Jury exhibition, photograph, n.d. Clarence J. Bulliet Papers, Archives of American Art, Smithsonian Institution.

new group, the Neo-Arlimusc.[39] At last he would have his Gallery of Modern Artists, now expanded to embrace all the arts. If the No-Jury Society's precedent was the Paris Independents, Weisenborn's new club recalled Les XX. The grandiose goals of the group were to draw Chicagoans interested in art, literature, music, and science into a single organization—hence the odd name, which combined the first two letters of those four words. Weisenborn's first planned event was, almost inevitably, a costume ball, held at the Merry Gardens on Chicago's north side in January 1927.

In an open letter to members of the Arts Club, Weisenborn stated his goals and hopes for Neo-Arlimusc: "The Arts Club . . . brings to the city international exhibitions unique even in America, and it provides an individual gathering place for members. . . . [But] there is needed a more informal meeting ground for the actual workers in the arts; a smaller place where artists, writers, musicians, and scientists may foregather and work out

5.8 Frances Strain, *Cabaret,* oil on canvas. Appeared in No-Jury Exhibition Catalog, n.d. Emil Armin Papers, Archives of American Art, Smithsonian Institution.

ideas mutually."[40] The meetings were to be held in Weisenborn's north side studio.[41] Sam Putnam, who followed the development of Neo-Arlimusc from Paris, enthusiastically announced that its proposed roundtable discussions "would mean nothing less than the coming of civilization"[42] to Chicago.

Harriet Monroe, while equally enthusiastic about the idea, was appalled by the title Weisenborn had concocted. Later in the year she joined Anderson in threatening a lawsuit if the name were not changed. Monroe called Neo-Arlimusc "inartistic, even juvenile," while the dour Weisenborn insisted it was "clever and appropriate."[43] Whatever its merits, the name stuck.

Events the first season included a spring exhibition on the theme "The Nude in Art,"[44] and a fall show whose subject was

"Chicago—the Real Modern Expression of Our 1927 Civilization" at which it was reported that "the pick of the No-Jury Society seems to be represented."[45] Among many other evenings at Neo-Arlimusc during the spring of 1927, Weisenborn arranged for Maxwell Bodenheim to speak on "What is Wrong with the American Novel," and Douglas McMurtrie to discuss "Modernism in Typography." The following January, the young Walter Blair spoke on "Early American Humor."[46]

Weisenborn started a fund to remodel the ground floor into a more usable space. He sold one dollar raffle tickets for his portrait of Clarence Darrow, first shown at the No-Jury exhibition of 1923, and offered photographs of the portrait autographed by Darrow to purchasers of ten chances (see fig.4.3).[47] The major fundraising event, however, was a midnight revel called "Alley Oop Chicago." Held on November 26, 1927, at the Playhouse Theater in the Fine Arts Building, the evening featured music by John Alden Carpenter and choreography by Ruth Page, while Bulliet offered autographed copies of his new book *Apples and Madonnas*.[48]

Enough money was raised through these various schemes, that remodeling could begin by late November with a reopening optimistically planned for January 1, 1928.[49] An isometric drawing of Weisenborn's ideas for the new space was published in November with the description, "In all essentials, such as form, color, texture and dimensions, a dynamic unity is suggested rather than the static or merely potential expression usually to be found in rooms which are to serve mass purpose."

When Weisenborn discovered that the German art critic Julius Meier-Graefe was stopping in Chicago as part of an American tour,[50] he pushed for completion of the gallery and quickly organized an exhibition of Chicago art in Meier-Graefe's honor. Weisenborn assembled works by many of Chicago's leading modern painters (excluding the new leaders of the No-Jury Society, with whom he was apparently still feuding). Marguerite Williams reported that Weisenborn "has gotten together . . . some of the high spots of Chicago modernism's early days along with what he thinks to be some of the most hopeful material of today."[51] On display were drawings by Stanislaus Szukalski; many of the nudes shown the previous year at Neo-Arlimusc; paintings by Weisenborn's latest "discovery," Seymour de Koven; Tennessee Anderson's *Hallelujah*, which critic Eleanor Jewett called "an outrage upon decency";[52] sculpture by Emil Armin, including *The Prophecy*; and even a work by Ivan Albright. Carl Hoeckner's provocative painting of a decade earlier, *The Homecoming* (fig. 5.9), which Bulliet called "a genuine masterpiece," was included in this retrospective of Chicago modernism.

On February 21 and 22, Meier-Graefe visited the Art Institute, the Arts Club, the Eddy Collection, and finally, Neo-Arlimusc.[53]

5.9 Carl Hoeckner, *The Homecoming of 1918,* oil on canvas, 1918–19. Courtesy, Atelier Dore Inc. and Carl Hoeckner Jr., San Francisco.

With Hoeckner acting as translator, and the German consul at his side, Meier-Graefe surveyed the new hall and its contents. Unfortunately, several decades had passed since the aging critic had automatically embraced every adversarial art group he encountered. By the standards of his beloved Cézanne, according to Bulliet, Meier-Graefe "failed to find anything significant" in the room,[54] and wished instead to return to the El Grecos at the Art Institute. Neo-Arlimusc continued through the summer of 1928; but gradually Weisenborn turned his interests elsewhere and the club faded away.

The momentum established in the 1920s began to wane after 1928, dissipating completely during the 1930s. Although the exhibitions of the No-Jury Society continued for many years, this organization, like its New York counterpart, lapsed into a kind of conservative provincialism. By the late 1940s, with the universal acceptance of European modernism, Chicago's energetic fight for an indigenous form of twentieth-century art had been all but forgotten.

The 1920s thus remain a decade apart from those that preceded and followed it. The progressive art groups that arose in those years, including the Cor Ardens, the No-Jury Society, and Neo-Arlimusc, not only presented alternative choices to the Art Institute, but were part of the general burgeoning of the local scene. Ironically, these organizations served as models for a host of conservative groups, including the Association of Chicago Painters and Sculptors, founded in 1923 and headed by Frank V. Dudley; and the South Side Art Association, organized in 1925, whose honorary president was Lorado Taft. The decade also saw the formation of such support groups as the Business Men's Art Club in 1920 and the Chicago Galleries Association in 1925.[55] Yet it was the independent societies, with their grandiose schemes—and their two vigorous, sometimes strident, defenders in the press—that loosened the perceived stranglehold of the Art Institute and brought renewed artistic life into the city.

CHAPTER SIX

"Of the Which and the Why of Daub and Smear": Chicago Critics Take On Modernism

SUE ANN PRINCE

Modernism in Chicago was as mercurial as it was controversial. A term that did not denote a specific style, it was a generic, catch-all word loosely applied by critics to many different kinds of art. Its meaning depended on the writer and the context. It usually referred to one of three general artistic categories: avant-garde European work beginning with the post impressionists—especially Cézanne, Gauguin, and Van Gogh—and continuing through cubism, post cubism, Duchamp, Matisse, expressionism, and as the years went on, surrealism and constructivism; contemporary local artists whose work had assimilated some aspect of the European avant-garde; or contemporary artists whose innate rebelliousness and belief in individualism pitted them against the generally conservative stance of the Art Institute. In this last case, the term did not necessarily denote abstraction or even post-cubist tendencies; the naturalistic figures by Macena Barton (fig. 6.1) were considered modernist along with the post-cubist renderings of Rudolph Weisenborn (see fig. 5.4).

By 1910 certain underlying assumptions about making and viewing art prevailed in Chicago, having been formulated and nurtured by the local philanthropists who had founded and still governed the Art Institute. Self-righteous and civic-minded, these bourgeois patrons valued art for its social utility: They wanted to educate and elevate the masses to the finer things in life, in short, to support an art that was "good for the people."[1] Inherent in that good was a theory of art which implied order and beauty along with a disciplined adherence to apparently infallible, universal laws—in other words, everything that nineteenth-century academic art had to offer. In the early teens their ideals still prevailed, promulgated by the people they hired to

6.1 Macena Barton, *Salomé*, oil on canvas, 1936. Macena Barton Papers, Archives of American Art, Smithsonian Institution.

run the Institute and its School and in general by their own power as leaders of the city's social and cultural elite. As long as they controlled the scene, art would be safe, comfortable, definable, controllable, and morally correct.

The goals of these patrons were furthered by contemporary mores. A few days before the opening of the Armory Show, a police order forced an art dealer to remove from his store window a copy of *September Morn*, a traditional painting of a nude by Paul Chabas (see fig. 1.9). It was reported that the city's official art censor, acting on behalf of the mayor, was to bring suit against the proprietors of the art store for "exhibiting and offering for sale a certain indecent picture of a nude woman."[2] Almost simultaneously, the newspapers also reported that Art Institute officials, more specifically, Director William M. R. French, had removed a painting from an exhibition of contemporary Scandinavian art at the Art Institute. The painting, *Summer Day* by Bernhard Folkestad, now apparently lost, depicted a poultry scene in a barnyard.[3] In both these cases, morality was the issue, not aesthetics.

It was against this backdrop of self-righteous civic leadership and moral censure that modernism came to town. Contrary to popular belief, it came prior to the Armory Show in three exhibits at Thurber's gallery—Jerome Blum in 1911, and Arthur Dove and B. J. O. Nordfeldt in 1912. The reception to Blum and Dove was mixed but, relatively speaking, positive. Several arts writers interviewed the artists and sympathetically if naively explained what they were trying to do. Nordfeldt's talent was praised more highly than that of Blum or Dove.[4]

Modernism also came to town in the aforementioned "Exhibition of Contemporary Scandinavian Art," held at the Art Institute from February 25 to March 16, 1913. Boldly colored distortions by such artists as Edvard Munch were displayed along with traditional works. A writer for the *Chicago Inter-Ocean* decided to explain, tongue-in-cheek, the mysteries of the radical art to his readers. He began:

> Listen, my children, and you shall hear
> Of the which and the why of daub and smear . . .

He proceeded to poke fun at the expressionism of certain contemporary works and concluded, "After the Scandinavians, the Cubists Thrice Welcome!" He was, of course, referring to the upcoming Armory Show.[5]

A few sympathetic observations were written about the Scandinavian work but they had little impact, as reaction to the nordic exhibition was drowned in the deluge of sensationalist headlines announcing the coming of the Armory Show already on view in New York.[6]

The sensationalism in the New York press predisposed Chicago reporters to ridicule the upcoming show. It gave them time to draft carefully their amusing, derisory comments, which in the comfort of seventy-five years' hindsight, provide us with a wealth of quotable material. During the New York show, Chicago headlines such as the following seemed to multiply weekly: "Insurgent Exhibit in New York: Examples of Freak Art"; "Futurist Fakes, Cubists Colics"; "Hit Mud with Brick: Result, Cubist Art."[7] Cartoonists had a heydey, and writers devised descriptions of particular works that easily rivalled New

York's famous "explosion in a shingle factory" comment about Marcel Duchamp's *Nude Descending a Staircase.*

Mistakes in names, designations, and historical facts were relatively frequent. Picasso was Paul rather than Pablo, Matisse was a futurist who let other people finish his canvases, and Van Gogh's ear-cutting saga was frequently exaggerated or distorted.[8] Three events in particular provided grist for the reporters' mill. Art Institute Director French chose to be out of town during the exhibition. A copy of Gertrude Stein's short piece "Portrait of Mabel Dodge in the Villa Curonia" arrived at the Art Institute a few days before the opening. Reporters were called in to review the work, which was promoted as an example of cubist literature. When they read the likes of "That is what is done when there is done what is and the union is won and that division is the explicit visit," they were stunned.[9] The text's incomprehensibility, needless to say, served only to fuel the hostility toward the coming cubist paintings. The third media event was an attempted burning in effigy of Henry Hair Mattress at the end of the show. In fact, the effigy was not burned because of dissension among the participants, but three mock Matisse works were set on fire.[10] While all three incidents provided spectacular headlines, they did not generate any thoughtful assessments of the art on view.

During the course of the exhibition, moral indignation was spouted by non-arts reporters and occasionally by art critics. Representations of the nude were particularly suspect. A *Tribune* editorial claimed, "The nudes pervert the ideal of physical perfection, obliterate the line which has heretofore distinguished the artistic from the lewd and obscene, and incite feelings of disgust and aversion."[11] H. Effa Webster, of the *Chicago Examiner* expressed similar outrage, deriding Gauguin's nude in *The Spirit of Evil*, which she felt was "as obscene as it is vile . . . The woman's face is detestably detestable in its evil leer."[12] Yet another article discussed the importance of barring children from the show.[13]

In looking beyond the sensationalism of the headlines and the unparalleled moral outrage of non-arts writers, however, we find Chicago's response to be more thoughtful, complex, and sophisticated than is generally acknowledged. The three major critics at the time were George B. Zug, assistant professor of art history at the University of Chicago, who wrote for *Chicago Inter-Ocean* until its demise in 1914; Lena May McCauley, a Chicago society woman who had written for the *Chicago Evening Post* since 1900; and Harriet Monroe (fig. 6.2), who wrote for the *Chicago Tribune* for several years through the early teens. Monroe was a matron who, despite her conservative roots in Chicago's high society, founded *Poetry* magazine in 1912, a progressive publication that became the focal point of the city's literary avant-garde for several years.

Sue Ann Prince

6.2 Harriet Monroe, photograph, ca. 1910–20. Department of Special Collections, The University of Chicago Library.

George Zug seems to have approached the show almost as though it were the subject of a doctoral dissertation. He went to New York to see it, studied avant-garde work in Paris and claimed to have read everything that had ever been written about it. Before the Chicago opening he wrote: ". . . as far as their technique and knowledge of nature go, as far as their design and workmanship go, such men as Van Gogh, Gaugin (*sic*), and Matisse are in the class with the young person; they have apparently never learned to paint."[14] Zug's judgments, which he explained at length, were based on an unyielding but informed belief in academic standards. He usually maintained a dry, humorless academic tone, but when he found himself unable to contain his disdain for modernism he would burst into emotional, judgmental attacks. Once, at the end of a long diatribe against the modernist aesthetic, he resorted to name-calling, labeled cubist works "freak products," and concluded, "Let others take cubism seriously, but for myself I am convinced that it is merely refuse for bunko artists."[15]

After the opening of the show, Zug became even more negative, citing Kenyon Cox and other New York- or Paris-based critics with whom he agreed. He read *For and Against*, a pamphlet distributed during the show that presented arguments for and against modernism, but he claimed it had not converted him. Something did have an impact, however, because at one point he suddenly accepted post impressionism. Offering no explanation, he declared that it had "a real purpose" and was "a genuine endeavor worthy of respectful attention . . . the beginning of something new and positive."[16] He continued to rail against Matisse and the cubists, but never again berated the post impressionists in print. Zug's lengthy articles were authoritative and negative in tone. However, unlike so much of the negativism surrounding the show in Chicago, his judgments were aesthetic not moral, steeped as they were in the history of art.

Lena May McCauley's first signed article about the show, which appeared four days before the opening, was upbeat: "The air is alive with questions—what are the impressionists, the post impressionists, the cubists and futurists?"[17] Perplexed by the issues herself, she dodged giving an opinion, quoting instead dispassionate definitions of the major modernist movements written by the art editor of the *Boston Transcript*. The neutral, safe tone of her article was significant: neither angry nor prematurely close-minded, it was characteristic of her stance. In several articles as early as 1910, she moralized about accepting the new: "There are some things we may not understand because we have not quite learned the language of the artist," she wrote, "but that is no reason why we should throw stones at his work . . ."[18] The day before the show opened to the public, an unsigned article in the *Chicago Evening Post* echoed those sentiments. It warned readers not to laugh modernism away: "It is too deeply and too widely grounded in the great art centers of the world . . . it at least embodies a spirit of individualistic revolt that ever wins the respect of men. This spirit American art can least of all afford to reject. We need it keenly right here in the art schools of Chicago."[19]

During the show McCauley discussed the lives of the post-impressionist painters objectively, in contrast to other writers whose accounts twisted the facts into exaggerated, sensationalist stories. Despite her desire to accept the outré, however, Matisse, Rousseau, and Kandinsky remained beyond her reach. She did not understand the non-academic message of their art, but at least acknowledged that a change of criteria was in the offing. Significantly, she never condemned the artists or their morality.[20]

The third major critic, Harriet Monroe, was refreshingly sensitive, curious, and open. Probably the first to discuss post impressionism in the Chicago press, on the occasion of the Jerome Blum show two years earlier, she had already proven her interest in modernism. Her response to Blum, Dove, and Nordfeldt had been thoughtful even though she did not understand them completely and was certainly not ready to proclaim them the equals of the old masters.[21]

Monroe, like Zug, went to New York to see the Armory Show and wrote about it for *Tribune* readers on February 16, the earliest Chicago review. She was clearly excited by the stimulation her New York viewing had provided: "The show has an air of cosmopolitanism never before attained in this country except at world's fairs, and it is less bound by academic standards. Even the cubists seem to be playing interesting games with kaleidoscopic polygons of color; even Matisse is dancing a wild tango on some weird barbarous shore."[22] A month later Monroe wrote another lengthy article with the stated purpose of preparing her readers, citing and discussing Clive Bell's theory of significant form and drawing upon French critics who championed the new art.[23]

Monroe studied the show throughout its run, writing lengthy articles at least once a week, usually in the Sunday edition. Her opening day article reveals her a little less enthusiastic than in New York, perhaps because her own comprehension of such painters as Matisse and the cubists was tentative.[24] But within a week Monroe had become exasperated with the show's detractors. She wrote, "The conservatives have little to say and they can't keep their tempers long enough to say it."[25] A few days later she struck out against their anti-intellectualism: "We are fighting one of those battles of the intellect—those of us who have any—which are common enough in Paris, but altogether too rare in our provincially shortsighted and self-satisfied community . . . It is to be deplored that our discussion is not always quite urbane . . . Better the wildest extravagances of the cubists than the vapid works of certain artists who ridicule them."[26] Accusing American art of becoming pallid and photographic, she explained that the new art represented a revolt against nineteenth-century realism and a search for new beauty and truth.

Along with Matisse and Duchamp, cubism was the most difficult aspect of the show for the Chicago critics. Monroe's approach was cautious, but it reveals her ability to think analytically and independently. Questioning what she perceived as too much reliance on formula, she feared the cubists might back themselves into a corner. She wrote: "They are too literary, too bent on telling a story, even though the terms in which they tell it are new and different. There is nothing so dangerous as a theory of either art or life, for both art and life are bigger than any theory . . . These cubist pictures . . . are so completely the product of a theory that there is little picture left."[27] Elsewhere she remarked: "These Cubist pictures seem to me, as I grow more familiar with them, a curious example of the logical exactness and consistency of the latin mind, its way of carrying an idea to its legitimate conclusion, regardless of the contradictions and whimsicalities which always, in real life, prevent a mathematically exact result."[28]

Monroe's comments reveal a relatively sophisticated understanding of the cubist works. Underlying all her reviews were a developing sensitivity to modernism, a strong sense of history, an understanding of the need for experimentation, and an acceptance of the inevitability of change. There is some indication that she vacillated in her opinion of modernism. According to the artist Manierre Dawson, for instance, she once said she had not seen anything good in the show.[29] It is true that her enthusiasm for it was not as great as that of her radical literary colleague, Floyd Dell. However, she was already in her fifties, a veteran of an earlier generation of artists, and a writer for a notoriously conservative newspaper with a very different audience. Her articles in the *Tribune* reveal that she was far more astute than has been acknowledged by historians; they were consistently more measured, analytical, and positive than that of nearly any other American newspaper writer, whether in Chicago or New York.

It was undoubtedly the glut of sensationalist headlines, the cartoons satirizing the show, and the accusations of immorality that brought a record-setting 189,500 Chicagoans to see it.[30] One article reported that a landscape architect blamed the degeneracy of the cubist works on the artists' poor housing in Paris. Such a story was more interesting and certainly more fun to read than real criticism.[31]

Over the years, historians have focused on the bizarre sensationalism and negativism of such articles to the detriment of critics like Monroe. One contemporary journal, *Current Opinion*, reported that Monroe had accused Matisse's works of being "the most hideous monstrosities ever perpetrated in the name of long-suffering art."[32] This statement has never been documented in a primary source; if Monroe made it, it was uncharacteristic of everything else she wrote. Yet it was quoted from *Current Opinion* by Milton Brown in his definitive study of the Armory Show and has been repeated many times by others as an example of the ignorance of Chicago writers. Indeed, sensationalism not only overwhelmed the examples of intelligent criticism that were written in Chicago in 1913 but has also clouded the historical record.[33]

Neither Monroe nor Zug continued to write criticism beyond the early teens. While McCauley remained at the *Chicago Evening Post* until 1930, she was eclipsed by two younger critics, Eleanor Jewett of the *Chicago Tribune* and C. J. Bulliet of the *Post's Magazine of the Art World* and later of the *Chicago Daily News*. Both Jewett and Bulliet wrote for more than twenty-five years. While there were other writers on modernism prior to 1940—Samuel Putnam (fig. 6.3), Ernest Heitkamp, Paul Gilmore, and Fritzi Weisenborn—none of them lasted as long or had as much impact as these two critics. Jewett and Bulliet were equally vigorous in their respective opinions about modernism; both wielded considerable influence and power and built a large following over the years. In addition, both provoked considerable anger on the part of their detractors. However, no two critics could have been more unalike in character, personality, upbringing, and viewpoint.

Jewett was the great niece of Colonel Cyrus McCormick, inventor of the reaper and president of the International Harvester Corporation. A part of Chicago's wealthy cultural and social

6.3 Frank Stella, *Sam Putnam,* drawing or print, photograph taken from *The New Hope,* August 1934, p. 4. Photo courtesy Paul Kruty.

elite, in the same McCormick family that published the *Tribune,* she was provided a private education at the Chicago Latin School and a year at Miss Nixon's finishing school in Florence, Italy (fig. 6.4).[34] Bulliet (plate 17), on the other hand, was born and raised in Corydon, Indiana, a typical small midwestern town near the Kentucky border. Neither of his parents was well educated; his father owned a plant food fertilizer business.[35]

Neither Jewett nor Bulliet had formal training in art history and neither set out to be an art critic. Jewett attended the University of Illinois for two years and the University of Wisconsin for one summer. She studied agriculture as her intent was to become a gentlewoman-farmer. According to her son, she was the only woman in the program, however, and she dropped out when the class began the chapter on animal breeding. Bulliet graduated Phi Beta Kappa from Indiana University with a major in English and minors in astronomy and mathematics. Known for his extensive reading, inquisitiveness, and writing ability, he served as editor of the school newspaper.

Jewett ended up in journalism when she discovered that starting a farm was too expensive. She joined the *Chicago Tribune* staff in 1917, and it is reasonable to speculate that it was her Mc-Cormick family name that landed her the position. Bulliet, on the other hand, worked his way up, beginning his career in journalism as a police reporter for the *Louisville Herald,* moving on to become a press agent for a theater company, a copy editor and reporter for the *Indianapolis Star,* and eventually, in 1924, the director of the *Magazine of the Art World,* a weekly art supplement to the *Chicago Evening Post.*

Aside from taking on a career, Jewett did what was expected of a Chicago society woman: she wore the right clothes, married, raised four children, and upheld the moral virtues of her puritanical upbringing. Despite the opportunity to become sophisticated and broad-minded intellectually, she remained a provincial at heart, a city girl who would have loved a purer life on the farm. Bulliet, on the other hand, was a country boy. Lacking in social graces, he nonetheless ended up in the city where his craving for culture could be satisfied. An intellectual, he was apparently careless in appearance. Debilitated by obesity, lameness, and eventually toothlessness (which he refused to correct with false teeth)—conditions that were all due to more than one chronic illness—he did not appear "cultured" (fig. 6.5). In short, he was the walking antithesis of Eleanor Jewett.

Bulliet's rejection of Jewett's moral self-righteousness was more than intellectual. He did not live with his wife and son in Indiana, but alone in a hotel apartment in Chicago, his liaisons with women artists occasionally becoming a cause célèbre in Chicago's art world. His curiosity was voracious; he was interested in all the arts and frequently also served as drama and music critic. He was passionately interested in a host of subjects that must have been distasteful if not downright horrifying to Jewett—transvestites and others who exhibited sexually deviant behavior, as well as egomaniacs like Hitler. He read profusely on the subjects, clipped articles, kept extensive files, and used the material for short stories and other writings, many of which were never published.

When Jewett began writing for the *Tribune* in 1917, she first worked as a feature writer for the Sunday section. Her early articles on the art beat, which appeared late that year, reveal an extreme naïveté about art; she liked "pretty" pictures that told a story—portraits, landscapes, and traditional, illustrational pictures of mothers and children. She often wrote short, sentimental poems and rhapsodic descriptions about pretty paintings she admired, making no attempt to explain their aesthetic or historical content.

Individualism was acceptable to Jewett as long as it did not conflict with the status quo, which meant, broadly speaking, the style of the nineteenth-century French Academy. For her, the academic meant fidelity to nature and included anything from a Hudson River landscape to American impressionism, as long as the objective luminism of the latter did not go too far into daubs and smears. It never occurred to her to question academic standards. In a review of *Modern Tendencies in Sculpture* by Lorado Taft, for example, she wrote: "You are impressed from cover to cover that here is a man who knows his subject. You are safe with him. What he says, you may believe. His cup of knowledge is raised to your lips; you may drink without fear—the water in the cup is pure."[36]

Jewett's reactions to modernism over the years echoed, reiterated, and exploited all the negative reactions to the Armory Show in 1913. She wistfully hoped modernism would go away, and for years she continued to assert that it was either a passing fad, or worse, a temporary disease like the measles or the mumps.[37] Her early use of the term modern, or modernist, generally designated contemporary artists or art activities of any persuasion. It had no pejorative connotation.[38] But by 1923 Jewett was distinguishing between modernists and contemporary painters who worked in a traditional vein. By the mid-twenties her dislike of modernism had turned to indignation and her pronouncements of incompetence had turned to judgments of immorality. She was equally outraged by avant-garde European works in the Birch Bartlett Collection at the Art Institute and by local contemporary works in the No-Jury exhibitions. She labeled Cézanne, Gauguin, and Van Gogh "brutal, primitive, and childish";[39] Matisse's works were "atrocities";[40] the work by locals was the result of "variously diseased schools of art thought."[41]

In 1924, about the time that Jewett was solidifying a viewpoint that would intensify throughout the rest of her career, she was

NOVEMBER, 1930

THE TRIB

ELEANOR JEWETT

6.5 Clarence J. Bulliet in his study, photograph, ca. 1950, photograph taken from *Courier Journal* magazine, March 30, 1952. C. J. Bulliet Papers, Archives of American Art, Smithsonian Institution.

6.4 Eleanor Jewett, photograph, reproduced on cover of *The Trib,* an in-house publication of the *Chicago Tribune,* November 1930. Eleanor Jewett Papers, Archives of American Art, Smithsonian Institution.

confronted with the arrival of Bulliet at the *Chicago Evening Post*. She had more than met her match. Bulliet was well versed in all the arts, especially drama. Given his predisposition toward the new, his sensitivity to contemporary aesthetics, and his belief in individualism and artistic freedom—which unlike Jewett's, had no limitations—he supported modernism from the start.[42]

In the first few paragraphs of his lead article in the inaugural issue of the *Post's Magazine of the Art World* (fig. 6.6), Bulliet unknowingly both set the stage for a battle over modernism and launched the magazine on a liberal course paralleling that of the *Friday Literary Review*, the *Post's* corresponding literary supplement whose first editor had been the radical socialist Floyd Dell.

Discussing a visit to the Birch Bartlett Collection, Bulliet called Picasso a "picturesque Spanish genius," said the *Girl and the Goldfish* by Matisse was "destined for immortality," and praised André L'Hote's *Women of Avignon* at length.[43] His mailbox was deluged with emotional letters the next week, both pro and con. Bulliet began to understand that he had unwittingly engaged in a battle: Lena May McCauley, the editor of his own magazine, had an uncommitted, middle-of-the-road approach to modernism, and Jewett was strongly opposed to it. Neither was well-informed. Appalled by their ignorance and narrow-mindedness in matters pertaining to art, he decided to become a critic himself, in addition to directing the magazine.

Bulliet voraciously read everything he could find on art and modernism, transmitted his newly found knowledge to his readers, and attacked his opponents relentlessly, causing a continual stir in Chicago's art world. He was on a campaign to smash the taboos he felt had been entrenched in Chicago since the 1893 fair.[44] Within three years he wrote a book on modernism titled *Apples and Madonnas*. Its startling opening sentence read, "An apple by Cézanne is of more consequence artistically than the head of a madonna by Raphael."[45] The book sold out six editions—perhaps in part because Bulliet's outrageous, entertaining writing style engaged the attention of the general public as well as that of art fans—and it was chosen for the White House library in 1933. Bulliet had indeed established himself as a strong if lonely voice for modernism in Chicago.

Jewett and Bulliet came to a head-on collision over an exhibition of Ivan Meštrović's work in May 1925. Bulliet understood the dramatic intent and impact of the artist's work and, though he acknowledged that Meštrović was a lesser genius than Cézanne, Picasso, or Matisse, he exuberantly called him, with some exaggeration, the "most spectacular figure in modern

6.6 Premier issue of the Tuesday art supplement of the *Chicago Evening Post Magazine of the Art World*, October 7, 1924, front page. C. J. Bulliet Papers, Archives of American Art, Smithsonian Institution.

THE CHICAGO EVENING POST
~Magazine of the~
ART WORLD
Published every Tuesday

TUESDAY, OCTOBER 7, 1924.

CHICAGO AS THE ART CENTER OF AMERICA

Freedom of Spirit of West Preserved

By Lena M. McCauley.

The Art Magazine of The Evening Post greets its readers.

Owing to its thousands of friendly subscribers in cities and villages from the Atlantic to the Pacific, the Gulf of Mexico to the Canadian boundary, the editor has faith that there is a reading public sufficiently devoted to the fine arts to welcome the news that the Art Magazine of The Evening Post will offer more generously than in the past.

x x x

The Art Magazine is the development of an acquaintance with the history of the Art institute, the art dealers and the art schools since the American renaissance in art which dawned upon the nation thirty-five years ago with the inception of the World's Columbian exposition. This is the thirty-fifth year of The Chicago Evening Post and the twenty-fifth year of the association with it of the present art editor, who returned from Europe after schooling at the Art institute and study under eminent teachers. In the passing quarter of a century every week The Evening Post has used what space it had at command to inform its public at large of exhibitions, museum happenings, the special work of artists and the development of the artistic side of Chicago.

x x x

Chicago is the logical art center of America, according to students of the tide of affairs. New York and Boston, in alliance with London and Paris and the European continent, express the cosmopolitan point of view. The New York Metropolitan museum, the National academy and Boston and its Harvard affiliations remain leading authorities. Washington city has a wealth of artistic interests in the National gallery and its future, the plans of the Smithsonian, the new Freer gallery, the Corcoran and the riches of architecture and city planning. Art history is well established east of the Alleghenies and commands high regard.

Chicago, having no old-world tradition or colonial history, has grown with and beyond the developing middle west. A chain of noble art institutions, the Carnegie at Pittsburg, the museums at Cleveland, Toledo and Detroit, at Cincinnati and Youngstown, are at the east, the Delgado museum at New Orleans, the City museum at St. Louis at the south, powerful wealth-building art organizations at Denver, Omaha and Kansas City to the west, a great foundation at Minneapolis at the north, and here and there museums at Indianapolis, Memphis, Springfield, Ill.; Milwaukee and a projected one at Aurora, all seek the ways of art education and the solace of the beautiful for the people. Chicago strategically situated, as the second city of the nation, audaciously extending its art collections and educational opportunities, is the art center of the nation.

x x x

The Art institute of Chicago has an attendance of about 1,000,000 persons annually from all parts of the world. It is not a sacredly guarded mausoleum of antiques and modern exhibitions. It is an open house, hospitable, with welcome to man, woman and child without regard to race or to condition of society. The Art institute, founded by men who made their fortunes in Chicago, is animated by the generous outlook of good will and enterprise characteristic of the Chicago citizen and known as the "Chicago Spirit." The president, trustees and the director of the Art institute (once a student there) are vitally interested in the upbuilding of the institution for the uses of the public. Where else is there a museum to which will come over 6,550 visitors in the few hours of a pleasant Sunday afternoon in August? Where is the museum to which flock tens of thousands of men and women from the city and the suburbs annually to make a success of its exhibitions? Where else do children in the public schools and art societies, great and small, talk of our "Art institute"?

x x x

The Friends of American Art and gift collections have assembled one of the finest galleries of American painting in this country or anywhere. The old masters' gallery and well-chosen private collections give a survey from the primitives, thru the eras of Rembrandt, Velasquez, the English, Barbizon, Dutch, Flemish, modern French to the latest work of note.

The Field museum in Grant park contains many art objects relating to nations of the past. The Luther Laflin Memorial Museum of Natural History, the Chicago Historical society, public library, the Newberry and Crerar libraries, the University of Chicago at the south and the Northwestern university at Evanston on the north are all alive in the modern spirit of the open door to the student and the dispersal of ideas favorable to the understanding of the fine arts.

x x x

Chicago itself, without boasting, is an artistic city in its aspirations. The city plan, the magnificent piles of modern architecture in office buildings and hotels, the park systems adorned with sculpture by Augustus Saint Gaudens, Daniel Chester French, Lorado Taft and various moderns, the city hall, federal building and new Merchants Trust bank with mural paintings by Frederick Clay Bartlett, William Van Ingen and Jules Guerin all point to a delight in the fine arts of building, painting, sculpture and landscape architecture. Whatever efforts there are appear in the light of today. The exhibition of posters advertising attractions on the north shore at the public library evidence a desire on the part of traction lines and business to use the language of art.

Art dealers in Chicago are animated by the friendly Chicago spirit. The House of O'Brien began its career in 1855, when Martin O'Brien came to this city with a few pictures and had a vision of its future. Other galleries date back longer than a quarter of a century. The interest in fine prints, etchings and engravings developed with the late Albert Roullier, who came from New York longer ago than three decades to become a leader in the art world. The handsome galleries with window displays from 7th street south to as far north on Michigan boulevard present an ever changing exhibit of the best pictures on the market, the bronzes and rare objects. Chicago is, in fact, a distributing center in the fine arts of furniture, interior decoration, painting, sculpture and the like. Buyers come a day's journey to exhibits. Valuable canvases are shown here a day and go to museums or collector buyers. Oriental antiquities of great value for museum purposes are dispersed by an authority of recognized standing from Chicago as the continental center in art trade. All these galleries have an open door for the visitor, for who knows when they may entertain an angel unawares? Educating an enjoyment for the fine arts is preparing the soil for business later.

x x x

The Art Magazine of The Chicago Evening Post has facilities for giving the news from the several great organizations, the Municipal Art league, with its representation from 12,000 women in the city and suburban clubs, the commission for the encouragement of local art; the Public School Art society, adorning Chicago school buildings; the Friends of American Art; the Antiquarians, and the various art societies including artists and patrons. The products and personalities of the art schools, of which about ten have national importance, interest the multitude of the alumni and families scattered from coast to coast and some from across the seas. These will read the Art Magazine.

x x x

The present art editor, substituting for Miss Isabel MacDougall, a gifted writer, then in Europe, in September, 1900, wrote a weekly column. Miss MacDougall decided to live in New York, returning for a short time to be art editor of the Record-Herald, after which she was editor of a magazine and went east to live. Her service to The Evening Post laid a foundation for serious reporting and commentary on the fine arts in Chicago and in America. The present editor, special writer and assistant to Victor Yarros, literary editor, an art student as well as writer on art, succeeded to the place of Miss MacDougall, and has built The Evening Post contribution to literature and news from a single column to the space of two pages in winter season. The volume of news and criticism in the field has led in 1924 to the pages of a magazine.

The Art Magazine of The Evening Post will endeavor to keep an open mind for the appreciation of the newer developments of painting, sculpture and design. Its policy will be to stimulate educational efforts and to support whatever is offered in exhibitions for the enlarged outlook on life, the culture of taste and those movements which will add to beauty, the joy of the citizen, and make Chicago not only "a city beautiful" but enterprising in the higher spirit that will make it a better home for its people.

The Art Magazine will welcome the assistance of its readers and offers an open forum for discussion of matters of value in the public mind.

Overlooking the Grand Staircase Art Institute of Chicago.~

Cubism in Lhote Here on Display

By C. J. Bulliet.

Now that the hullabaloo of cubism has died down—the tumult and the shouting receded so far in the distance as to be heard only as an indistinct, confused murmur—Pablo Picasso's nightmarish fantasy begins to appear as the substance of more ethereal dreams. The theory of the picturesque Spanish genius, in spite of all its outward trimmings of lunacy, was sound at the core—a method of frigid composition, delicate and decorative as blue-cold rock crystal, and mystic as death. It was in its fantastic extremes that it became absurd, as Picasso himself recognized. He abandoned the absurdities that reached their climax about 1914-15, but the assertion generally made that he forsook the method itself is hardly borne out by photographs of his work as late as 1922.

One of the most adroit retainers of the cubist ideas in modified form is Andre Lhote, who contributes an amazing nude to the Paris Salon des Tuileries, 1924, and an excellent example of whose work is now on exhibition at the Chicago Art institute in the Birch-Bartlett collection. "Women of Avignon," the canvas here is called, and it holds its own even in competition with Seurat's famous "Sunday on Grande Jatte," already taking on the air of an "old master" which hangs directly opposite; with two Matisse studies of women, one of them, the girl and the goldfish, already destined for immortality, and with characteristic landscapes by Derain and Gaugin.

x x x

In Lhote's fascinating study of the two Avignon women are retained many of the angles and planes of the cubists, and even strong suggestions of the cubes themselves, which led Matisse to name "Cubisme" the bizarre school of Picasso. The garments offer easy opportunity for the treatment, but the method is carried out easily, too, and adroitly, in the difficult faces and the hands. In the nude in the Paris salon, according to black and white reproductions that have reached America, Lhote finds no difficulty in applying triumphantly the treatment to the entire figure.

Tho it is the cubistic element that introduces, as a matter of fact, the suggestion of the grotesque in the Lhote figures when the observer compares them with "true-to-nature" conceptions, it is this very element that apparently operates in just exactly the opposite way. Lhote makes such use of his planes and angles in his skillful blendings of light and shades in his distribution of color that it appears to the observer that were it not for these planes and angles there would be confusion thrice confounded.

x x x

M. Lhote's nude in the Tuileries salon suggests somewhat in pose Goya's immortal La Maja—the "desnuda" twin—who haunts forever, like Mona Lisa, anyone who beholds her in the Madrid Prado. Lhote's semi-cubist "La Maja" has not the infinite charm of Goya's all-too-human duchess, but in the bizarre and fantastic play of lights and shadows there radiates from the angles and corners of her face and form something very human and very appealing, even if cold. The Avignon women, too, at the Art institute, are human—more warmly so than the Parisian—in spite of their sphinxlike air of calm, stolid mystery. Even the sphinx, in some moods, isn't bad company.

x x x

Andre Lhote is a theorist as well as a painter, and his gifts of the pen rival those of the brush. Perhaps

Continued on Page 11.

sculpture." Bulliet understood and explained at length the expressive distortions of Meštrović's *Crucifix* (fig. 6.7), tracing its heritage to pre-Renaissance renderings of the Christ.[46] He saw in Meštrović an emotional sincerity, an example of "expressionism," a term that, like Sheldon Cheney, Bulliet sometimes used synonymously with modernism.

Jewett, on the other hand, was outraged. Unable to combat Bulliet on aesthetics, she lamblasted Meštrović's religious works on moral grounds:

> It sickens you—those long, rasping, crooked hands of the crucified Savior . . . those feeble, imbecile, drawn faces of the angels . . . the wasted attenuated Egyptian heads of Virgin and Child. . . . Why such sculpture should be permitted to be exhibited in a public gallery . . . passes the understanding. It is a vicious influence. The mastery of technique and independence of thought, the qualities that make it great enough to command an almost universal chant of praise, those should not be enough to blind one to its malignity.[47]

No mention of Bulliet was ever made in Jewett's columns, but his sensitive, unabashed support of the European modernists was clearly a threat to her, as was his book *Apples and Madonnas*. It is reasonable to speculate that the increasing vehemence of her criticism in the late twenties was a response to that threat, as was her occasional wavering of opinion on modernism, and her refusal to accept a free copy of the book (she returned it to the publishers with a cryptic rejection note that read, "Sorry—I do not care to accept this book.").[48]

Bulliet's impact on the art world was considerable. His *Magazine of the Art World*, which had both out-of-town subscribers in addition to local *Post* subscribers, was the largest weekly art publication in the country, offering a section of extensive news and reviews on each of the following: current exhibits in Chicago, activities in New York, art in other American cities, the art scene in Europe, antique furniture and interior decoration, commercial art, and news about art dealers. He allowed many viewpoints: McCauley's conservative column ran on the editorial page opposite his freewheeling "Artless Comment on the Seven Arts," in which he frequently attacked his opponents, sometimes by name. His work soon attracted the attention of Peyton Boswell, editor of *Art Digest*, and Bulliet began writing articles for that publication and occasionally for *The New York Times*.

Bulliet continued to arm himself with more knowledge, persisting in his dogged support of modernism and in his desire to educate his readers in it. He spun the European modernists' lives and goals into lengthy, anecdotal, and sometimes gossipy tales, both for the *Magazine* and for his subsequent books, of which there were seven on art.[49] In 1932, when the *Chicago Daily*

6.7 Ivan Meštrović, *Crucifix*, wood, 1916, The Meštrović Crikvine, the Chapel of the Holy Cross, Split, Yugoslavia.

News took over the *Post*, the *Post's Magazine of the Art World* ceased publication. But Bulliet became critic for the *News* and increased his local readership eightfold.

The Century of Progress exhibition, the blockbuster event of the 1930s in Chicago, was extremely significant in its matter-of-fact, chronological inclusion of modernist masterpieces along with old master works. Ironically, however, it was a non-event in the critics' battle over modernism. Press coverage was extensive but dealt mostly with other aspects of the fair and the exhibition. Jewett focused on the old masters and summarily dismissed the new ones.[50] Bulliet treated old and new masters equally. His newspaper articles about individual works of art in the fine arts exhibition were wildly popular and were published in a two-volume book called *Art Masterpieces from a Century of Progress*, which sold more copies than any other single book in Chicago that summer, aside from one novel.

Throughout the thirties, Jewett and Bulliet maintained their respective stances in regard to modernism. According to Katharine Kuh, a Chicago gallery owner, Bulliet was "the only Chicago art critic during the years of my gallery who had the faintest idea of what I was trying to do . . . the only one that I even considered taking seriously. Without him, we would have had nothing."[51]

Meanwhile, Jewett found support in Thomas Craven's books, which she reviewed at length. Her anti-modernist attitude intensified and shifted in emphasis, moving from immorality to abnormality. She came to view modernist works as products of insanity, which reflected a diseased mind or worse yet, a diseased soul. She found Rudolph Weisenborn's figures "degenerate and brutalized" and concluded that the artist himself was "brutal at soul!"[52] Likewise, after a trip to the east, she wrote of Matisse's paintings in the Cone Collection in Baltimore: ". . . all of Matisse's lines point to sex. It would be a gorgeous orgy were the women mentally more vigorous, spiritually more awake, and physically better proportioned. As it is one thinks the only fit place for them is the psychopathic ward . . ." She went on to say that they had a "pronounced affiliation to the mentally diseased and deficient."[53]

Jewett's will to protect Chicago from the evil influences of modernism would eventually lead her to support Josephine Hancock Logan's "Sanity in Art" movement, founded after the 1936 Annual Exhibition of American Painting and Sculpture at the Art Institute. Jewett served on the Board of Trustees of the organization, whose purpose was, in Logan's words, to bring "rationalism, sanity and soundness" back into art and to work toward "the restoration of real art and a resumption of progress along the line of established and universal principles . . . to help rid our museums of modernistic, moronic grotesqueries . . . masquerading as art."[54]

Logan's book, *Sanity in Art*, was filled with contradictions. She insisted she did not aim to restrict artistic freedom but nonetheless moralized about how artists should practice their art, which was of course according to academic rules. It was the culmination of Jewett's viewpoint and brought on what was probably the

6.8 Roy Nelson, caricature of Clarence J. Bulliet, n.d., but probably early 1930s.
C. J. Bulliet Papers, Archives of American Art, Smithsonian Institution.

final, major round in Chicago's battle between nineteenth-century academic standards, which were tied to an underlying self-righteous morality, and a new modernist aesthetic (fig. 6.9 and 6.10).

As would be expected, Bulliet was appalled by the Sanity in Art movement, which acquired members nationally. That Logan disagreed with his taste in art was not the issue; it was her desire to restrict artistic freedom—the creative rights of the individual—that enraged him. What he had always respected in the

6.9 Portrait of Josephine Hancock Logan, photograph, n.d. Archives of the Art Institute of Chicago. © 1989 The Art Institute of Chicago. All Rights Reserved.

modernist ethos was its respect for individualism. In a scathing, passionately written article, which appeared just before the opening of the movement's first show, he compared Logan's militant aims to those of Hitler. "Mrs. Logan would turn back the art clock in Chicago to about the time it ticks out in Berlin and

6.10 Cover of *Sanity in Art*, book by Josephine Hancock Logan, founder of the Sanity in Art organization, 1937. Photo courtesy, Sue Ann Prince.

Munich and lately in Vienna." He went on to say that Hitler blamed the Jews, Logan the French. But, he concluded, "Hitler has an axeman; Mrs. Logan only has her little book."[55] That book had an immediate impact, however, causing one local artist to render a savage depiction of Logan in a painting titled *Horsefeathers* (fig. 6.11).[56]

Paralleling the nationwide interest in developing an authentic American art in the thirties, both Jewett and Bulliet became more and more interested in the production of a genuine local art. Bulliet wrote a significant and comprehensive series of articles called "Artists of Chicago, Past and Present." Launched in 1935, the series examined the lives and careers of living and dead Chicago artists of all persuasions, beginning with C. P. A.

6.11 Lester Ambrose, *Horsefeathers*, oil painting, 1937. Painting deriding Josephine Hancock Logan. Photograph from the C. J. Bulliet Papers, Archives of American Art, Smithsonian Institution.

Healy; 106 articles were written over a four-year period.[57] They remain a major source on Chicago's early art scene.

As time went on, however, Bulliet became disillusioned by the dearth of first-rate Chicago art and by the prevailing social realist style of American art in general. He railed against derivative modernist work—"pewee Picassos, midget Matisses, dinky Derains, dilly Dalis, fifth-rate Frenchmen in disguise," as he called them.[58] By the late thirties, even Jewett mimicked his discouragement. Bulliet's disillusionment was evident in his 1936 book, *The Significant Moderns and their Pictures.* He hit his readers with a startling introduction in which he declared that modernism was dead. He claimed that the movement had run its course, from Cézanne to Picasso, and that it now consisted of puny imitations. He blamed the Depression and what he termed the "world-wide tendency toward a bristling, bragadoccio nationalism"—Hitler, Mussolini, Stalin, and the conformism of Roosevelt's WPA—for the decline of the modernist impulse.[59] Jewett was gleeful. She, who had wished all along that modernism would disappear, reported that even its most ardent supporters had declared it a thing of the past.

Modernism, as defined here, was not dead. It had been accepted into the mainstream in Paris and New York, and it had become institutionalized in Chicago in 1933 at the Century of Progress exhibition. The local battle for and against it continued, but it began to ring hollow. Jewett's outrage became outdated and Bulliet's defenses no longer seemed necessary. The battle was winding down, exhausted by its own repetition, by a lack of relevance, and overwhelmed by external forces—an economic depression and another war.

From 1910 to 1940, Jewett and Bulliet exemplified the pros and the cons of Chicago's battle over modernism: Jewett prolonged for thirty years the whole battery of objections introduced at the time of the Armory Show, from charlatanry, ugliness, and incompetence to foreignism, immorality, and insanity. She represented what was perhaps the biggest stumbling block for modernism in Chicago—an underlying self-righteous, puritanical morality. Bulliet, picking up where Harriet Monroe left off, relentlessly crusaded for the modernist cause by offering an informed though quirky sensitivity to the new art of the twentieth century. He championed the independent, creative spirit of the European avant-garde and nurtured that same spirit wherever he found it in Chicago. He stood for the individualism that defined Chicago modernism more than anything else.

By 1940, neither critic had convinced the other of much, and Chicago had not yet resolved its collective position on modernism. But each of these critics had given the other a reason to carry on the battle, and, in the final analysis, it was the battle—the dialogue—that perhaps reveals the most about the coming of modernism to Chicago.

CHAPTER SEVEN

Modernism and Design in Chicago

LLOYD C. ENGELBRECHT

In the period before 1940 few cities offered more opportunities for the development of modern design than did Chicago. Entrepreneurs created an industrial basis for design, active design reform organizations sprang up, innovative ideas in design education emerged, and no less a figure than Frank Lloyd Wright served as a forceful though largely absentee spokesperson for the modernist position on design. Yet little or no inspiration or reinforcement from the local fine arts scene occurred, and no identifiable design idiom was spawned in Chicago during the early twentieth century. There is, indeed, no easy way to characterize design in Chicago from 1910 to 1940 except to say that it was eclectic, offering everything from hard-to-read Sears, Roebuck catalog entries (fig. 7.1) to progressive graphic design, innovative equipment for the home such as faucets (fig. 7.2), and some daring interiors. Although there was some truly original and creative design, it was rare.

In order to understand modern design in twentieth-century Chicago, it is necessary to look at the development of its industry in the previous century. In 1832 when Chicago was a mere village of 150 people, events were set in motion that transformed the city into the westernmost outpost of the Industrial Revolution. Its industrial development was partly due to its location but it was also partly the result of the efforts of a type of entrepreneur who was attracted to Chicago—the kind of person who was particularly adept at taking advantage of the new capabilities opened up by the Industrial Revolution. As the city grew from a village to a major industrial center, these entrepreneurs offered unusually rich opportunities for creative and innovative design.

As early as 1832, George Washington Snow originated the bal-

7.1 Faucet shown in a
Sears, Roebuck and Com-
pany Golden Jubilee catalog
of Fall/Winter 1936–37, size
of portion shown as originally printed, approxi-
mately 3-¼ in. × 2-¾ in.
Courtesy, Sears, Roebuck
and Company.

Our Leading Mixing Faucet Value

The finest faucet of its type made! Would
easily cost $4.50 elsewhere. It has every desir-
able feature. Renewable seats, quick compres-
sion—opens to full stream with quarter turn.
Swing spout has removable anti-splash strainer
which removes foreign particles from water; removable self-drain-
ing brass soap dish. Indexed brass handles. Fits any openings
between 7¾ to 8¼ in. center-to-center. Female threads for ½-
in. pipe connection. Made of heavy brass, perfectly machined
with deep, accurate, leakproof threads. Triple coated—copper,
nickel and an extra heavy coat of chromium. Will never rust,
tarnish, pit or peel. Shpg. wt., 5 lbs. 8 oz.

$3⁶⁹

42 D 1636 . . . . $3.69

7.2 Alfonso Ian-
nelli, faucet for
Mueller Plumbing
Company, 1936.
Photo courtesy, Fons
Iannelli. Chicago
Architecture Foun-
dation.

loon frame and used it as a structural system for building a warehouse located just a few feet north of the present building of the Art Institute of Chicago.[1] Sigfried Giedion, a Swiss art historian who was fascinated with Chicago's history, pointed out that it was the balloon frame, making use of newly available machine-cut nails and other products of industrialization, that transformed wood construction into an industry: "The balloon frame marks the point at which industrialization began to penetrate housing."[2] Giedion also pointed to some of the innovators, men such as Swift, Armour, and Wilson, who brought the young city of Chicago to a unique position among early centers of meatpacking.[3] Some of the key factors in the mechanization of meatpacking had appeared elsewhere, but only in Chicago did meatpacking attain a scale that transformed a huge section of the country to the west of Chicago, stretching from Texas to the Canadian border, into what Giedion called "a gigantic reservoir of cattle."[4] These factors included intensive use of rail transportation, refrigeration, and the packaging of cooked beef in metal cans.

The industrialization of agriculture depended on another Chicago innovator as well, an inventor who turned his talents to farm machinery and later established the firm that more than any other prospered in the nineteenth century by the opening up of agricultural acreage. This innovator was Cyrus Hall McCormick, who knew the secret both of making things work and of exploiting them.[5] McCormick assuredly was not a designer. When his reaper was displayed at the Great Exhibition in London in 1851, a writer in *The Times* (London) referred to it as "this cross between an Astley chariot, a wheel barrow and a flying machine."[6] McCormick expanded the *scale* of the manufacturing in not only agricultural but also other types of machinery and thus enhanced opportunities for designers in later generations.

It was also in Chicago that manufacturers utilized the potential created by the need for large-scale production of uniforms during the Civil War to develop an industry out of men's ready-to-wear clothing. Two Chicago companies—Sears, Roebuck and Montgomery Ward—expanded the practice of mail-order merchandising to unprecented levels through efficient marketing of mass-produced items made available in virtually limitless quantities as a result of industrialization.

The businessmen who made innovative use of industrialization, thereby creating a bridge between the worlds of industry and design, did not only exist in Chicago's earlier years. A later example is Walter Paepcke (1896–1960), who as a young man became president of a family business, the Chicago Mill and Lumber Company. In 1926 Paepcke organized the Container Corporation on his belief that paper and fiber cartons would replace wooden boxes and crates for most uses. The success of this new venture vindicated his faith in the growth of paper packaging.

The firm's functional and well-designed containers show that Paepcke quickly realized the importance of good design to his firm.[7] In 1937 the Container Corporation began its highly regarded series of advertisements. An early example was created by the French graphic designer A. M. Cassandre. The simple wording clearly stated Paepcke's faith in paper and fiber packaging: "Folding cartons, corrugated and solid fibre cases for every industry" (fig. 7.3).

While industrialization brought many benefits, it had its disadvantages. Among them were labor-intensive operations and large, impersonal workplaces. The resulting tedium and hardship for workers brought about occasional outbreaks of violence and recurring incidents that resulted in repression and death, including two in the late nineteenth century: the Haymarket Square bombing in 1886, which grew out of a dispute at the McCormick Harvestor Works, and the Pullman Strike of 1898.[8] The harsh working conditions that led to such strikes were a strong if indirect factor in the development of design in Chicago and its establishment as a center of the Arts and Crafts movement. This movement adopted key tenets of the English Arts and Crafts movement such as its opposition to inhumane working conditions and its stress on the quality of the work experience. John Ruskin (1819–1900) had resoundingly denounced work experiences which dehumanized workers by demanding that they "make their fingers measure degrees like cogwheels, and their arms strike curves like compasses."[9] William Morris had called for an end to the kind of labor that was "mere wearing away of body and mind" and instead called for labor which could give "pleasure in our work."[10]

By the 1890s Chicago had become one of the most active centers of Arts and Crafts activity outside England. This was principally due to the efforts of the Chicago Arts and Crafts Society, founded in 1897, and the Industrial Art League, organized in 1899. The constitution of the Chicago Arts and Crafts Society, published in 1898, directly reflects Ruskin's and Morris's attitudes toward labor, as well as an awareness of actual working conditions in Chicago's factories. One of its stated aims was:

> To consider the present state of the factories and the workman therein, and to devise lines of development which shall retain the machine in so far as it relieves the workman from drudgery, and tends to perfect his product; but which shall insist that the machine no longer be allowed to dominate the workman and reduce his production to a mechanical distortion.[11]

Still another concern of the Arts and Crafts movement, as Chicago social critic Thorstein Veblen (1857–1929) noted, "came out of a revulsion against the besetting ugliness of what was present

7.3 A. M. Cassandre, advertisement for Container Corporation of America, July 1937. Photo courtesy, Lloyd Engelbrecht.

before the eyes."[12] The remedy sought by those active in the Arts and Crafts movement was an emphasis on high quality products that combined serviceable and pleasing elements. It was a problematic goal in the short term because it emphasized handwork, which was expensive, but in the long run it survived as part of Chicago's continuing Arts and Crafts legacy.

In Chicago as elsewhere, the Arts and Crafts movement was beset with inner contradictions. Its emphasis on handwork, for instance, seems unrelated or even antithetical to industrialization. Yet some Chicago industrialists had ties to the movement. One was Julius Rosenwald, a major executive and share-owner in Sears, Roebuck, which dealt in mass-produced items that could be illustrated in catalogs and sold in vast quantities. A supporter of improving the education of designers for mass production industries,[13] Rosenwald was nonetheless a close friend of Jane Addams, one of the most influential members of the Arts and Crafts movement in Chicago.[14]

Frank Lloyd Wright (1857–1959) is one of the best examples of a creative person who was strongly influenced by the Arts and Crafts movement but who also was frustrated by its internal contradictions. As late as 1939, Wright still vividly remembered a particularly bitter battle nearly forty years earlier within the Chicago Arts and Crafts Society over his criticism of the group's emphasis on handicraft. Wright recalled that even Oscar Lovell Triggs, then a University of Chicago professor of English, rejected his arguments. Wright later claimed that because he felt so "badly set down" by the encounter, he was driven to articulate his ideas in his now famous essay of 1901, "The Art and Craft of the Machine."[15] In it he eloquently defended his conviction that "in the machine lies the only future of art and craft" and deplored the absence of manufacturers in the Chicago Arts and Crafts Society because "without the interest and cooperation of manufacturers, the society can not begin to do its work."[16]

The Association of Arts and Industries, founded in 1922, concentrated on the improvement of manufactured goods in the Chicago region. Its members included manufacturers, bankers, department store executives, publishers, art patrons, artists, architects, and designers. A major force in Chicago design during the 1920s and 1930s, the Association became a focal point—even a battleground—for discussions about modern design and design education. Yet it offered no clear attitude toward modernism. Two of its initial board members were conservative artists: the painter Oliver Dennett Grover and the sculptor Lorado Taft.[17] More significantly, William Nelson Pelouze (1865–1943), the president of the Association from its inception until 1936, was known to have a very conservative taste in the fine arts.[18] He was also the head of the Pelouze Manufacturing Company, which made scales and electric heaters. Although Pelouze's public statements stressed the value of good design for a strong U.S. position in international trade, he merely reiterated commonplace arguments that dated as far back as the mid-nineteenth century. He also called for "an industrial art school where the trained designer upon graduating is ready to report for duty to any of the many industries requiring such trained artists or designers."[19]

Artist and designer Norma K. Stahle (1891–1950), the executive director of the Association of Arts and Industries during its entire existence, managed most of the group's affairs and was probably the most influential person in the group's internal deliberation. Nothing is known of her ideas on design or design education, other than what can be gleaned from newspaper accounts or the few pieces of her correspondence that survive. Since she no doubt worked closely with Pelouze, the statement in her first letter to Moholy-Nagy in 1937 that "we have always subscribed to the plan of the Bauhaus"[20] seems somewhat exaggerated. This indication of an underlying sympathy with the modernist position, at least in design, is borne out by other letters in which she indicates admiration for Wright and his ideas[21] and by her interest in the activities of two pioneering west coast modernists, Rudolph Schindler and Richard Neutra.[22]

Whatever the opinions of its leaders, the Association sparked interest in the issue of modernism through lectures, debates, and panel discussions. In 1925 it played a role in bringing the educator Charles R. Richards to Chicago for a series of lectures at the Art Institute. His talks presented a comprehensive overview of developments in European industrial art since the beginning of Industrial Revolution.[23] In November 1927 the Association organized a debate on the issue of modernism. Alfonso Iannelli, who had tried to introduce a modernist influence to the Art Institute when he taught there from 1923 to 1925 and again in 1927, led a team of three to defend the proposition "Resolved, that the hope of art expression lies in the modern movement, or, whether or not artists of the present should completely discard the forms of the past and work only in the spirit of the modern movement."[24] Iannelli emphasized the contradiction between contemporary architectural designs for prominent Chicago structures such as the Field Museum and Soldiers Field in a neoclassic style and the design of automobiles, department store window displays, and advertisements in a modern style.

Leading the opposition toward the modernist position was Marion Hickman Gheen, a member of the Association's Board. She responded that unless modern art "reverts to classic forms it has nothing to stand on by itself" and called an example of Iannelli's own work classic: a figure over a doorway at Immaculata High School in Chicago (fig. 7.4). Gheen's response is difficult to understand in view of that particular example of Iannelli's work and of what is known about her own work. Iannelli's figure is more medieval than classic; in fact, his faucet of 1936 (see fig. 7.2), could more easily be called classic, if classicism is understood in the general sense of refinement and restraint. An example of Gheen's own work, a dining room of 1931 (fig. 7.5), could be considered classic in the same sense. But the dining room is not classic in the sense of the stylistic revival of the Field Museum, for example. In fact, Gheen's dining room shows no evidence of any revivalist style—the type of design so strongly denounced by the modernists.

The Association solicited Frank Lloyd Wright to articulate the modernist position on at least two occasions.[25] Although Wright

7.4 Alfonso Iannelli, sculpted figure over a doorway, Immaculata High School, Chicago (architectural design by Barry Byrne), 1921–22. Photograph taken from *The Western Architect*, February 1925.

7.5 Marion Hickman Gheen of Miss Gheen, Inc., "Modern Dining Room," photograph, 1931. Photo courtesy, Lloyd Engelbrecht.

had left the Chicago area permanently in 1909 and had built infrequently there after 1914, it is clear that his views were crucial to the city's proponents of modernism. Reliance on his ideas may have been due in part to the high esteem European modernists held for him (even long before Americans recognized his importance), an esteem that deeply impressed Iannelli during a three-month visit to Europe in 1924.[26] When Stahle invited Wright to participate in an Association-sponsored debate in May 1932, she wrote him a letter that stated clearly how important she considered his acceptance. She said, "We can't play Hamlet without Hamlet."[27] The topic of that panel discussion, moderated by Iannelli, was "Is Modern Architecture Livable?" Wright was the only one of the four speakers who thought so. He declared, "Old architecture is no good anymore; it's dead," and went on to praise Louis Sullivan, who Wright declared had "originated modern architecture, which later spread to Europe." Architect Alfred Grander led the opposition by arguing that modern architecture lacked what he called "hominess" because it was "brittle, hard, superbly sanitary but like a hospital."[28]

All that can be concluded from the available evidence on the Association's debates is that by the early thirties there was considerable disagreement about the merits of modern design. Some design-conscious Chicagoans supported modernism; others felt uneasy about it, yet they were not very adept at articulating what it was about modern design that made them uneasy.

One result of these polemics was the organization of the short-lived Designers' League in 1931. Its membership included designers, architects, and artists. Wright himself was a member.[29] Its stated purpose was "to carry on the impulse to modern expression that originated in Chicago in the work of Louis Sullivan [and] Frank Lloyd Wright," because, it proclaimed, "this age has a character of its own that is given expression by an honest solution of practical needs in modern materials." Wright's central importance in Chicago to the concept of modern design and its development is apparent again. Since the League's specific aim was "to promote the use of good design and the employment of high-class designers and craftsmen in the manufacturing industries of midwest America," it seemingly duplicated the endeavors of the Association of Arts and Industries. It is tempting to speculate that its organizers felt a more steadfast champion of modernism was needed.

While the merits of modernist design were hotly debated among design professionals, it is ironic that the general public accepted modernism in design more easily than in the fine arts. Design had an advantage over the fine arts; perhaps because it was perceived by conservatives as involving functional matters rather than purely aesthetic ones, the conservative taste often imposed on the fine arts did not always carry over into the realm of design. Chicago critic Clarence J. Bulliet (1883–1952) pointed out in 1931 that Chicago department stores, which all maintained their own art galleries then, concentrated on art that was, in his words, "soft and soothing—something to rest the 'tired business man'—a [Camille] Corot or a [Jean-Jacques] Henner." But Bulliet pointed out that in the same stores "advertising departments were eagerly adapting for their own purposes the discoveries of Matisse and Picasso." Later the same year in reviewing an exhibition of paintings by Fernand Léger, Bulliet pointed out that "the practical decorators and the architects are helping themselves to the discoveries of Picasso, Braque, and Léger for practical purposes."[30]

Ideas about design education as well as the merits of modern design were continuously challenged. As far back as the turn of the century, Oscar Lovell Triggs (1865–1930) of the Industrial Art League called for industrial education that integrated work experience using real objects and processes with a broader range of studies.[31] Although the Association of Arts and Industries did not directly implement Triggs's educational ideas, its general emphasis on the importance of design education can be traced to his lingering influence, as can the statements Stahle made to a newspaper reporter in 1936 in favor of giving design students "actual materials to handle in machinery, textiles and furniture" over the "Art Institute method" which she described as an attempt "to teach by drawings on paper."[32]

The Association presented exhibitions and design competitions as well as lectures and debates. It also generated two important educational efforts for which it is still remembered today. First, there was a project to provide funds to the School of the Art Institute to strengthen and increase its efforts to educate students who would then work in industry.[33] The results of these efforts fell short of the Association's expectations. Even out-of-towners, such as Connecticut-based Sheldon and Martha Candler Cheney, took note. They reported that after "years of timid advance and retreat [by the School of the Art Institute], the effort to be machine-minded had become so feeble that the Association of Arts and Industries withdrew from the arrangement and, in 1936, set to work to plan its own independent school"[34] which opened in 1937.[35] To organize this school the Association turned to a major figure in European modernism, Laszlo Moholy-Nagy (1895–1946), who named the school The New Bauhaus: American School of Design.[36]

Although the New Bauhaus was closed by the Association of Arts and Industries after the 1937–38 academic year primarily for financial reasons, Moholy went on to establish his own school, the School of Design in Chicago. With the support of Walter Paepcke, it evolved into the Institute of Design, or "I.D." The most immediate impact Moholy had on design practice in Chicago was in the area of graphic design. His greatest impact in the long run came from his version of the Bauhaus foundation course at the New Bauhaus and at its successors. At the Bauhaus in Germany Moholy had been one of three principal teachers in the foundation course and was the first to write about it extensively.[37] Instead of trying to bring each student to a preconceived ideal result, as traditional education in art and architecture had sought to do, the course concentrated on stimulating and nurturing each student's creative powers.[38] Because so many of Moholy's students became active after World War II as teachers in newly expanded college and university departments of fine arts, architecture, and design, his influence was felt most strongly after his death in 1946 (the foundation course is still widely used in the education of artists, architects, and planners).[39]

Moholy's efforts in design education encompassed more than the foundation course. A broad range of courses including design, film, photography, music, philosophy, biology, and other academic subjects, as well as guest lectures (one by Bulliet) on a variety of topics. If Moholy and Triggs had ever met, Moholy probably would have considered the older man a bit old-fashioned; nevertheless, Moholy was the first to put into practice on a continuing basis the educational ideas Triggs had argued for more than three decades earlier. The impact was profound. A student of a night class taught for the Art Directors' Club of Chicago in 1938 by Gyorgy Kepes, another European modernist at the New Bauhaus, wrote:

This course, attended by art directors, artists and designers, had more effect than anything else on the progress of design in Chicago. Previous to that, we had all been used to designing by looking through books and magazines and getting ideas—that is, taking someone else's. This whole new revolutionary concept of *thinking*—taking the required elements, the medium, the audience, the purpose, and arriving at a solution from inside out, was real liberation, and we were just ripe for it.[40]

Given the opportunities provided by industry, the legacy of the Arts and Crafts movement, design organizations, and the innovative educational ideas that were brewing in Chicago during this period, it is no surprise that the design scene was a lively one. As for the products that came out of that scene, however, the quality and style varied greatly.

One highlight emerged in graphic design in the pioneering work of Douglas C. McMurtrie (1888–1944), a leading historian of printing and the only theorist of the New Typography movement in Chicago. The New Typography movement had begun in the early 1920s in the Soviet Union, the Netherlands, and Germany and had quickly spread at least as far as Chicago by the time McMurtrie published his 1929 book *Modern Typography and Layout*. In it McMurtrie argued that "the development of abstract design in the fine arts . . . has had the greatest influence on the applied arts."[41] Examples were given of designs by Moholy, El Lissitzky, and other European modernists, but no mention was made of their paintings nor of those of the influential Russian Suprematist Kasimir Malevich or the even more influential Dutch De Stijl painter Piet Mondrian. The omission of these artists echoes the complete lack of awareness in Chicago of the international constructivist movement, which would not be seen in the city until 1934.[42]

A scholar but not an elitist, McMurtrie was interested in the application of design in the commercial world. In his book he illustrated a food store advertisement he had happened to see, which he found so "modern, distinguished and readable" that it startled him.[43] He also included an advertisement he considered bad, a *Chicago Tribune* ad for a department store that combined a modern type face (Stygian) for the display but a "rather conventional" layout of illustrations and text.[44] McMurtrie's own work (fig. 7.6) displays a sense of sureness and sophistication that justifies ranking him as highly as the better known modernists of Europe whose work he cited.

One of McMurtrie's legacies is the Society of Typographic Arts, which he helped found in 1927. It was the only group that rivalled the Association of Arts and Industries in fostering an awareness of modern design in Chicago. Underlying its organization and activities was the growth of printing, publishing, modern typography a

MODERN TYPOGRAPHY A

Ultra-Modern [McMurtrie]. Ludlow Typograph Company.

modern typograph

MODERN TYPOGRAPHY

Ultra-Modern Bold [McMurtrie]. Ludlow Typograph Company.

modern typography and layo

MODERN TYPOGRAPHY A

Parisian. American Type Founders Company.

7.6 Douglas C. McMurtrie, "Ultra-Modern" and "Ultra-Modern Bold" typefaces for Ludlow Typograph Company, photograph, ca. 1929. Photograph taken from *Modern Typography and Layout* (Chicago: Eyncourt Press, 1929).

and advertising in Chicago in the early years of the twentieth century, which created an increased demand for graphic designers. Because Chicago's printing industry specialized in professional and trade journals, catalogs, advertisements, telephone directories, and railroad timetables,[45] it was relatively unhampered by the forces of tradition that haunted book production, and thus presented opportunities for design innovation similar to those in Chicago industries discussed above. But those opportunities more often than not were squandered. As McMurtrie observed, the opportunities provided by improvements in printing technology often resulted in what he called "a high degree of technical facility in a style of an age of the world far removed from our own."[46]

The Century of Progress Exposition of 1933 and 1934 was, like McMurtrie's work, another high point for Chicago. It had an enormous effect on public taste in design, prepared the way in Chicago—and to some extent nationally—for the acceptance of emergent modern styles, and proved that a large undertaking could be accomplished without reference to historic styles (except in quaint enclaves, such as the "Italian" village). Indeed, later evaluations of the main exhibition buildings of the Exposition have castigated them as "pallid and superficial,"[47] but nevertheless have credited them with achieving "a consistent, if not especially distinguished, standard of modern design throughout."[48]

One particular section of the Exposition, the Home Planning Group, was especially significant. It contained small exhibits by designers, manufacturers, and suppliers that stressed specific applications to present living conditions. A series of model houses included designs that were in some ways more adventurous than those of the large exhibition buildings elsewhere on the fairgrounds. Those of modernist architect George Fred Keck (1895–1980) were the most daring. The twelve-sided "House of Tomorrow," shown in 1933, included tubular steel chairs designed by Leland Atwood, of Keck's office, and executed by the W. H. Howell Company of Geneva, Illinois (fig. 7.7).[49] Keck's "Crystal House" of 1934 made use of another tubular steel chair designed by Atwood (fig. 7.8), executed by the Chicago Workshops, Inc.; this one very directly brings to mind European work of Mies van der Rohe and Marcel Breuer.[50]

Emily Genauer, writing in 1939, maintained that the furniture, the interiors, and the architecture of the Chicago fair constituted a determining influence in recent American taste. She

7.7 George Fred Keck, "House of Tomorrow," dining room, photograph, 1933. Photo courtesy, Hedrich-Blessing, architectural photographers, Chicago.

also claimed it paved the way for the wide public acceptance of the model houses, decorative exhibits, and furniture shown at the New York Fair in 1939. Genauer wrote:

> Up to the time of the Chicago exhibit, the consciousness of America's millions had not been appreciably dented by modern decoration. It had been little more than a phrase suggesting possibly the arty ateliers of Paris and New York . . . beyond application to one's own normal scheme of living.
>
> Then the Fair on the shores of Lake Michigan was opened, and countless Americans visited the row of model houses. . . . They found modern decoration good. For the country-wide popularity of the new style dates from the time they came upon it accidentally in Chicago, admired its simplicity, its directness,

7.8 George Fred Keck, "Crystal House," dining room, photograph, 1934. Photo courtesy, Hedrich-Blessing, architectural photographers, Chicago.

its straight simple lines and chunky forms, and most of all, its patent livableness.[51]

The fair also illustrated that Chicagoans did not make a neat distinction between International Style design, as represented by Mies, Breuer, et al., and the Art Deco design championed at the fair, even though Alfred Barr of the Museum of Modern Art in New York vehemently insisted that there was a clear difference. Barr did not consider Art Deco modern enough for his museum. That the distinction was not always clearly made in Chicago, (and perhaps not as often in New York as Barr might have liked!) may have affected the way Chicagoans understood design. The exhibition of International Style European architecture, organized by Henry Russell Hitchcock and Philip Johnson for the Museum of Modern Art, was brought to Chicago by the Association of Arts and Industries in 1932 and shown in the galleries of Sears, Roebuck's State Street store along with models of buildings to be erected for the 1933 Century of Progress Exposition.[52] These fair buildings were basically Art Deco expressions of a sort deliberately ignored by Hitchcock and Johnson. Barr himself would not have wanted the models of these buildings shown in his museum and would no doubt have concurred with Wright in his vigorous criticism of the major buildings at the fair as "wholesale imitation, hit or miss, of the genuine new forms that occurred in our country in out of the way places many years ago."[53]

Chicago industry sometimes looked to the outside for designers. A. J. Snow, director of the design department for Sears, Roebuck, felt in 1936 that the firm was hampered by the "failure of a true industrial arts school to emerge in Chicago," and was "constantly on the alert to find talent with sufficient design promise to merit employment."[54] Thus the firm turned to out-of-town consulting or freelance designers such as New York-based Raymond Loewy (1893–1986). In 1934 Loewy designed the first of his "Coldspot" refrigerators for Sears, Roebuck. This proved to be his first major success as a designer, and Sears introduced new Loewy-designed models annually in following years. By 1936 Loewy had opened a branch office in Chicago.[55]

The establishment of the New Bauhaus in 1937 infused Chicago with new energy in design. Moholy was the best example of a Bauhaus personality in that he excelled in a mix of creative fields including fine arts, film, photography, and several fields of design—as well as writing and teaching. In his writings all aspects of his creativity were woven into a coherent whole, and modernism was revealed to Moholy's students and readers as a broad concept that permeated all aspects of life.

Though deeply involved in design, Moholy always remained active as a fine artist and continued to feel that he was a painter first.[56] Even today he is more widely and better known than any

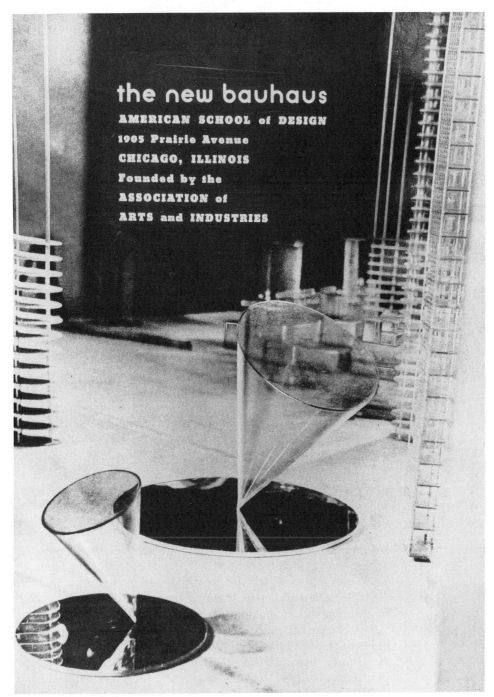

the new bauhaus

AMERICAN SCHOOL of DESIGN
1905 Prairie Avenue
CHICAGO, ILLINOIS
Founded by the
ASSOCIATION of
ARTS and INDUSTRIES

7.9 Laszlo Moholy-Nagy, cover for catalog of the New Bauhaus, 1937. Courtesy, Hattula Moholy-Nagy, Ann Arbor, Michigan. Photo courtesy, Lloyd Engelbrecht.

7.10 Laszlo Moholy-Nagy, emblem of the New Bauhaus, 1937, after a 1922 design by Oskar Schlemmer. Photo courtesy, Hattula Moholy-Nagy.

other Chicago artist of his or an earlier generation.[57] One long-range legacy of Moholy-Nagy's work in Chicago was his demonstration that the fine arts and design can reinforce each other, as demonstrated by the freshness and quality of his famed New Bauhaus catalog cover of 1937, which included sans serif letters that spelled "the new bauhaus" against a background taken from a futuristic photographic still of special effects he had created the year before for the film "Things To Come" (fig. 7.9). His logo for the school (fig. 7.10) was based on a similar design by Oskar Schlemmer for the Bauhaus in Germany. Gyorgy Kepes (b. 1906), another European modernist at the New Bauhaus, was a creative figure of comparable breadth. For a 1939 showing of both his design and fine arts work at the Katharine Kuh Gallery, he displayed his skill as a graphic designer in a striking catalog cover of simple black lettering against a rich blue background (fig. 7.11).

In summary, while there is much to admire in Chicago design before 1940, it seems that more should have been accomplished at the level of quality achieved by such exceptional figures as Keck, Iannelli, and McMurtrie. It is also noteworthy that no identifiable design image was spawned in Chicago comparable to those architectural idioms that resulted from exhilarating bursts of creativity such as the metal frame skyscrapers of Louis Sullivan (1856–1924) during the 1890s and the pathbreaking domestic architecture of Wright during the next decade. Yet the opportunities offered to designers by Chicago's extraordinary industrial development, the legacy of the Arts and Crafts movement, the awareness of design fostered by the Association of Arts and Industries and other groups were not by themselves enough for a vital design community to thrive in the city. In ret-

7.11 Gyorgy Kepes, cover for exhibition catalog for the Katharine Kuh Gallery, photograph, 1939. Courtesy Library of the University of Illinois, Chicago.

györgy kepes

september 26 - october 28
1939

Katharine Kuh Gallery — Chicago
540 North Michigan Avenue

rospect, it seems clear that three factors hampered design creativity in Chicago. First, as was perceived by many at the time, effective design education was only sporadically offered in Chicago between 1910 and 1940. Second, in the years following World War I Chicago architecture was no longer on the cutting edge and thus offered little inspiration to designers. Third, as noted above, there was little interaction with or creative inspiration from the fine arts.

CHAPTER EIGHT

The Little Review: Early Years and Avant-Garde Ideas

SUSAN NOYES PLATT

The Little Review, the longest lasting of the experimental little magazines of early twentieth-century America,[1] first emerged in Chicago as part of a larger climate of experiment and change in literature, poetry, politics, theater, music, and the visual arts. Founded in mid-1913 by Margaret Anderson, who was at that time an idealistic and little-known book reviewer and editor, the magazine provided an important outlet for the early avant-garde scene in Chicago. *The Little Review* has traditionally been famous for its pioneering publication of James Joyce's *Ulysses* in the late teens, but it first achieved significance for its presentation of early works by such soon-to-be-honored writers as Sherwood Anderson and Edgar Lee Masters, as well as for its reviews and reports on other radical activities in Chicago in the early teens. Margaret Anderson and her magazine emerged in the midst of this experimental group of writers as a result of a particular conjunction of individuals and events. The first of these events was the controversial Chicago showing of the International Exhibition of Modern Art, known in New York as the Armory Show.

In the early spring of 1913 the Armory Show, usually called the Post-Impressionist Exhibition, invaded the staid cultural circles of the city. At the beginning of its run, the director of the Art Institute of Chicago, William French, who had gone to California for the duration of the exhibition, heard from a self-respecting matron and mother that a distinguished "alienist" (expert in insanity) had visited the exhibition and declared the art to be the work of distortionists, psychopathologists, and geometric puzzle artists. The matron was concerned, she confided to Mr. French, for the moral and mental well being of her daughter.[2]

Yet, even as some members of the bourgeois sector of Chicago saw the exhibition as a threat to their moral security and tranquility, the literary, political, and artistic avant-garde responded eagerly to its challenge. The radical art of Paul Gauguin, Pablo Picasso, Henri Matisse, and Wassily Kandinsky invigorated and inspired an alert group of painters, writers, poets, and playwrights who had converged on Chicago in the years just before World War I. The central figure in this radical scene in early 1913 was Floyd Dell, a socialist and the editor of the *Friday Literary Review,* the book review supplement of the *Chicago Evening Post.* Dell, who made a sketch of himself naked as Adam (fig. 8.1) around the same time that he launched the new world of culture in Chicago, championed the Post-Impressionist Exhibition in his newspaper supplement during March and early April 1913. He claimed that it

> exploded like a bombshell within the minds of everybody who could be said to have minds. For Americans it could not be merely an aesthetic experience, it was an emotional experience which led to a philosophical and moral revaluation of life. But it brought not one gospel, it brought a half-dozen at least and from these one could choose what one needed.[3]

Dell bravely opted for the art of Gauguin because of its "bold color and primitive simplicity and serene vitality."[4] In doing so he won the praise of Harriet Monroe (see fig. 6.2), the only informed local art critic, as well as one of the few veterans of cultural concerns in Chicago who was responsive to the exhibition. She herself celebrated the experimental art repeatedly in order to offset the ridicule that it received from the rest of the press.[5] As the focal point for new ideas and issues in 1913, Dell received praise from established writers like Monroe, as well as vigorous complaints from other radical thinkers about the hopeless ignorance of the general public:

> A man with a grievance was in our office the other day. "Why," he demanded, with a bitter gesture, "do the people who go to the Art Institute to see the new pictures boast so loudly of their ignorance? Why do they so proudly parade the fact that they cannot understand what they see? One would think that ignorance was a rare and valuable thing, instead of being really quite common. They seem to imagine that it is they who are being put on public exhibition, instead of the pictures."
> He said other things too, with bitter gestures, but we will let it go at this.[6]

Such a complaint to Dell reflected the attitude of the nascent avant-garde artists and writers in Chicago. One member of that avant-garde was B. J. O. Nordfeldt, who, as one of the few post-impressionist painters in Chicago, educated Dell to the new vi-

8.1 Floyd Dell, *Self-Portrait (with Fig Leaf)*, sketch, 1911. Floyd Dell Papers, Newberry Library, Chicago.

sual art. As early as November 1912 Dell enthusiastically reviewed Nordfeldt's work in an exhibition at Thurber's gallery. He suggested a theme of freedom:

> Of course the main virtue of Nordfeldt's work is in his ability to paint what he wants to paint, freely, with a minimum of brush strokes and a maximum of effectiveness. . . . He has put his colors where he wanted them to go with a sure stroke, and that is the modern understanding of the word "art."[7]

During the week of the Post-Impressionist Exhibition, about five months later, Nordfeldt painted Dell's portrait, the artist's own most experimental work to that time, using a flattened background, asymmetry, and slightly fauve colors such as an acidic yellowish-pink in the background and a touch of green in Dell's face (plate 18). Dell was dressed in what was seen then as a modern look: a "high collar and black stock . . . a stick and gloves," a look suggested by the feminist Charlotte Perkins Gilman.[8] Dell was transfixed by the experience of being painted by a post impressionist and commented that "the arts do fertilize each other; they liberate each other from their own tradition. . . . The artistic effects characteristic of one medium of expression awakens a fruitful envy in the imagination of workers in another medium."[9]

Such a concept of the interdisciplinary stimulation and exchange of new ideas among creative thinkers was the crux of the avant-garde scene in Chicago in 1913. Dell, a socialist primarily involved with literature and politics (as suggested by his recently completed book *Women as World Builders,*[10]) was responsive to and fostered radical ideas in painting, poetry, theater, philosophy, and even his own personal life. In the spring of 1913, shortly after the Post-Impressionist Exhibition, Dell moved to a small interdisciplinary art community located in the storefronts at 57th Street and Stony Island Avenue, near Jackson Park (fig. 8.2). First erected for the Chicago Columbian Exposition of 1893, the storefronts had become a center for artists and intellectuals as early as 1903 when Nordfeldt and Thorstein Veblen first had studios there.[11] Dell expressed his radical social attitudes by having a separate studio from his wife, Margery Currey. He wrote of his bohemian life on 57th Street in a letter to a poet friend, Arthur Davison Ficke, who still lived in Dell's hometown of Davenport, Iowa:

> I have just returned to my ice cold studio, where I have built a fire with scraps of linoleum, a piece of wainscotting and the contents of an elaborate filing system of four years creation. . . . My room contains one bookcase and nine Fels-naphtha soap boxes full of books . . . a typewriter stand, a fireless cooker . . . and a couch with a mattress and a blanket.[12]

The austerity of his environment paired with the burning of his filing system marked a watershed in Dell's life as well as, metaphorically, in the avant-garde culture of Chicago. His catalytic ideas were a major stimulus for the emergence of Chicago's experimental scene. That scene first came into focus at the Jackson Park Colony in 1913 under the stimulus of Dell and Currey. It included Maurice and Ellen Browne, founders of one of the earliest avant-garde repertory theaters in America, who had been attracted to Chicago by Dell's writing in the *Literary Review.*[13] Several visual artists in addition to Nordfeldt, as well as various political and academic figures, also participated in the

8.2 B. J. O. Nordfeldt, *The Corner 57th Street Chicago, 1912*, etching, 1912. Photo courtesy Paul Kruty.

parties at Jackson Park given in the spring and summer of 1913 by Margery Currey.[14] Some of the visitors included Edgar Lee Masters, who was about to begin his classic book *Spoon River Anthology*, Vachel Lindsay, who was at that time gaining prominence after exchanging his poems for bread across the country, and Carl Sandburg, who was also just starting his career. Harriet Monroe and Henry Blake Fuller occasionally appeared, providing a link to the older generation of the cultural establishment known as the "genteel tradition."[15] Theodore Dreiser, by then settled in New York but revered by the Chicago community for his role in developing a new realism in literature, occasionally dropped in.

Margaret Anderson (fig. 8.3), the founder and editor of *The Little Review*, emerged from this scene of socialist politics, experimentation in literature, and liberal ethics not long after the furor of the Post-Impressionist Exhibition of 1913. She began her career as a peripheral part of the scene at the *Friday Literary Review* and subsequently at the 57th Street Studio.[16] Born in 1886, Anderson came to Chicago in 1908 from Columbus, Indiana to escape her suffocating family life, a life she had been rebelling against since her early childhood. After a series of escapades, she obtained regular employment as a literary editor of the *Continent*, a religious weekly; she also wrote reviews for Floyd Dell at the *Friday Literary Review*. She described Dell's entourage in her autobiography:

> Floyd Dell was surrounded by a literary group that gave promise of being the only one of interest in Chicago. I have always felt a horror, a fear and a complete lack of attraction for any group, of any kind. . . . But I was willing sometimes to see this one because Floyd Dell was in it—was it, rather.[17]

Dell was surprised by the idealism and enthusiasm of his young reviewer. He found her views to be so extreme that he sometimes ran a second review of the same book in order to balance her enthusiasm:

> her views, as expressed in 1911, had been, in fact, austerely idealistic, matching her starry-eyed, unearthly young loveliness, which was just too saint-like. She wrote well, if more enthusiastically than anybody had ever written before in the whole history of book-reviewing; an editor could not argue with her, for she stared him down with young limpid blue eyes which knew better than all his crass cynical wisdom.[18]

Dell brought Anderson to the 57th Street scene. In the late summer of 1913, inspired by the creative energy generated by Dell and his environment, Margaret Anderson officially announced her intention to found an interdisciplinary magazine that would report on the newest tendencies in art, drama, literature, and dance. Her decision was partially based on her feeling that her life had been entirely uninspired. In the midst of a sleepless night she suddenly had the inspiration to create a magazine and "to fill . . . it up with the best conversation the world has to offer."[19] That "conversation" initially was to be that of the Jackson Park artists, writers, and poets.

On the evening of Anderson's official announcement, a large

8.3 Margaret Anderson, photograph, n.d. *The Little Review* Archives, University of Wisconsin, Milwaukee.

group of these young modernists gathered at Currey's studio.[20] After an intense discussion *The Little Review* was born, borrowing its title from both the Little Theatre and the *Friday Literary Review*. Not long afterwards, Dell departed for New York where he would become the controversial managing editor of *The Masses* in Greenwich Village during the mid-teens. Partly due to Dell's departure, which resulted in the loss of publishing outlets for the avant-garde scene which he had stimulated, Anderson's small magazine became an important publication and supporter of what later scholars have come to call the Chicago Liberation.

One new arrival to Jackson Park, who responded vigorously to both the Post-Impressionist Exhibition and Margaret Anderson's magazine was Sherwood Anderson. Anderson came to Chicago in the spring of 1913 with his brother Karl who was on the organizing committee for the Art Institute show. Sherwood Anderson was deeply impressed by the radical art; years later he described his writing in terms that recalled post-impressionist painting.[21] As a newcomer to the avant-garde scene in Chicago,[22] Anderson viewed Margaret Anderson as a pivotal figure:

> In Chicago when you [Margaret Anderson] came, you were most needed. . . . I saw men and women of our unreal world become real to each other for a time. I saw men and women standing together. I saw belief springing up. . . .
> You gave a lot of queer isolated people a quick and sudden sense of each other. Something started. You walked about, being personally beautiful, as I dare say you are now. You talked with a quick rush of words. . . .
> You got us all together.[23]

Margaret Anderson emerged, thus, as one of the most charismatic visitors to the Jackson Street colony. She responded vigorously to the polemics of Dell in his *Literary Review* which favored a new world order. She rebelled against her bourgeois roots in the midwest, against the traditional life she saw around her, and made a stand for art as if it were a matter of life and death. Her enthusiasm and beauty, more than her intellectual sophistication, created *The Little Review*. The magazine supported the causes Dell championed: feminism, anarchism, socialism, modernism. It addressed futurism, the Little Theatre, and ultimately even poetry. As it began including poetry, *The Little Review* placed itself in competition with Harriet Monroe's magazine, *Poetry*, which was founded in 1912 as the pioneering publication of the early avant-garde poets in Chicago. A comparison of the two publications clarifies the unique nature of *The Little Review*.

Margaret Anderson could not have been more different from Harriet Monroe, a denizen of Chicago culture. Although both women founded little magazines, Monroe was over forty years old by the early teens and a veteran from another era of Chicago culture, that of the Little Room of the 1890s. The Little Room encompassed Lorado Taft, Ralph Clarkson, and Charles Francis Browne, all professors at the School of the Art Institute of Chicago who by 1912 were considered entrenched academics. Among the literary figures the Little Room included were Hamlin Garland and Henry Blake Fuller.[24] Monroe had become famous in Chicago while still a young woman by composing her "Columbian Ode," which was sung by five thousand voices at the Columbian Exposition of 1893. She was an informed art critic and had undertaken the brave project of publishing *Poetry* by the responsible means of subscriptions. Margaret Anderson was casual, youthful, and idealistic. She practically hypnotized her contributors into writing for *The Little Review*. Mark Turbyfill, a poet, dancer, and artist, described Anderson in his unpublished memoirs:

> I saw her hair glowing like a Burne-Jones aureole, her eyes opening wider in sapphire astonishment at my blindness. . . . She lifted her hand creatively into the air, brushing lightly the flower that nested on her blouse, and in that moment I saw the space above us gleaming, replete with the effulgence of the archetypal rose. It was the secret, the vision I longed for.[25]

In the same memoir, Turbyfill characterized Monroe as business-like when she offered him a contract to sign.[26] Anderson operated her magazine mainly on charm and sporadic donations; writers already established by *Poetry* magazine such as Vachel Lindsay donated their prize money to *The Little Review*; Eunice Tietjens, a poet who helped Harriet Monroe at *Poetry*, donated her diamond ring.[27] Although both Anderson and Monroe were important as editors of Chicago's experimental literature, and Monroe's courage to publish a magazine devoted to poetry was widely respected and supported, Anderson's radical editorial style made her magazine more eccentric and experimental as well as more exciting.

Initially solvent, Anderson rented an office in the Fine Arts Building on Michigan Avenue. A few floors below *The Little Review* office was Maurice Browne's Little Theatre, another focal point of avant-garde activities in downtown Chicago. The first issue of *The Little Review* appeared in March 1914. Anderson's opening editorial reflected her effusive energy and youthful belief that she could change the world:

> If you've ever read poetry, with a feeling that it was your religion, your very life; if you've ever come suddenly upon the whiteness of a Venus in a dim, deep room; if you've ever felt music replacing your shabby soul with a new one of shining gold; . . . if these things have happened to you and continue to happen till you're left quite speechless with the wonder of it all, then you'll understand our hope to bring them

nearer to the common experience of the people who read us.[28]

She also wrote an article on Ignace Paderewski that reflected her avid interest in music and piano playing. The opening issue included articles by participants in the Jackson Park colony such as Cornelia Anderson (Sherwood's wife), Margery Currey, Floyd Dell (by then already in New York), Vachel Lindsay, and Eunice Tietjens. It also published a letter solicited from John Galsworthy and included a long article by the magazine's primary backer, Dewitt C. Wing. Most significantly, it ran an article by Sherwood Anderson which harkened back to the inspiration of the Post-Impressionist Exhibition in calling for a "New Note" of "truth and honesty" rather than merely adapting the effects of the new:

> A cult of the new has sprung up, and doddering old fellows, yellow with their sins, run here and there crying out that they are true prophets of the new just as following last year's exhibit, every age-sick American painter began hastily to inject into his own work something clutched out of the seething mass of new forms and new effects scrawled upon the canvases by the living young cubists and futurists. . . .
>
> Something has happened in the world. . . . Old standards and old ideas tumble about our heads. In the dust and confusion of the falling of the timbers of the temple many voices are raised.[29]

The first issue set the tone of change and excitement, signifying a receptiveness to a new order that writers and artists felt emerging in Chicago in 1913–14. Although the leading post-impressionist painter, Nordfeldt, had left Chicago, Margaret Anderson reproduced the post-impressionist work of Jerome Blum and Raymond Jonson. Then emerging as a radical set designer for the Little Theatre,[30] Jonson would later become a central artist of the group known as the Transcendental Painters. Anderson also introduced the work of the recently arrived Polish sculptor Stanislaus Szukalski.[31] The Russian emigré Alexander Kaun, another member of the Jackson Park art colony and a friend of Margaret Anderson, wrote an article on "Futurism and Pseudo-Futurism." The magazine even printed Marinetti's futurist manifesto "War, the Only Hygiene of the World."[32] Quotes and an advertisement for the newly translated book by Wassily Kandinsky, *The Art of Spiritual Harmony*, appeared (fig. 8.4), along with pithy remarks by the popular art critic, Clive Bell. Margaret Anderson's campaign was to make a stand for intensity and authenticity in art and life. She wrote in the seventh issue:

> Our culture—or what little we have of such a thing— is clogged by masses of dead people who have no

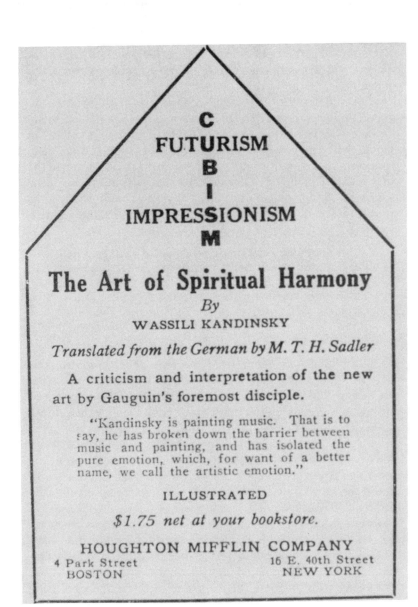

8.4 An advertisement for the English translation of Wassily Kandinsky's book, *The Art of Spiritual Harmony* (known in later translations as *Concerning the Spiritual in Art*), appeared in *The Little Review*, November 1914, p. 70.

conscious inner life . . . after one has chosen highly . . . his real struggle—and his real joy—begins. And only on such a basis is built up that intensity of inner life which is the sole compensation one can wrest from a world of mysterious terrors . . . of ecstasies too dazzling to be shared.[33]

The "inner life" to which Anderson referred may have been inspired partially by the ideas of Wassily Kandinsky. Anderson's choice of the culture of the "inner life" was based on the writings of poets such as Vachel Lindsay, Eunice Tietjens, and Edgar Lee Masters who appeared several times in the first few years of the magazine.

Yet to consider the "new note" of modernism only in the context of familiar names from the visual and literary arts is a violation of the spirit of Margaret Anderson's enterprise. Modernism also appeared in other forms. Political ideas such as anarchism were certainly an important part of modernism in Chicago in the early teens. The anarchist Emma Goldman was a favorite of the magazine; Anderson saw her ideas as applicable to the arts, as she expressed in an important editorial titled "Art and Anarchism" (fig. 8.5):

> An anarchist is a person who realizes the gulf that lies between government and life; an artist is a person who realizes the gulf that lies between life and love. The former knows that he can never get from the government what he really needs for life; the latter knows that he can never get from life the love he really dreams of.[34]

The Little Review also supported the idea of birth control and gave prominent coverage to the feminist Margaret Sanger's visit to Chicago.[35] Margaret Anderson described her commitment to feminism in general in the first issue: "Feminism? A clear thinking magazine can have only one attitude; the degree of ours is ardent."[36] In an early issue, *The Little Review* advertised Floyd Dell's book *Women as World Builders* and supported the feminists he wrote about such as Charlotte Perkins Gilman. Editorials promoted the ideal of a new world alive with change, even after the outbreak of World War I.

Anderson's initial success with *The Little Review* was the result of both the supportive and talented group of writers and political activists in Chicago as well as her own eccentric, spontaneous style. She fascinated the Chicago avant-garde with her antics such as publishing the magazine from the shores of Lake Michigan when she could no longer pay the rent for an office (partly because she had lost advertising revenues as a result of her public stand in support of Emma Goldman). When advertisers refused to buy space, she created ads in which she wrote "Carson, Pirie, Scott and Company ought to advertise something, though I don't know just what. . . . I think they resent even having to keep pace with the change in fashions."[37]

For two years the Chicago avant-garde modern scene sustained *The Little Review*. During this time it also began to publish the work of a group of experimental poets in Massachusetts and London such as Hilda Doolittle, Richard Aldington, and Amy Lowell. By the spring of 1916, though, many of the original members of the Chicago avant-garde associated with *The Little Review* had moved to Greenwich Village or otherwise dispersed.

Art and Anarchism

MARGARET C. ANDERSON

W HEN "they" ask you what anarchism is, and you scuffle around for the most convincing definition, why don't you merely ask instead: "What is art?" Because anarchism and art are in the world for exactly the same kind of reason.

An anarchist is a person who realizes the gulf that lies between government and life; an artist is a person who realizes the gulf that lies between life and love. The former knows that he can never get from the government what he really needs for life; the latter knows that he can never get from life the love he really dreams of.

Now there is only one class of people—among the very rich or the very poor or the very middling—that doesn't know about these things. It is the uneducated class. It is composed of housewives, business men, church-goers, family egoists, club women, politicians, detectives, debutantes, drummers, Christian Scientists, policemen, demagogues, social climbers, ministers who recommend plays like *Experience,* etc., etc. It even includes some who may be educated—journalists, professors, philanthropists, patriots, "artistic" people, sentimentalists, cowards, and the insane. It is the great middle-class mind of America. It is the kind of mind that either doesn't think at all or that thinks like this: "Without the violence and the plotting there would be nothing left of anarchism but a dead theory. Without the romance of it anarchism would be nothing but a theory which will not work and never can until nature has evolved something very different out of man. It is cops and robbers, hare and hounds, Ivanhoe and E. Phillips Oppenheim all acted out in life. It is not really dangerous to society, but only to some members of it, because unless every one is against it there is no fun in it."

There is no fun talking about anarchism to people who understand it. But it would be great fun to make the middle-class mind understand it. This is the way I should go about it:

What things do you need in order to live? Food, clothing, shelter. What things *must* you have to get life out of the process of living? Love, work, recreation. All right.

Does the government give you the first three things? Not at all. It isn't the government or law or anything of that sort that gives you food or clothes. It's the efficient organization between those who produce these things and those who sell them to you. And it isn't government that keeps

8.5 Margaret Anderson, "Art and Anarchism," article that appeared in *The Little Review,* March 1916.

Anderson began to think her cause was faltering. She commented despairingly: "I have been realizing the ridiculous tragedy of *The Little Review.* It has been published for over two years without coming near its idea."[38]

Precisely at this juncture Jane Heap appeared, the person who would be the mainstay of the magazine for the rest of its existence (fig. 8.6). The daughter of a supervisor at an insane asylum in Kansas, Heap had moved to Chicago around 1900 and completed an art degree at the School of the Art Institute of Chicago in 1905. Although Heap had been a participant in Little Theatre performances as early as 1912, she first met Margaret Anderson in the spring of 1916.[39] Her impact on the magazine was drastic and immediate. A brilliant and ascerbic conversationalist on any topic, she entranced Anderson. They became lovers (an early example of open lesbianism) and spent a summer talking about art and life in California, an experience recorded in some flamboyant cartoons that appeared in the September 1916 issue (fig. 8.7). That same issue contained the famous twelve blank pages in response to Margaret Anderson's declaration that she would rather print nothing than fall short of being fully creative: "*The Little Review* hopes to become a magazine of Art. The September issue is offered as a Want Ad."[40] Her intense interaction with Heap was at least partly responsible for her sense that the magazine was not sufficiently creative. At this same time, under the stimulus of Heap's art background, the magazine changed from its drab brown cover to brilliantly colored jackets and bolder typefaces.

In the winter of 1917 another editor joined the magazine and also wrought a radical change in *The Little Review*. Ezra Pound, who had been affiliated with *Poetry* magazine almost since its inception, decided to transfer to *The Little Review* in March 1917.[41] With Pound as foreign editor from London, the magazine began to publish the next generation of modern writing—the work of T. S. Eliot, Wyndham Lewis, and James Joyce. In that same winter *The Little Review* moved to New York, thus ending the Chicago history of the magazine, even though its own best-known chapter was just beginning. During the New York years the magazine was censured, suppressed, and even burned for publishing excerpts of James Joyce's *Ulysses* that were considered obscene; ultimately the editors were led into court and fined.[42] By 1921, with Pound's continued support and as a rebuttal to its repression, *The Little Review* became a conduit for avant-garde European painters and poets such as Jean Cocteau, Constantin Brancusi, and Fernand Léger.

From a naively enthusiastic protest against the status quo supported by the youthful modern thinkers in politics, art, and literature in Chicago in 1913, *The Little Review* became an important magazine of the international avant-garde by the early 1920s. From mirroring the post impressionism, futurism, and expressionism of the nascent Chicago modernist scene in the visual arts, theater, and literature, *The Little Review* ultimately en-

8.6 E. O. Hoppe, *Jane Heap*, photograph, n.d. *The Little Review* Archives, University of Wisconsin, Milwaukee.

Light occupations of the late here is nothing to edit.

8.7 Jane Heap, cartoons from *The Little Review,* September 1916.

gaged the central issues of the avant-garde literary and visual arts scene of London and Paris.[43] *The Little Review* had a longer, more complex history than most of the other "little" magazines of the early twentieth century, but its lasting roots were in the Chicago avant-garde scene of the early teens. Those roots emerged one last time in the numerous tributes from the early contributors in the final issue of the magazine published in Paris in May 1929. It was a long, exciting journey, but without the exuberant idealism spawned in Chicago in 1913, it never would have even begun.

CHAPTER NINE

The Katharine Kuh Gallery:
An Informal Portrait

AVIS BERMAN

A portrait, be it in words or images, can reveal a personality, clarify social and psychological relationships, fix a likeness, and document the subject's place in the world. These are the aims of my account of Katharine Kuh's years as an art dealer. The portrait of her gallery is based chiefly on the sittings I had with her while conducting her oral history for the Archives of American Art. Over the course of fifteen sessions, which began on March 18, 1982, and ended on March 24, 1983, I learned a great deal about Katharine Kuh's career as an art dealer from 1935–1942, and her later life and times as a curator at the Art Institute of Chicago, the art critic of *Saturday Review*, the eye behind the First National Bank of Chicago's acclaimed collection, a friend of artists, and a passionate lover and defender of art (plate 19). I hope, by quoting from and distilling Katharine's own words—the fruits of our sittings—to convey a firsthand sense of her gallery's color and spirit, its meaning to Chicago as the only private gallery in the city consistently devoted to advanced contemporary art, and the cultural climate in which she thrived and struggled as a pioneering dealer. I have supplemented the original oral history with more recent interviews and have also drawn upon the Katharine Kuh Papers in the Archives of American Art.

Katharine Woolf was born on July 15, 1904, in St. Louis, Missouri, and grew up in Chicago. She earned a B.A. at Vassar, received a master's degree in art history at the University of Chicago, and began a doctorate, also in art history, at New York University at night while holding down a daytime job at the American Association for Labor Legislation. In 1930 she returned to Chicago to marry George Kuh, a businessman. At that time, she recalls, there were five places where one could regularly see modern and progressive contemporary art, and the Art Institute was not one of them. The Chester Johnson Galleries handled impressionists, post impressionists, and early twentieth-century French art; the Increase Robinson Gallery showed Americans, many of them from Chicago; and the Roullier Gallery specialized in French art and fine prints. Thus it was rare to see vanguard art that was not French, save for two places that were far more courageous than any of the dealers—the Arts Club of Chicago (which is a story in itself) and the Renaissance Society of the University of Chicago. The Arts Club, for example, had a one-man show of Joan Miró as early as 1931; and in 1934 the Renaissance Society asked James Johnson Sweeney to arrange a show that made history—he selected works by Arp, Brancusi, Braque, Calder, Gris, Hélion, Léger, Miró, Mondrian, and Picasso. Some of these artists had not yet been widely recognized even in Europe.

The Kuhs lived in Highland Park, which Katharine found somewhat stifling after her life in New York. However, as the years went on, she began lecturing on art to private groups of sixteen to twenty people. They met in the houses of the various students, who usually organized the classes themselves and paid a dollar apiece to hear her. Katharine says, "I remember a woman in one of my groups. I had talked at great length on Velázquez. When the meeting was over and she was putting on her coat, she said, 'By the way, he sounds fascinating. If he should ever come to Chicago, I'd like to give a party for him.' I felt totally deflated, but in truth some very astute Chicago collectors got their start through those lectures and open discussions."[1]

The Kuhs' marriage broke up after five years and Katharine, in her innocence, decided to open an art gallery. She was determined to make it a center for the new and vital, explaining, "I guess I wanted to be a pioneer in my own backyard. And of course I wanted to strike out on my own. I needed to live a life I believed in, a life that was more challenging. I wanted to make a total break, and for a long time I had been fascinated by the avant-garde in art. These were heady years, with the emergence of one great movement after the next."

In the fall of 1935, Katharine took over Increase Robinson's gallery space, because Robinson was giving it up to become the supervisor of the local federal art project. The gallery was on the Near North Side, at 540 North Michigan Avenue, in the mezzanine of the Diana Court Building, which no longer exists. The building took its name from a fountain of Diana by Carl Milles in the court. The Katharine Kuh Gallery consisted of one long room, painted stark white; a free-standing wall divided it into a large front section and a small back area (fig. 9.1). The rent was $50 a month. This was in the middle of the Depression and, as Katharine says, "I had no financial backing whatsoever during

9.1 The Katharine Kuh Gallery, photograph, November 1940. On view are Oceanic sculptures from the collection of Wolfgang Paalen and watercolors by George Fred Keck. Katharine Kuh Papers, Archives of American Art, Smithsonian Institution.

the entire life of the gallery, a fact that insured my independence but also long hours and hard work because I couldn't afford help."

The gallery opened on November 4, 1935. Katharine had no stock of her own so she arranged to borrow a group of paintings from the New York dealer Marie Sterner.[2] None of the artists shown are remembered today or have amounted to much. They were clever, superficial artists who had appropriated School of Paris mannerisms, and Katharine was most unhappy with them. As she puts it, "They were well-bred, acceptable. Just what I didn't want. Only a blithe neophyte would have been brash enough to start a contemporary art gallery in the Middle West, at that time the home of entrenched conservatism."

Having to look at these paintings every day for a month was intolerable. Katharine decided she would show only artists whose work she believed in and was stimulated by, even if she could not sell it. These artists can be divided into roughly five categories, all of them strong choices: avant-garde European artists, such as Kandinsky, Klee, Léger, Albers, Picasso, Miró, Jawlensky, Archipenko, and Moholy-Nagy; progressive Chicago artists, such as Robert Jay Wolff, Julio de Diego, Rudolph Weisenborn, Charles Biederman, Gertrude Abercrombie, George Fred Keck, and Julia Thecla; advanced American artists based in New York, such as Alexander Calder, Gaston Lachaise, Isamu Noguchi, Lyonel Feininger, and Stuart Davis; Latin American artists, such as Carlos Mérida and Rufino Tamayo; and photographers, such as Edward Weston, Ansel Adams, and Eliot Porter. Katharine never expected to make any money from the gallery, but she did expect it to break even, which it eventually did. At its most profitable, the gallery supported itself but not her, which was fine with Katharine. She says, "The gallery was a creative enterprise for me and I was willing to support it with outside work, as I would have done for a child."

Katharine ran the gallery on a proverbial shoestring. She could not afford to have catalogs printed, so she made do with sending out announcement cards. She did everything herself, with a minimum of help. She brought her lunch every day and stayed in the gallery from morning until evening. If she needed to leave the city, she trusted her mother to replace her. Students from the School of the Art Institute, Katharine says, "helped me pack, unpack, and install exhibitions. We'd work until late in the evening, and I'd have a picnic supper in the gallery." One of those students was the California painter Emerson Woelffer, who later wrote to Katharine that helping her in the gallery was his first close encounter with important contemporary art.

In March 1936, Katharine began holding art classes at the gallery. "The classes really carried the gallery," she says. "They allowed me to do exactly as I wished. I was not a born saleswoman, and I usually got bored before a transaction was consummated. I'm afraid I was less interested in selling than in showing. My hope was to expand visual horizons in Chicago. My classes took place behind that dividing wall. If the telephone rang, I had to hop up and answer it while the class waited. If critics or customers came in, I had to get up and look after them. People put up with all that. They just waited.

"One time while I was teaching a class in modern art, I asked, 'Where's Mrs. So and So?' One of the other students said, 'Oh, she had a baby a few days ago.' I said, 'I didn't realize she was pregnant,' and the student replied, 'You're so used to distortions that you don't even recognize them.'"

Katharine made a substantial change in her exhibition policy as soon as she could, a fact attested to by her second show, in February 1936, of paintings by Le Corbusier, drawings by Picasso, and terra cotta sculptures by Noguchi. Whereas the *Chicago Tribune*'s story about the forgettable opening show was headlined, "New Gallery Has Moderns That Please,"[3] the paper did not feel that way for long. Once artists of truly radical sensibilities were on view, its reviewer, Eleanor Jewett, was no longer so delighted. She commented on this second show, in regard to

Le Corbusier: "One hopes he does not build like he paints." Similarly, she wrote, "The Picasso drawings are cheerfully futile."[4] But not everyone was scared away. Elizabeth Paepcke bought a Le Corbusier painting and Claire Zeisler purchased a sculpture. Zeisler was Katharine's most enthusiastic client—as time went on, she acquired several Klees, a Picasso, and an Albers. Katharine describes her as "the most independent, perceptive person in Chicago where art was concerned. She came in, understood, enjoyed, and even bought. She gave me courage. All this was before she became a distinguished artist in her own field."

Katharine's resolve to show only experimental art—in her words, "artists who introduced us to new worlds"—would put her in direct conflict with the predominant taste in Chicago. As one local writer observed in 1937, "With the exception of the Arts Club, . . . the Katharine Kuh gallery is the only Chicago gallery willing to display the canvases of these ultra-moderns."[5] The gallery's few supporters were a tiny but receptive group consisting of professors, art students, artists, and a sprinkling of intellectuals who bought occasionally. For example, former Senator S. I. Hayakawa of California was teaching in Chicago when he bought a large circus drawing by Alexander Calder in 1937. It cost $36, and he paid for it in three monthly installments—Katharine's commission was one-third of the total price, so one can imagine how much money she made from all this. (Not included in this educated group were the curators from the Art Institute, who never, Katharine hastens to say, bought a single object from her gallery in all the years she ran it.)

Shortly, this circle of appreciators would expand to include the European emigrés who had fled the Third Reich and settled in Chicago—Mies van der Rohe, Laszlo Moholy-Nagy, Gyorgy Kepes, Hugo Weber, and many others. These men, who by their own work and teaching were transforming the art life of Chicago, were familiar with the art Katharine showed and gave her the emotional and intellectual backing that had rarely been provided before. The gallery also received good press notices from C. J. Bulliet, the liberal art critic of the *Chicago Daily News*. But this coterie was still miniscule.

The gallery's most vocal opposition came from the two art reviewers—Katharine refuses to dignify them with the name of critic—of the *Tribune* and the *Herald and Examiner*. Not only were they both grossly ignorant when they took up their jobs, but they also did not bother to educate themselves in preparation for their new assignments. Is it any wonder that they were both violently anti-modernist? Eleanor Jewett of the *Tribune* was a great-niece of Colonel McCormick, the publisher of the paper. She needed a job, so she was given the post of art critic. The art critic for the Hearst paper, the *Herald and Examiner*, was Paul T. Gilbert, who Katharine says "was really a sports writer. His wife did the footwork. He never came; he never saw a show. He sent her and she reported back. He and she knew nothing about art and they damned everything that *she* saw. He'd just write. He never looked—he was too busy with golf."

The more dangerous antagonist was Jewett. In Katharine's words, "She became a terrible enemy of the gallery. Here we were living in a marvelous period when the great artists from Europe were developing a new visual language, really a new philosophy, and she was hell-bent on destroying them. The *Tribune* had an enormous circulation and most people in the city really took it as the word of God. They were, I'm afraid, in complete agreement with the reactionary critics." To illustrate what Katharine went through, two excerpts from typical reviews follow.

Gilbert on Josef Albers, who was given a show by Katharine in 1937, when he was still practically unknown in this country: "Whatever the cognoscenti may profess to see in them, the layman, even by a stretch of the imagination, will be unable to discern the remotest suggestion of anything on land or sea. And, perhaps, he would do well not to try." [6]

Jewett on Paul Klee, whom Katharine began showing in 1938 and almost every year thereafter. Klee was an artist for whom Jewett reserved her special contempt: "Mrs. Kuh is extremely proud of it [her Klee show] and considers it one of the most important shows her gallery has brought to Chicago. . . . [She] speaks of the 'exquisite and imaginative quality of the work.' Of this you must judge in person . . . It seems to us as tho [*sic*] when a man has spent such time and effort in wiping out all intelligence from his work that it is highly improper for the spectator to read meaning into it. Therefore, out of respect, we will desist from effort." [7]

In November 1936, the gallery mounted a large show of photographs by Ansel Adams, becoming the first art gallery in Chicago to show fine photography. By then the gallery had already gained some renown, because Adams wrote to Katharine from California requesting an exhibition. He was having a show with Alfred Stieglitz at An American Place in New York and thought it would be nice if he could have one in Chicago at the same time. If the work was good enough for Stieglitz, it was good enough for Katharine—but although Stieglitz was getting $100 a print, she dared ask no more than $25.

When Adams came east to Chicago, he was thin, nervous, and broke. Katharine didn't sell more than three or four prints. She remembers, "Ansel said he would be tremendously grateful if I could get some portrait commissions for him. We had a very good time together. After dinner one night, we went to one of those machines that took three or four pictures for a dime and we both had ours done (fig. 9.2). He was 34 and I was 32.

9.2 Ansel Adams, photograph, November 9, 1936, when he and Katharine Kuh had their pictures taken in an automatic photo machine. Katharine Kuh Papers, Archives of American Art, Smithsonian Institution.

"I did get him a commission from an older woman, Rosette Lowenstein. She was interesting looking—very autocratic and intelligent. He enjoyed photographing her. She wore pince-nez glasses that were very much a part of her personality. He insisted that she keep the glasses on. He made fine searching portraits of her and developed all the trial prints. She didn't like them because, I presume, they didn't flatter her. They really zeroed in on her. That unnerved her and she told me, 'I can't bear to look at myself.' That was that—she rejected every one of them, and Ansel didn't ask her for a cent." Adams gave Katharine some of the proofs, which she later donated to the Art Institute of Chicago.

After the Ansel Adams show, the gallery had a Christmas exhibition with scroll drawings by Noguchi, a group of paintings and drawings by several Chicago artists, plus small works by

Léger, Lurçat, Pascin, Matisse, and Picasso. Prices ranged from $5 to $100, and public reaction was as usual. In a review subtitled "Moderns Are Weird," Gilbert concluded, "Drawings by Leger are nightmares, while Paschin's [sic] watercolors can be taken seriously only by extremists."[8] And during the run of the show a woman walked into the gallery, looked around, and commented, "I don't see how you find the time to do all these and still run your gallery."

Beginning in about 1937 the gallery began to benefit from the influx of artists, designers, and architects who had left Central Europe and were settling in Chicago. That year, Katharine remembers, "I was sitting at my desk as usual when this very strong, heavyset man walked in. He asked, 'Are you Katharine Kuh?' in a thick Russian accent. He then said he was Alexander Archipenko. He wanted to know if I would handle his work, and I jumped at the opportunity because he was an artist I had long admired. He was a little shocked that I was so dégagé, inexperienced, and unchic, and especially concerned that I didn't have any entourage to do the dirty work. All the same, he had a number of shows with me and he was one of the few artists that I really was able to sell in Chicago (fig. 9.3). His students, many of whom were rich women, would rush to buy his work."

Not long after meeting Archipenko, Katharine received a visit from the German art dealer Carl Nierendorf, who also just appeared in the gallery. "He had a suitcase with him," she recalls, "and in that suitcase he toted around small pictures—everything unframed, matted, and carefully packed into the suitcase. Among them were several Paul Klees, and I flipped. In those years, Klee's paintings meant more to me than any other artist's because I found that his wonderful private world was based on the most subtle ideas and symbols. For me they opened an intangible view of life as they gently debunked all pretensions. Nierendorf, who had fled Hitler and would later become an important New York dealer, lectured me on this occasion. He said, 'Mrs. Kuh, you should dress better. You should put your hair up'—I wore my hair down tied back with a ribbon—'You should look more like a grande dame. You're never going to sell a picture this way.' Well, I didn't change my hair or my clothes, but nonetheless he lent me the Klees and we did business together until the gallery closed."

A love of Paul Klee's work was a bond shared between Katharine and Mies van der Rohe, who arrived in Chicago in 1938. Katharine and Mies became friends, and she later sponsored him for U.S. citizenship. She recalls, "He would come to my Klee shows and study each one for about ten minutes. He would walk around the gallery, saying in that deep voice of his, 'Wunderbar! Wunderschoen! Wunderbar!'"

In contrast to Mies's deeply sympathetic response, Katharine

9.3 The Katharine Kuh Gallery during the run of an Archipenko exhibition, photograph, n.d. Katharine Kuh Papers, Archives of American Art, Smithsonian Institution.

remembers the time two other Germans—Mr. and Mrs. Thomas Mann—came in during a Klee show. "The minute he walked in," she says, "I recognized him. They seemed to take it for granted that no American understood German and began talking. Mrs. Mann could only repeat, 'Schrecklich! Schrecklich!' (Dreadful! Frightful!) To which Thomas Mann nodded and said, 'Ja, ja, schrecklich.' I was so sad that the man who had written *The Magic Mountain* couldn't understand Paul Klee."

Katharine says that Mies, Archipenko, Moholy, and their faculties and students, who poured into the gallery month after month, gave her a second wind and the validation to keep going. Such support was genuinely needed, for the cultural climate had become not more but less tolerant of her gallery. Jewett attacked more immoderately as time went on, as artists like Kandinsky and Léger and Klee began to be seen at the gallery year after year. This antipathy was also tied up with Jewett's being a cog in Sanity in Art, a rabid movement of art vigilantes begun by

Josephine Hancock Logan in 1936. The object of Sanity in Art was to have solely the most reactionary art, and only American art at that, shown, bought, or collected in Chicago. Its adherents fought every new idea tooth and nail. One would be tempted to joke that Sanity in Art was a synonym for "Inanity in Art" if the group had not exerted such a baleful influence or been so vicious in pursuing its agenda. The Katharine Kuh Gallery was targeted for harassment and there were three or four menacing encounters. Members of Sanity in Art began by writing Katharine nasty letters and then graduated to in-person visits. In her words, "A committee would march into the gallery, a committee of three, and they looked like characters in a cartoon by Helen Hokinson because they were always big, bulky women wearing hats. I'd be alone in the gallery—I had many hours when I didn't have a single visitor—and they would pound in. They would literally pound in, and then they'd start berating everything. If a customer by chance came in, they berated him or her—and the poor customer fled."

Katharine had one experience during an exhibition of work by Carlos Mérida, whom she used to show nearly every year, from 1938 onward. She got to know him well after she started teaching over the summer at an art school in San Miguel de Allende, Mexico, where the artist also taught. Her gallery was closed during the summers, and teaching in Mexico, as well as running an employment bureau part-time for the Art Institute in the winter, were two other ways Katharine financed the business. Through knowing Mérida and living in San Miguel, Katharine also met Rufino Tamayo and Edward Weston and absorbed Mexico to the bone. She says that the genesis of *Death is Incidental*, a drawing by Mérida that she showed in the gallery and later gave to the Solomon R. Guggenheim Museum, was profoundly Mexican and exemplified the personal association between her and many of her artists. Katharine recalls, "Carlos and I were sitting on a bench in the plaza when a horse-drawn wagon drove by with blood spilling out from the corpse of a dead Indian. We later learned that he had tried to steal a chicken. Carlos said, 'In your country, death is accidental; in Mexico, it is *incidental*.'"

To return to Mérida and Sanity in Art, "During one of his shows," Katharine says, "he was sitting in my gallery across from me and reading the newspaper. Three of these women appeared. At first they thought he was a customer, though why they thought a customer would be sitting there reading the paper, I can't imagine. Then they realized he was the artist. What they didn't know was that Carlos was stone deaf. He couldn't read lips so he just stood there. He thought they were excited because they were so entranced with the show. He was beaming, and the more he smiled the more heated they became. He actually thought they were in love with his work. The next thing I knew, he picked up the head lady's hand and kissed it fervently. She didn't know what was happening. The women were overwhelmed with confusion, and they departed in total befuddlement.

"But it wasn't always as funny, and I decided to talk to a lawyer. He told me, 'All you have to do is go over to the telephone and quietly call the police if you have a customer.' One day they came in when I was working with a person who seemed serious. The ladies kept up a rapid fire of angry comments, so I called the police. The women were escorted out of the gallery because they were interfering with the operation of a legitimate business, which was against the law. They never returned after that."

One memorable instance of local ignorance worked very well for the gallery. On January 19, 1937, the architect Leland Atwood (plate 20) hurried into the gallery to ask Katharine if she were going to the auction of the estate of the pioneering Chicago collector, Arthur Jerome Eddy, which was to take place the next day. Katharine was not even aware of the sale because it was being held, she says, "in an unknown little auction house on Wabash Avenue" with no fanfare whatsoever. She, Atwood, Bertha and Daniel Catton Rich, and Molly and John Thwaites (the British vice consul and an ardent connoisseur of contemporary art), all went together. It immediately became clear that the auctioneer had no idea of what he was selling. Katharine recalls, "The first thing he said was, 'What am I bid for this Timpansky?' It was a handsome expressionist Kandinsky, a 1909 landscape of Murnau with a church, which I found quite marvelous. The auctioneer suggested $20. I nodded, and he said, 'Sold.' He asked me my name and because I didn't want to say who I was, I replied, 'KK.' Then, one of the great *Improvisations* of 1912 came up, and John Thwaites got it for $155. The price was bid up a bit because his wife became so excited that she had bid against him.[9] The next Kandinsky to come up was an early fauve painting of Murnau. The auctioneer said, 'Anyone willing to give $5 for this?' I raised my hand and he said, 'To KK.' Then whenever no one else wanted a work, he would say, 'How about KK?' as a joke, and I would say yes. He thought I was crazy. So I got ten pictures for $110—including the two Kandinskys, four Jawlenskys, two Man Rays (a rayogram and a painting, each for $10), a Gabriele Munter, and an early color lithograph by Bonnard."[10]

"Some time later I called an architect I knew named James Eppenstein and asked him if he thought he could sell the expressionist Kandinsky to one of his clients. I asked $350 and he bought it immediately. Later he called me to say that he and his wife loved the picture so much that they weren't going to sell it. I said 'Bravo!' and told them that they wouldn't regret it—to hold on to the painting because it was going to be worth a lot more." As a footnote, in November of 1987, James Eppenstein's children sold their father's Kandinsky at Christie's in New York.

The painting went for nearly twice the presale estimate—it was bought for $2.4 million.

The gallery presented the purchases from the Eddy estate in September 1938 and followed this exhibition with another outstanding one—a solo show of Joan Miró, which included such seminal paintings as *Dog Barking at the Moon*, now in the Philadelphia Museum of Art, and *The Farm*, which was later bought by an Oak Park native named Ernest Hemingway. Works of this caliber were available, yet nothing was sold. Negative reviews stirred up so much resentment that someone—never identified, but thought to be associated with Sanity in Art—threw a whiskey bottle through the plate glass window of the gallery. In reporting the incident, Gilbert, in *The Herald and Examiner*, called Katharine—the victim—"the leader of the leftists,"[11] implying that she brought the vandalism on herself. In her review, titled "An Old Blotter Becomes Art in Miro Exhibition," Jewett charged the artist with taking an ink-splotched piece of blotting paper, framing it, and exhibiting it as art.[12]

Nevertheless, Katharine went on undeterred, making no concessions and trying to persuade the public that art was not limited to traditional classifications. In January 1940, she gave Moholy a comprehensive show, but it was not appreciated. The reviewers, with the exception of Bulliet, said that his work—the constructions and the photograms—was not art. In honor of Lyonel Feininger's seventieth birthday, she gave him his first solo show in Chicago. Katharine also organized several theme shows she hoped would be provocatively educational in making their points. "Order and Clarity in Art" featured suprematist, purist, constructivist, and neo-plastic paintings by El Lissitzky, Léger, Ozenfant, Mondrian, Albers, and Kandinsky. The centerpiece of "Color in Modern Art," an exhibition devised to illustrate the functional and emotional use of color, was a version of Franz Marc's *Blue Horses*. Besides this great work, the gallery displayed two other paintings by Marc, as well as examples of Miró, Kandinsky, and Chagall. "Leaders of Cubism" celebrated the epochal early achievements of Picasso, Braque, Juan Gris, and Roger de la Fresnaye. In October 1941, through her friendship with Kepes, he and Katharine organized a highly unusual survey of avant-garde advertising, which showed that commercial design had intrinsic artistic merit. Some of the designers represented were Moholy, Kepes, Herbert Bayer, Herbert Matter, and Paul Rand. Katharine says she was so pleased with this show that she forgot she had a gallery—after all, nothing was for sale.

It was not the small profits or the poor sales or the savage opposition that stopped Katharine, but a global conflict. After America entered World War II, works of art could no longer be shipped across the Atlantic, and she could not stay in touch with the European artists that she wished to represent. In April of 1942, the Katharine Kuh Gallery closed its doors. But although the gallery's life was over, its founder's long and distinguished career had really just begun.[13]

Appendix: Checklist of Exhibitions at the Katharine Kuh Gallery

1935

November 4	The gallery opened with a loan exhibition from the Marie Sterner Gallery, New York: Brabo, Ebihara, Ferat, Edy Legrand, Marembert, Pruna, Sureda
December	Rubin, Karl Zerbe

1936

January	Raymond Jonson, Keith Martin, Charles Rain, Charles Sebree; Aristide Maillol, Guitou Knoop
February	Le Corbusier, Picasso, Isamu Noguchi
April	Fernand Léger, André Bauchant, André Derain, Valentine Prax, Kirsta, Lurçat, Jean Hugo, Picasso
May	Gertrude Abercrombie, Emmanuel Viviano (to 6/13)
October	Annot, Jacobi
November	Ansel Adams (11/2–11/21)
December	Noguchi; Abercrombie, John Stenval, Jonson, Hans Werner, Julia Thecla; Hugo, Léger, Lurçat, Pascin, Matisse

1937

January	Anthony Angarola
February	Benjamin Kopman
March	Peter Takal, Picasso
April	Abercrombie, Rudolph Wiesenborn
May	Alexander Calder, Gaston Lachaise, Léger; Alexander Archipenko, Viviano
September–October	Josef Albers, E. Misztrik de Monda (this exhibition was then loaned to the Renaissance Society)
November	Le Corbusier
December	Archipenko

1938

January	Jonson; exhibition of 54 paintings and drawings (among them, works

1938

January	by Picasso, Archipenko, Lurçat, Léger, Noguchi, Le Corbusier, Takal, and Jonson) loaned by the gallery to the Isaac Delgado Museum, New Orleans
February	Archipenko
March	Carlos Mérida
April	Chagall, Beckmann, Grosz, Kandinsky, Klee, Kopman, Léger, Nolde, Rouault: a loan exhibition borrowed from J. B. Neumann's New Art Circle
May	Rita Stein, Abercrombie, Nicola Ziroli
September–October	Selections from the Arthur Jerome Eddy auction: Kandinsky, Jawlensky, Man Ray, Gabriele Munter, Chaubaud; Léger, Derain, Lyonel Feininger, Klee
November	Joan Miró
December	Rufino Tamayo; architectural model of "Suspended House" by Paul Nelson

1939

January	Edward Weston
February	Stuart Davis
March	Archipenko
April	Mérida
May	Abercrombie, Raymond Breinin, Sebree
September–October	Gyorgy Kepes
November–December	Paul Klee

1940

January	Laszlo Moholy-Nagy
February	Lester O. Schwartz
March	Abercrombie, Hofer, Léger, Lurçat, Matisse, Mérida, Modigliani, Picasso, Rivera, Sebree, Kurt Seligmann, Dora Slobe
April	Robert Jay Wolff
May	Léger
October	Emil Nolde
November	Oceanic sculpture from the collection of Wolfgang Paalen; George Fred Keck
December	Klee

1941

January	Archipenko, Jawlensky, Lurçat, Mauny, Mérida, Moholy-Nagy, Wolff, Kepes; "Color in Modern Art": Franz Marc, Miró, Léger, Kandinsky, Chagall, Klee (1/28–mid March)
March	Weisenborn
March	"Leaders of Cubism." Braque, Picasso, Gris, de la Fresnaye (3/17–4/6)
April	Archipenko
May	Lyonel Feininger
September	"Advanced Guard Advertising": Frank Barr, Herbert Bayer, Lester Beall, McKnight Kauffer, Kepes, Herbert Matter, Moholy-Nagy, Paul Rand, Ladislaw Sutnar
October	Picasso, Takal
November	Charles Biederman; Anni Albers
December	Picasso; Julio de Diego

1942

January	"Order and Clarity in Art": Kandinsky, Léger, El Lissitzky, Albers, Mondrian, Ozenfant, Jawlensky; Eliot Porter (1/23–3/14)
February	George Fred Keck, Viviano
April	Archipenko

The gallery closed before the end of April 1942.

CHAPTER TEN

Traditions and Trends:
Taste Patterns in Chicago Collecting

STEFAN GERMER

"**M**odernism" never came to Chicago. The term was coined retrospectively when it was all over. In 1936, Chicago critic Clarence J. Bulliet declared, "The art movement that was . . . known during the first quarter of the present century as modernism has run its course. It began with Cézanne and it ended with Picasso."[1]

The feeling of closure which Bulliet expressed was common in the 1930s.[2] By then the avant-garde movements had become history, and it was thus a time of retrospectives and surveys: it was within that cultural climate that the term "modernism" was created. Starting with the post impressionists, the concept of modernism subsumed all recent artistic movements into one project that teleologically led to abstraction.

The retrospective impulse that had shaped the concept could be felt behind the establishment of the Museum of Modern Art (MoMA) in New York in 1929. This impulse also brought Chicago the Century of Progress exhibition in 1933 and 1934, and found perhaps its most authoritative formulation in the 1936 MoMA show, "Cubism and Abstract Art." In the catalog of that show, Alfred Barr described the formative conditions of modernism:

> The pictorial conquest of the external visual world had been completed and refined many times and in different ways during the previous half-millenium. The more adventurous and original artists had grown bored with painting facts. By a common and powerful impulse they were driven to abandon the imitation of natural appearance."[3]

Abstraction, Barr argued, had been the logical consequence of a thousand-year-old pictorial culture, and instead of being a rupture with tradition it was its necessary fulfillment.

Three years before the MoMA show, Chicago presented its definition of modern art. While less ambitious than Barr's in the presentation of contemporary developments, the exhibition at the Art Institute shared the same modernist premises. It was held in conjunction with the Century of Progress fair and was intended to enlist the artistic avant-garde movements in support of the concept of an all-encompassing process of modernization—the exhibition's central message. The exhibition opened in a city which had been severely hit by the Depression. The shock of the 1929 stock market crash had created a need for an affirmation of the industrial, scientific, and artistic potential of the age. It was within this ideological context that the concept of modernism was further elaborated.

The Art Institute exhibition of 1933 presented the evolution of art in a chronological survey from the thirteenth century to the production of the present day. Cézanne was shown as a pivotal figure for the genesis of modern art, and the paintings of Matisse and Picasso were hung side by side with the works of Gauguin, Toulouse-Lautrec, and Van Gogh, thereby establishing a direct connection between post impressionism and early-twentieth-century art. This presentation meant a selective reinterpretation of art history and marked the final step of the integration of the early-twentieth-century avant-garde movements into the museum institution.[4]

Twenty years before the Century of Progress exhibition, in 1913, the Armory Show had polarized supporters and opponents of modern art in Chicago. Matisse had been ridiculed by Art Institute students. Now he was recognized as one of the leading representatives of contemporary art. Marcel Duchamp's *Nude Descending a Staircase*, which had been the scandal of the Armory Show, was presented in 1933 as an important document of cubist painting.

Indeed, the integration of all that had appeared outrageous, radical and revolutionary in 1913 was achieved by way of its historicization, the making of avant-garde art into a part of the art historical canon. This integration of the new, culminating in the 1933 exhibition, had been prepared for long before. The expansion of the art historical canon was the achievement of a group of five collectors. It is to Martin A. Ryerson, Arthur Jerome Eddy, Frederic Clay and Helen Birch Bartlett, and Annie Swan Coburn (figs. 10.1, 10.2, 10.3, and 10.4) that Chicago owes its collections of modernist paintings. Together with Joseph Winterbotham, who had endowed a fund for the acquisition of recent European art in 1921, these five collectors shaped Chicago's perception of modern art.

This "Modernist Five"—as one might call them—was an odd

10.1 Portrait of Martin A. Ryerson, photograph, 1904. Archives of the Art Institute of Chicago. © 1989 The Art Institute of Chicago. All Rights Reserved.

group consisting of a millionaire-connoisseur, a lawyer in the defense of everything modern, a man who had renounced a business career in order to become a painter and his artistically inclined wife, as well as a withdrawn lady who at age fifty-four had started to build a collection which the German art critic Meier-Graefe would later respectfully call "one of the best I ever saw."[5] For all five collectors, assembling works of art was more than just a fashionable pastime: it was a conviction, an end in itself. In this way these modernist collectors differed from the collectors of the previous generation.

10.2 Arthur Jerome Eddy, photograph, n.d. Private collection.

Ever since the fire of 1871, art enthusiasts in Chicago had been concerning themselves with contemporary art. Between 1890 and 1930, one can roughly distinguish four different types of art collectors in the city, those interested in the *contemporary*, the *modern*, the *modernist*, and the *avant-garde*. Each of the four types differed in his or her definition of modern art, and in the role that art collecting played in his or her lifestyle. While the focus here will be on the modernist and avant-garde collectors, who were the most important during the period under consideration, a look at their predecessors will serve to clarify both continuities and generational differences in their attitude toward art.

For a contemporary collector, art was primarily a status sym-

Stefan Germer

10.3 Frederic Clay Bartlett and Helen Birch Bartlett, photograph, n.d. Archives of the Art Institute of Chicago. © 1989 The Art Institute of Chicago. All Rights Reserved.

bol. First-generation millionaires and *arrivistes*, such as Chicago's streetcar king Charles T. Yerkes, wanted paintings which would function as unmistakable indicators of their economic success. Consequently they bought paintings which looked expensive, preferably by artists who had already won fame abroad. For these collectors modern art did not imply any specific aesthetic program, but was defined by its mere contemporaneity and its opposition to old master painting, the general term used for all pre-nineteenth-century art. When Yerkes commissioned paintings by the French salon artists Bouguereau and Détaille in 1892, he thought of himself as collecting modern art.[6]

The second type, the modern collector, had a different understanding of modern art. As an example, at the same time that Yerkes bought his Bouguereau painting, Bertha Palmer assembled nine of Monet's recently completed *Haystacks*. For her, "modern art" was not defined by its opposition to older works but was distinguished by its own characteristics. The term came to embrace the latest in art and in fashion, and consequently Bertha Palmer would not confine herself to established standards, but rather visited artists' studios and current exhibitions, consulted with experts and subscribed to the major magazines in order to explore the recent developments. In this latter situation, art collecting became a way of life, and the paintings served as a backdrop for grand-scale social events held in the picture gallery of the Palmers' Lake Shore Drive castle. Both Bertha and Potter Palmer bought, traded, and sold pictures partly to upgrade their holdings and partly to profit from the interest in French impressionist art they had helped to bring about. In 1893 Potter Palmer confided to the American painter Theodore Robinson that he wanted to buy pictures "that he wouldn't lose on,"[7] while his wife had manipulated the market for her own gain all along. Collecting was a luxurious fad for the Palmers; consequently the sums they spent on paintings were accounted for together with the expenses for dresses, jewelry, and flowers in Bertha Palmer's account books.

The "Modernist Five" under discussion here defined their role in direct opposition to the ostentatious collecting style of the Palmers. They also rejected the philanthropic concepts of a man such as Art Institute President Charles L. Hutchinson, who sought to employ art for public benefit. While these commonly held oppositions united the group, the nature of their actual acquisitions reveals two distinguishable attitudes among them. Martin A. Ryerson, the Bartletts, and Annie Swan Coburn can be characterized as modernist, while Arthur Jerome Eddy must be considered avant-garde. Eddy was unique in his interest in the recent and not-yet-established as well as in his cultivation of a theoretical understanding of modern art, which radically set his collecting style apart from his peers.

To extra-artistic uses of art, the "Modernist Five" opposed a concept which defined art as an autonomous entity. This definition had important consequences, not only for the collectors' understanding of modern art but also for their comprehension of art history in general, for it directed their attention mainly to the formal aspects of the art works. A focal point for the formulation of the new attitude towards art was the World's Columbian Exhibition of 1893. Arthur Jerome Eddy formulated his ideas about impressionist painting there and envisioned a more spiritual kind of art. In his 1893 review of the exhibition, Eddy wrote:

It is one thing to paint the exterior of things, it is another thing to paint the soul of things, it is still another and greater thing to paint the soul, one's own soul into the soul of things. Art is representation plus the man, rather than subject matter or technique.[8]

Eddy proclaimed thus an aesthetic approach to art, defining subject matter and technique as less important than the emotional intensity of an art work. Art had to reflect nature according to an inner necessity, not just reproduce its outer appearance.

In its emphasis on the expressive qualities of the art work, Eddy's concept paralleled those ideas which Roger Fry and Clive Bell would declare some sixteen years later to be the essence of post impressionism. Eddy differed from these British aestheticians, however, in his understanding of art as a means of spiritual communication rather than as an autonomous formal entity. While Eddy's idea ultimately points back to a symbolist mysticism which ideally wants to rid itself of all form,[9] Fry was searching for "the emotional significance that lies in things" and Bell defined "significant form" as the main concern of the post-impressionist artists. The difference between Eddy and these theoreticians becomes clear in Fry's "An Essay in Aesthetics" of 1909, in which he wrote:

We must . . . give up the attempt to judge the work of art by its reaction on life, and consider it as an expression of emotions regarded as ends in themselves. And this brings us back to the idea . . . of art as the expression of the imaginative life.[10]

The theories of Fry and Bell became influential in the teens and provided the basis for a first wave of formalist criticism in the twenties; however, their concepts would have been only of academic interest had Fry and Bell not supported their views with examples of works by Cézanne, Van Gogh, and Gauguin, thereby making post impressionism into an aesthetic paradigm.[11]

By way of their writings and through the influential exhibitions at the Grafton Gallery in London in 1910–11 and 1912, these theoreticians of post impressionism formulated a history of modern art which started with Manet and subsequently explored what Fry had dubbed the "expressionistic" reaction to impressionism in the works of Cézanne, Van Gogh, and Gauguin. Fry summarized the result of the work of these artists as "the re-establishment of purely aesthetic criteria in place of the criterion of conformity to appearance—the rediscovery of the principles of structural design and harmony."[12] In Fry's opinion, the avant-garde movements of the early twentieth century had continued the formalization begun by the three post-impressionist masters.

The post-impressionist paradigm defined a specific aesthetic project and gave a logical and coherent account of the development of modernist art. Thus it was of great interest for all of Chicago's modernist collectors, and we know from the listings of the contents of their libraries[13] that all of them were familiar with the formalist interpretation of art history. The post-impressionist paradigm provided these collectors with a rationale as well as a guide for making their selections. In contrast to the earlier collectors, whose choices had often been dominated by status preoccupations, the "Modernist Five" collected with an art historical agenda in mind.

The post-impressionist paradigm, however, was not devoid of social implications. Given the level of connoisseurship it required, it presupposed a collector whose social position allowed him the cultivation of his aesthetic sensibility. This sensibility then came to function as a very sophisticated indicator of social status, since it appeared in the form of an almost "natural" gift, allowing the collector to take his distance from the vulgar ostentation of earlier collectors. Such a refinement in class definition was in keeping with the social position of the "Modernist Five." Though Ryerson was the only millionaire among them, all possessed considerable means, and four of the five collectors enjoyed the amenities of inherited wealth.

Between 1890 and 1930, Martin A. Ryerson, Arthur Jerome Eddy, Frederic Clay and Helen Birch Bartlett, and Annie Swan Coburn explored the confines of the post-impressionist paradigm through the activity of collecting. The most important phase in the collecting career of each of them followed that of one of the others, but they in part overlapped. Martin A. Ryerson dominated the Chicago scene from the 1890s to the end of the first World War. Arthur Jerome Eddy began to collect at the same time as Ryerson but made his most important acquisitions in the years surrounding the Armory Show, when he rapidly built an avant-garde collection to which he kept adding until his death in 1920. Annie Swan Coburn and the Bartletts made their most important acquisitions in the 1920s. Each of the five had a significant impact on Chicagoans' understanding of modernism.

Martin A. Ryerson's interest in art evolved over the years. Being by far the wealthiest among the collectors considered here, he did not have to confine his activities to one area. His collecting began in the 1890s with conventional landscape painting, followed by Dutch seventeenth-century art and impressionist pictures. By 1920, Ryerson had assembled a collection of major impressionist paintings, including Renoir's *Girl at the Piano* (acquired in 1911) and Manet's *Bullfight* and *Young Woman with a Round Hat* (acquired in 1912). After 1920 his real enthusiasm shifted to post impressionism and led to the purchase of Cézanne's *The Gulf of Marseille Seen from L'Estaque* (acquired in 1920) and Gauguin's *Why are you angry?* (acquired in 1925).

Ryerson's taste in these years is well documented in a small notebook he kept, in which he recorded the names of the painters and the prices of works he was interested in.[14] In addition to Cézanne and Gauguin, whose names recur often after 1920 in the notebook, Ryerson noted the names of other post impressionists, in particular those of the symbolist Redon, of the nabis Vuillard and Bonnard as well as Denis, and of the fauve artist Vlaminck; he eventually acquired paintings by all of these artists.

His change from impressionist to post-impressionist art followed the general trend in those years. We may even surmise that in his selection Ryerson followed the examples of Annie Swan Coburn and Frederic Clay Bartlett, who had already turned to post-impressionist painters. In the case of Toulouse-Lautrec, however, Ryerson did not follow the lead of his peers; although recording the prices of available works, Ryerson did not pursue the acquisition of any of them, perhaps because Lautrec's somewhat sketchy technique and his choice of subject matter did not agree with the collector's conception of painting.

Ryerson cherished the abstract formal qualities of an artwork, and over the years built a collection which was held together by a concern for decorative quality, color harmony, and painterly excellence. These concerns can already be seen in Ryerson's impressionist purchases, during the course of which his taste evolved from Lepine's *Canal St. Martin* to a thorough appreciation of Monet's work that began with the acquisition of his *Red Road near Menton* in 1891 and continued unabated throughout the teens, finally leading the collector to visit Monet at Giverny in 1920. The acquisition of paintings such as *Waterlilies* (1906, acquired in 1914), *Waterloo Bridge* (1903, acquired 1914), *Charing Cross Bridge* (1901, acquired 1916) and the *Parliament of Westminster* (1899–1904, acquired 1916) shows Ryerson's understanding of the importance of series painting for Monet's work. These canvases were acquired within five to ten years after their creation, and this interest may have directed Ryerson subsequently to earlier series—such as the 1877 *Gare St. Lazare* series, of which he bought one example in 1913.

Ryerson's purely formal interest in art allowed him to establish connections within the oeuvre of one painter; in addition it made him aware of similarities between recent and older works of art. Thus, his interest in formalism freed him from socially imposed taste patterns, and led him to the re-evaluation of areas long neglected by art history. Ryerson's collecting career included two instances of such rediscoveries: the first was the acquisition of El Greco's *Assumption of the Virgin* for the collection of the Art Institute in 1906, and the second was his discovery of early Italian Renaissance painting that culminated in the acquisition of Giovanni di Paolo's *Scenes from the Life of St. John the Baptist.* Certainly, both acquisitions must be seen within a history of the formation of the modernist sensibility, since the precondition for these re-evaluations was the new formalist aesthetic. While El Greco was particularly dear to both Fry and Bell, who saw him as a forerunner of modern art in general and of Cézanne in particular,[15] Bell described the modernity of the early Italian primitives thus:

> . . . primitive art is good . . . for, as a rule, it is also free from descriptive qualities. In primitive art you will find no accurate representation; you will find only significant form.[16]

Ryerson's conception of art as an autonomous entity, an understanding which had informed his collecting, also inspired the way in which he displayed his holdings. In Ryerson's house the visitor was led from the ground floor rooms, where the modern paintings were hung, to the library on the second floor, which the collector had transformed into a sanctuary of early Italian art. Overwhelmed by this sequence, a visitor described his impression thus:

> What first impresses one in the Italian room is the superb decorative effect of the whole—the dignity and beauty imparted to the room itself by the twilight of colour shot through with gleams of gold. . . . However various [the pictures] may be in other ways, they are all alike in this: they hang neighborly on the wall, no one interfering with the other, dusky and gorgeous, they flatter the eye with their perfect concord.[17]

The arrangement was unobtrusive, but carefully calculated. Instead of Bertha Palmer's sumptuous picture gallery, which employed art for social purposes, this one was a scholarly treasure trove, in which each object was considered for itself. The austerity of the room must have made the earlier form of conspicuous consumption look vulgar.

In contrast, Arthur Jerome Eddy, the second key collector of the period between 1890 and 1920, preferred striking, unusual juxtapositions of paintings. In his house, the paintings of Manet and Whistler hung together with those by Kandinsky and the young American artist Albert Bloch. A basis for the comparison of Eddy and Ryerson is provided by the fact that both were of the same generation—Ryerson was born in 1856, Eddy three years later—and both were graduates of Harvard Law School. Initially, their collecting interests were the same. Like Ryerson, Eddy had started with a reassessment of impressionism and in 1894 acquired Manet's *Draped Philosopher,* a painting by Renoir, and Monet's *Snow Effect at Falaise.*[18] From early on Eddy was oriented toward an art which was interesting for the expressive quality of its formal elements alone. This interest made him responsive to Whistler, whose work he had first seen at the World's Columbian Exhibition of 1893. For Eddy, Whistler occupied a transitional position which the collector described thus:

> In the clearness of his vision and the faithfulness with which he painted the things and people with which he came into contact, Whistler was an Impressionist—an Impressionist long before Monet—but in his search after color and line music, in his attempts to do things beyond and above nature, he was a Post Impressionist.[19]

Eddy's sensitivity to artists who did things "beyond and above nature" and his interest in "color and line music" motivated his purchases at the Armory Show in 1913. While the World's Columbian Exhibition of 1893 had been a formative experience for Eddy, the Post-Impressionist Exhibition (as the Armory Show was referred to in Chicago) gave his collecting its definitive orientation. At the New York and Chicago presentations of the exhibition, Eddy bought a total of twenty-five artworks, surpassed in number only by the forty-one of New York's "noble buyer" John Quinn,[20] but unsurpassed in audacity and awareness of artistic significance. Eddy's acquisitions ranged from Vuillard lithographs to Duchamp's *King and Queen Surrounded by Swift Nudes* and included works by Gleizes, Villon, Picabia, Dunoyer de Segonzac, and Brancusi.

In his book *Cubists and Post-Impressionism*, published a year after the Armory Show exhibition, Eddy gave an account of late-nineteenth- and early-twentieth-century art, thereby justifying his choices. His explanation, defense, and interpretation of modern art remained tied to the post-impressionist aesthetic. Following Fry, Eddy defined art as autonomous, and like Bell, he understood it as the expression of the artist's self, stating that abstraction from empirical reality heightened the emotional impact of an artwork.[21] The interest in the decorative qualities of an artwork explains Eddy's enthusiasm for the paintings of Amadeo de Souza Cardoza, as well as his acquisitions of such fauve reinterpretations of Cézanne as Derain's *Forest at Martiques* and Vlaminck's *Rueil*.

The expressive current was represented in Eddy's collection by the Blue Rider group, and particularly by Kandinsky. Eddy had been fascinated by the artist's *Improvisation No. 30* (fig. 10.5) at the Armory Show and subsequently went to Munich, where he acquired works by the Russian as well as by his associates Franz Marc (*The Bewitched Mill* [fig. 10.6]), Gabriele Münter (*Still Life with Queen*), and Alexei Jawlensky.[22] Eddy's visit to Munich was the beginning of a thorough exploration of Kandinsky's work, which led him to buy eighteen of the artist's paintings and

10.5 Wassily Kandinsky, *Improvisation No. 30*, oil on canvas, 1913. Arthur Jerome Eddy Memorial Collection, 1931.511. © 1989 The Art Institute of Chicago. All Rights Reserved.

to include long excerpts from the artist's tract *On the Spiritual in Art* in his book *Cubists and Post-Impressionism*. While Eddy's expressionist bias had helped him to discover and understand the Blue Rider group and Paul Klee, at that time both equally unknown to the American public, it blocked his access to cubist

10.6 Franz Marc, *The Bewitched Mill*, oil on canvas, 1913. Arthur Jerome Eddy Memorial Collection, 1931.522. © 1989 The Art Institute of Chicago. All Rights Reserved.

painting. Although Eddy quoted the critical champions of cubism and Gleizes and Metzinger at great length in his book, his own views on the subject remain somewhat obscure.

While he proclaimed that cubism was best suited to "illustrate a discussion of the philosophy of post impressionism,"[23] he considered Picasso's and Braque's cubist pictures an impasse, writing the following about cubist abstraction:

> The result is a picture so scientific, so abstract, it appeals to but few, and excites no emotions in anyone, because it was not the result of an emotion in the artist.[24]

Clearly, Eddy's views were shaped by the poor representation of Picasso's and Braque's work at the Armory Show. In keeping with his general aesthetic orientation, he acquired only such cubist works as were either compatible with his decorative ideals (such as Picabia's *Dances at the Spring*) or satisfied his taste for the spectacular and expressive (like Duchamp's *King and Queen Surrounded by Swift Nudes*).

Eddy's importance for the promotion of modern art in Chicago and the United States was nevertheless paramount. He belongs to the same pioneering group of avant-garde collectors as John Quinn, Lillie Bliss, Katherine Dreier, and Walter Arensberg. Considering the boldness of his acquisitions, it is hard to believe that he and Martin A. Ryerson were of the same generation. Despite a common background, their collecting interests took opposite directions: while Ryerson had expanded the post-impressionist paradigm into the past, proclaiming the modernity of the Italian primitives, Eddy had extended it forward in time to encompass contemporary art.

These differences were not just a matter of temperament but were indicative of diverging conceptions of the collector's social role. In part, this difference can be explained in sociological terms. Inherited wealth had enabled Ryerson to withdraw from business in the early 1890s and to devote himself exclusively to his scholarly and philanthropic interests. Liberated from business duties, Ryerson crafted for himself the role of the gentleman in leisurely pursuit of the arts and sciences. Study, travel, and exploration were part of this concept: Ryerson consciously avoided the merely fashionable and topical. As a successful corporation lawyer, Arthur Jerome Eddy became involved in a kind of collecting that was in keeping with his business activities rather than being an escape from them.

Disposing of considerable, yet much more limited resources than Ryerson, Eddy made "educational capital"—his theoretical understanding of the concerns of contemporary art—and intellectual flexibility his main "assets." Consequently, old master painting never held his interest, and the already-explored post-impressionist works—whose increasing prices required larger and larger sums of money—were for him merely a transitional phase. At a time when rising prices precluded the acquisition of pre-nineteenth-century art for most collectors, Eddy proclaimed they should instead turn to the art of their own time and through their support disclose the "Rembrandt of their age" to the public. He firmly believed that the work of art remained the property of its creator even when it passed into private possession, obligating the collector to become an active supporter and promoter of the artist whose work he owned. Like Ryerson, Eddy saw the collector as an explorer, but an explorer of the new.

Both Martin A. Ryerson and Arthur Jerome Eddy adopted the formalist aesthetic and extended it to areas other than the post-impressionist period for which it had been originally conceived. Annie Swan Coburn, and Frederic Clay and Helen Birch Bartlett, however, operated in a different culture climate. After the First World War and during the twenties, modern art became recognized as a legitimate and profitable field of collecting. This period witnessed the rise of such major collectors of impressionist and post-impressionist works as Samuel Courtauld of London, Helene Kröller-Müller of Otterlo, Oskar Reinhardt of Winterthur, and their American peers Chester Dale, Duncan Phillips, and Alfred C. Barnes.

The international competition created by these collectors led to a phenomenal expansion of the art market, and while prices for art objects rose in almost all fields, the increasing demand for impressionist and post-impressionist masters made these the dominant figures of the modern art market, soon to be joined by Matisse and Picasso.[25] In the twenties, the post-impressionist paradigm became not only the almost universally accepted theoretical explanation of the genesis of modern art, but also an important sales argument for those Parisian art dealers, who—like Bernheim-Jeune, Paul Rosenberg, and Paul Guillaume—combined stocks of impressionist and post-impressionist works with those by Matisse, Vlaminck, and Dufy, as well as by Soutine, Modigliani, and Utrillo.[26] A 1923 exhibition organized by Félix Fénéon at the Bernheim-Jeune showrooms[27] presented works by Bonnard, Camoin, Cross, Derain, Dufy, Jongkind, Marquet, Matisse, Modigliani, Roussel, Van Dongen, Signac, and Vlaminck as a safe investment grouped under the telling title, "*On propose*" ("We suggest"). In this fashion post-impressionist art and its twentieth-century offspring were marketed and the paradigm described here became institutionalized.

For aspiring collectors such as Annie Swan Coburn and the Bartletts, this meant that they operated in a field which had already been mapped by art historical discourse, structured by art dealers, and accepted by other collectors. Such previous mapping allowed these inexperienced new collectors to form museum-quality collections within a relatively short amount of time, and often without the help of professional advisors. For instance, Annie Swan Coburn started her collection in 1910, after her husband's death, with arbitrary acquisitions of works by American artists such as Betts, Hassam, Weir, Ryder, and Whistler. She soon realized that by concentrating her resources on French impressionist and post-impressionist art, she could form a collection which would have both internal coherence and art historical significance.

Focusing on the period between 1860 and 1900, she assembled groups of works by Monet, Renoir, Manet, and Degas. Her selections from among these painters' works were intended to demonstrate the variety of aspects within each oeuvre. The sampling of Monet's work extended from the 1867 *Beach at Sainte-Adresse* to a 1908 canvas from the Venetian series and included typical pieces from the haystack, Vétheuil, and poppy field suites. Coburn limited her acquisition of Renoir's paintings to the years between 1878 and 1885, centering these around *On the Terrace*, which she had bought from the private collection of Durand-Ruel in 1925 for the then extraordinarily high price of $100,000.[28] The acquisition of Manet paintings as varied as the 1862 *Lange Boy* and the 1879 *Illustrated Journal* reveals the art historical interest underlying Coburn's selection, as do the choices from Degas's work, which extended from the relatively early *Uncle and Niece* to the *Millinery Shop* of 1882. Following the art historical logic of the post-impressionist paradigm, Annie Swan Coburn added examples of each of Fry's founding figures of modern art to her collection: Cézanne's *Auvers-sur-l'Oise* hung side by side with Van Gogh's *Sunny Midi* and Gauguin's *Incantation*.

In making her selections, Annie Swan Coburn profited from the fact that her field of interest had already been mapped, and thus collecting had become less a matter of discovery than of the systematic exploration of the established paradigms. The preselection of this area allowed her to concentrate on the high-quality pieces available. Well-read in art history and well-connected with the leading New York art dealers, Coburn knew the market situation for impressionist and post-impressionist art and could thus operate independently from advisors or experts. Occasionally, Art Institute Director Robert B. Harshe—who urged her to buy a study for Manet's *On the Balcony* in 1925[29]— or curator Daniel Catton Rich would make suggestions; usually, however, Annie Swan Coburn decided for herself. Each of her purchases was carefully planned and had to be considered and reconsidered, as with Toulouse-Lautrec's *Augusta*, which she visited repeatedly at Wildenstein's New York branch before deciding to buy it in 1926, after almost a year of deliberation.[30]

Operating in the highly competitive market for impressionist and post-impressionist art in the 1920s required money in addition to knowledge and connections; Annie Swan Coburn spent considerable sums on her pictures. Monet's *Cliffwalk,* for example, cost her $18,000, while she paid $24,000 for Renoir's *Lady Sewing* and $38,000 for Degas's *Uncle and Niece.*[31] Clearly, Coburn would not have spent such extraordinarily high sums on her paintings had she not intended them to form an institutional collection which would ultimately be placed in a museum. Dealers like Joseph Durand-Ruel had understood their client's intention, and when he congratulated Annie Swan Coburn in a letter on the acquisition of Renoir's *On the Terrace* in 1925, he pointed out that the picture would make a magnificent addition to the Art Institute's holdings.[32] These plans notwithstanding, Coburn maintained a casual and relaxed attitude about her collection. More than one visitor returned from the delightful disorder of her Blackstone Hotel apartment, where pictures sat on the floor in addition to cluttering the walls, raving about the Cézanne stored under Coburn's bed.[33]

While the institutional character of the Coburn collection thus remained veiled until its bequest to the Art Institute in 1932, it was known from the beginning that the Frederic Clay and Helen Birch Bartlett collection was destined for the Art Institute. In keeping with the educational zeal of many collectors of that period, the Bartletts wanted their pictures to "carry the message of Modern French Art to a wider public."[34] Prior to the acquisition of Seurat's *Sunday Afternoon on the Island of La Grande Jatte* in 1924, they were perceptive but casual collectors looking for pieces to embellish their various residences. In keeping with the conservative aesthetic that informed Frederic Clay Bartlett's own painting, they selected paintings by Lhote, Lotiron, Utrillo, Modigliani, and other Ecole de Paris painters who had been presented to them as undisturbingly modern.

With the acquisition of *La Grande Jatte* the Bartletts changed the scope of their purchases. They proceeded to surround Seurat's painting with a selection of major post-impressionist works, including Toulouse-Lautrec's *At the Moulin Rouge,* Gauguin's *Day of the God,* and Van Gogh's 1886 *Montmartre, Bedroom at Arles,* and *Madame Roulin Rocking the Cradle.* Cézanne was represented by his 1895 *Basket of Apples,* which Bartlett had acquired for $50,000 in 1925–26. This still life remained the only Cézanne in the collection, since the two other paintings by the artist which Bartlett had considered as additions—*The Boy in a Red Waistcoat* and a self-portrait of the painter—failed to meet the collector's expectations when they were hung tentatively with the other pictures in 1927 and 1928.

Because of their importance for the elaboration of the post-impressionist aesthetic, Bartlett had tried to secure Manet's *Bar at the Folies-Bergères* (which had been the central piece of the first Grafton Gallery exhibition in 1910–11) and had instructed Robert B. Harshe to bid for Seurat's *Circus* at the sale of the John Quinn collection in 1924.[35] Both attempts, however, failed: Quinn had bequeathed the Seurat to the Louvre, while Manet's painting went to Bartlett's London rival Samuel Courtauld. The acquisition of two figure paintings and a landscape by the Swiss artist Ferdinand Hodler, whose work Bartlett had discovered on a trip to Switzerland in 1924, was unusual in a post-impressionist context and unique for an American collector. The purchase of these Hodler paintings remained, however, an isolated incident in Bartlett's collecting career. When the Lucerne dealer Theodore Fischer offered Bartlett three of Hodler's most important pictures in 1926[36]—*The Day, Enchanted Woman,* and *Holy Hour* (fig. 10.7)—the collector declined, a decision perhaps motivated by the realization that these paintings differed from his other Hodlers in their explicit symbolist content and were thus less compatible with the post-impressionist aesthetic underlying his collection.

In its decorative harmony, the Birch Bartlett collection had a programmatic intention and a specific aesthetic message. By way of combining the works of the post-impressionist masters with those of contemporary painters such as Derain, Lhote, Modigliani, and Utrillo, it meant to present art history in such a fashion that these undisturbingly modern artists appeared as the legitimate continuation of the older tradition. It was in this fashion that these same artists had been marketed by the Parisian dealers, who also included certain phases of Picasso's and Matisse's work in their presentation of recent art history.[37] A work from Picasso's "blue period" such as *The Old Guitarist* fit well into this scheme, as did Matisse's *Woman Before an Aquarium,* since in the 1920s Matisse's work was marketed as a reconciliation of avant-garde innovations and a tradition defined as specifically "French."[38]

With the donation of the collection to the Art Institute in the memory of Helen Birch, who died in 1925, Frederic Clay Bartlett made his interpretation of art history public. That this gift had a programmatic character and was indeed to be understood as the manifesto of a specific aesthetic conviction became evident when Bartlett submitted, along with the donation, a plan for its installation. Following the ideas of the neo-impressionist painter Paul Signac in his book *D'Eugène Delacroix au Neo-Impressionisme,*[39] Bartlett demanded that his collection be displayed in a gallery stripped of all decorative moldings and painted white. The paintings were to be presented in uniform white frames (see fig. 12.7).

Apparently Bartlett intended to underscore the modernity of the art in his collection while simultaneously defining it in exclusively formal terms. In its exclusion of outside reality from the museum space, the installation of the Birch Bartlett collection marked the triumph of the aesthetic attitude which had guided

10.7 Ferdinand Hodler, *Holy Hour,* oil on canvas, 1907. The painting was offered to Frederic Clay Bartlett, but he declined. Kunsthaus Zürich.

all of these modernist collectors; it was emblematic of an approach that regarded art as autonomous and understood its development principally in formal terms. This understanding, which found its most influential formulation in the post-impressionist paradigm, provided a coherent account of the genesis of modern art. The paradigm had subsequently been elaborated by art theoreticians, employed by art dealers, and followed by art collectors before Bartlett made it the basis of his museum presentation.

Since Bartlett's concept for the installation of his collection continued the organizational model of the collector's museum from which the Art Institute was trying to distance itself, his plan was not adopted.[40] Nevertheless, the aestheticizing attitude behind it became instrumental for the integration of avant-garde art into the museum.

The aestheticizing attitude underlying Bartlett's collection was equally important in the shaping of the other collections considered here. While it was effective as the basis for these private collections, it was problematic as the basis for a public collection because it reduced the social content of avant-garde art to an aesthetic issue and cancelled out the radical impulses which had been crucial to the formation of many of the late-nineteenth- and early-twentieth-century art movements.

In bequeathing to Chicago splendid additions to the existing holdings of impressionist art, the "Modernist Five" left a slightly unbalanced account of the evolution of modern art. With the exception of Eddy, they focused their attention on French art, underrating or simply ignoring the contributions of German, Italian, Russian, and American artists. Despite subsequent donations and museum acquisitions which have somewhat rectified the imbalance, one of the characteristic features of the Art Institute's collection remains this biased account, restricted in its Francophile orientation and reductive in its aestheticizing interpretation of modern art. It was in this fashion that these five Chicago collectors brought modernist art to the city.

CHAPTER ELEVEN

"In the Highest Efficiency": Art Training at the School of the Art Institute of Chicago

CHARLOTTE MOSER

In 1911, two years before the Armory Show came to Chicago, the prominent New York artist and critic Kenyon Cox delivered the annual Scammon Lectures at the Art Institute of Chicago. His series of lectures, entitled "The Classic Point of View," was drawn from his book of the same name published that year. As one of America's last great apologists for the neo-Renaissance style espoused by the Ecole des Beaux-Arts, Cox was on very friendly terrain at the Art Institute. When he defined the "classic spirit" as the search for perfection, the love of clearness, reasonableness and self-control, and above all, the love of permanence and of continuity, he uttered artistic values deeply felt at the Art Institute.[1]

Nowhere at the museum did Cox's words find greater agreement than at the School of the Art Institute, whose catalog included a tribute from Cox on the first page from 1919 until 1927. Reverence for the antique and the idealized depiction of the human figure, for the technical expertise of past masters, for the image of the Renaissance artist as a worldly *homme d'affaires* had permeated School curriculum since its founding in 1866 as the Chicago Academy of Design. Rigorous drawing and painting from plaster casts of classical sculpture were required of students until the early 1920s because it was believed, according to long-time faculty member Charles Francis Browne in 1916, that this study nurtured the artistic judgment necessary to bring "beauty and character" to one's art.[2]

Beauty and character, along with other moral qualities such as truth and nobility, were fundamental to Chicago's understanding of art at the turn of the century. Such values, which epitomized the nineteenth-century academic art tradition, had first become entrenched in Chicago during the World's Columbian

Exposition of 1893. The fair and the cultural ideals it represented so profoundly shaped the city's identity as it evolved from a sprawling frontier settlement to an urban center that, a generation later, its proclamations about high art remained intact. As Chicago's oldest and most prestigious art school, the School of the Art Institute carried the banner of the academic art tradition well into the twentieth century and may have continued to do so indefinitely had it not been for three cataclysmic events in the life of the institution. The first, called by one observer the "bomb of Modern Art exploding in the galleries of the Art Institute,"[3] was the arrival of the Armory Show in Chicago in 1913. The second occurred the following year with the death of William M. R. French, founding director of the Art Institute in 1882 and the School's first dean. The third was World War I, which wrenched Chicago as it did the rest of the country into confronting the new social and economic conditions of the twentieth century.

Together these elements plunged the School of the Art Institute into a thirty-year period of uncertainty in which the conservatism of its heritage modulated, slowly and often painfully, into a more contemporary attitude toward art. During these years, the School often found itself bandied about between the different, often contradictory definitions of modernity then prevailing in Chicago. These differences would not be sorted out until after World War II when a unique visual interpretation of modernism emerged at the School in what is now known as imagism. Nevertheless, some of the seeds for that later development were planted during the tumultuous years from 1910–40. The effort to establish an industrial arts school at the Art Institute in the 1920s increased the emphasis on design theory as it related to industrial production in the modern age—one of the most provocative aesthetic concerns of the early twentieth century. This emphasis made a lasting impact on School curriculum and its teaching methodology, even after plans for an industrial arts school were abandoned.

At the same time, another artistic philosophy was introduced which encouraged greater emotional expressiveness, a quality noticeably absent from earlier School instruction. This occurred through a series of visiting professorships at the School beginning with George Bellows in 1919, followed by visits in the early 1920s by Randall Davey and Leon Kroll. Through these three artists associated with New York's Ashcan School, a style emerged in the mid-1920s which united the School's traditional emphasis on illustrational realism with a heightened emotional response to everyday reality. The result was a local version of American Scene painting developed in the 1920s and later seen in the city's WPA murals and easel paintings of the 1930s.

Some of the conflicts the School ultimately had with modernism can be traced to the School's charter and, more specifically, to its relationship with the museum. In 1882, when the old Chicago Academy of Fine Arts was reorganized as the Art Institute of Chicago, the founding and maintenance of a school of art and design were its first priorities, a reflection of the spirit of South Kensington and the English design reform movement then sweeping across the country. The preservation and exhibition of collections of art objects came second. When the museum moved into its new building at the close of the World's Columbian Exposition, the school occupied prominent space that was only later used as exhibition galleries. In these years when exposure to aesthetic activity was considered critical to improving the moral character of Chicago, the mission of the School and that of the museum were virtually identical.[4]

Indeed, the popular image of Chicago at the turn of the century as a cesspool of moral decrepitude may have played a role in shaping the dominant aesthetic attitudes at the School of the Art Institute. There were other art schools in the midwest, notably the Academy of Art in Cincinnati where Frank Duveneck had established a stronghold for the Munich School of painting. Other regional art schools existed as training components of midwestern art museums. However, by 1910, partially due to the far-reaching effects of the Columbian Exposition, the city of Chicago occupied a mythic role in the urban fantasies of the rural midwest, fantasies of the "big bad city" popularized in contemporary fiction by such Chicago writers as Theodore Dreiser and Upton Sinclair. Drawn to the exoticism of city life as much as to the education Chicago would offer, art-struck midwestern youths could choose from two Chicago art schools: the commercially oriented and sometimes technically more progressive Chicago Academy of Fine Arts founded in 1902, or the high-minded, classically oriented, long-established School of the Art Institute. A more bohemian alternative to these institutions apparently did not exist, stimulating a handful of artists' collectives in Chicago in the early part of the century.

Improving students' moral fiber seems to have been built into educational theories practiced at the School of the Art Institute in the early part of the century. Demanding "thoroughness and industry" was highly regarded as a way both to train students for the work world and to produce high levels of aesthetic achievement in their work. To this end, the School's statement of purpose until 1918 claimed "to maintain in the highest efficiency the severe practice of academic drawing and painting from life, from the antique, from objects and around this practice, as a living stem, to group the various departments of art education."[5] A paternalistic, often overly protective system existed at the School, which was later compared by Leon Kroll to a "reformatory,"[6] whereby students were required to participate in monthly "concours" modeled on the beaux-arts plan. In these "concours," student accomplishment was judged against rigorous faculty criteria which, before World War I, permitted little personal expressiveness. Proper artist decorum was also dictated. In the 1918–19 School catalog, prospective students were informed that only those who respected "the character of the craft for which they are preparing and who will conduct themselves accordingly" need apply.[7]

The dilemma of whether to become a trade school or remain a fine arts school was a constant source of concern at the School during the first two decades of the twentieth century. Skill at illusionistic rendering, which the School promised to teach in an efficient and presumably expedient manner, was then applicable to both the fine arts and the commercial arts. While some seventy-five percent of the 822 students enrolled at the School in 1913 claimed to want to learn artistic trades,[8] the School faculty in reality found its students to be "green and raw" and "full of ambition" but not knowing what they wanted.[9] By offering both commercially oriented courses in design and illustration as well as academic courses in anatomy and perspective, the school allowed students who were unsure of their direction to sample both routes before embarking on a four-year program. The School of the Art Institute also offered tantalizing access to the museum's collection of old master paintings which the rival commercial school, the Chicago Academy of Fine Art, founded by Carl Werntz, could not provide.

A typical student experience was that of Raymond Jonson, who became one of the city's most prominent abstract artists in the 1920s. When Jonson came to Chicago in 1910, he was one of those "green" students who wanted to learn an artistic trade. He enrolled at the Chicago Academy of Fine Art with the hope of becoming an illustrator, the school's specialty. However, two months later he wrote in a letter, "Real art seems the only thing now. . . . I went over to the Institute, only two blocks from school, and inquired concerning night classes (in anatomy). . . . Tell Papa his boy, if he ever amounts to anything, will not be a cartoonist but an artist. . . . Art, real art, for me."[10]

In the classic mode, the basis for "real art" at the School of the Art Institute was expertise at making anatomically correct renderings of the human body. John Vanderpoel, who taught figure drawing from 1888 until his death in 1911, had enormous impact on shaping artistic attitudes at the School (fig. 11.1). A talented and impassioned teacher who had trained in Paris at the Academie Julien and who believed profoundly in the beaux-arts tradition, Vanderpoel influenced a generation of students at the School from Georgia O'Keeffe to B. J. O. Nordfeldt. He had become one of the nation's leading authorities on rendering the human figure when his 1907 book *The Human Figure* was adopted as a standard art school text. A vehement opponent of post-impressionist art who routinely attacked modern artists in his classes, Vanderpoel inspired a loyal following among his students, and over the years a large body of Vanderpoel lore devel-

11.1 Portrait of John Vanderpoel, photograph, 1911. Vanderpoel actively denounced modernism until his death in 1911. Photograph taken from the *Bulletin of the Art Institute of Chicago*, July 1911, p. 3. © 1989 The Art Institute of Chicago. All Rights Reserved.

oped. One popular story recounted how, during his student days in Paris, he had once drawn six toes on a figure when none of the other students had noticed that the model, in fact, had an extra toe.[11] Toes returned as a point of contention at the Armory Show, perhaps not entirely coincidentally, when the investigator for the Senatorial Vice Commission claimed that one of the women in Matisse's painting *Luxury* had only four toes, viewed no doubt as a reflection of the artist's own bestiality.[12]

Advanced studios at the School leaned heavily on Vanderpoel's neo-Renaissance emphasis on the human figure. The sculpture department, established by Lorado Taft and later headed by Charles Mulligan, trained artists to produce classicizing works for a city which had remained sculpture-mad after the Columbian Exposition. Portraiture, a commercially viable artistic pursuit in Chicago at the turn of the century, was a popular subject at the School. It was taught by Ralph Clarkson, the Chicago portrait painter favored by the city's social set; Karl Buehr, an Academy of Rome trained artist who taught from 1893 until the 1930s, and George Oberteuffer, a virtuoso portrait painter in the manner of John Singer Sargent, whose influence dominated in the 1920s.

Landscape painting, an important component of the region's artistic identity at the turn of the century, also had particular significance in Chicago. The leading landscape teacher at the School was Charles Francis Browne, an arch-conservative spokesman for a traditional artistic style. Other faculty who taught landscape painting during these years were Albert Krehbiel, Frederick Fursman, and DeForrest Schook.

Finally, in 1912, John Norton began teaching decorative design and mural painting, the latter a practice which was called "the hope of painting in America."[13] Norton, who worked with Frank Lloyd Wright on murals for the Midway Gardens, was for many years the most active progressive voice on the faculty (fig. 11.2). From his student years at the School, Norton had rebelled against the academic restrictions of the curriculum. Around 1900, he was part of an ad hoc student alliance to defend modern artists routinely ridiculed in Vanderpoel's classes. Calling themselves the Beetles, this little coterie of students consisted of Norton, Albert Krehbiel, Harry Townsend, Harry Osgood, and B. J. O. Nordfeldt.[14]

When Norton joined the faculty, he brought with him independent ideas about how art should be taught. In a faculty survey taken in 1916, he claimed not only that insistence on cast drawing undermined the creative development of students but that it damaged their ability to understand the relevance of their education. "At the end of four years, he may be an intelligent draftsman, a fair technician and able to match any color, but as a creative artist he is worse than when he entered. His training has all been for the glory of the instructor whose class grows larger. The brains of the students cannot be tacked up for public inspection each month and so there is little way to learn whether or not the mental process of the students are improved."[15]

Norton's viewpoints, however, went unheeded by the overwhelmingly conservative faculty and museum administration. When the museum turned to the School for jurors for its two annual juried shows—the Chicago and Vicinity show and the American show—it was typically the more distinguished, more conservative faculty members who were asked to serve and who effectively discouraged the inclusion of modern works in the shows. By the time of the Armory Show in 1913, the views of Vanderpoel and Browne that prevailed at the School provoked one of the most intense responses to the Armory Show anywhere in America. Walt Kuhn, one of the show's New York or-

Charlotte Moser

11.2 John Warner Norton, *Light and Shadow,* oil on canvas, ca. 1924. Norton was one of the most progressive teachers at the School of the Art Institute. Gift of Friends of American Art, the Art Institute of Chicago. © 1989 The Art Institute of Chicago. All Rights Reserved.

ganizers, wrote that "the instructors at the Institute are mad through" and one "threw a virtual fit condemning Matisse."[16] Students at the School went further, staging a mock trial of a fictional artist named "Henri Hairmatress" whose effigy was stabbed and dragged around the Art Institute terrace. Such theatrics were fairly standard practice at the time among the Art Institute students, who regularly staged elaborate schoolwide pageants. The student lampoon of the show was not an isolated incident. Two weeks earlier, a less public burlesque of the show was held at the Cliff Dwellers Club, a prestigious male artists' club whose membership included the director and most of the board members of the Art Institute.[17]

The Armory Show came to the Art Institute with the reluctant support of Director William M. R. French. Then seventy years old, French was ambivalent about the show and had made plans to be away from Chicago throughout its run. Brother of the leading American neo-Renaissance sculptor Daniel Chester French and himself a former anatomy instructor at the Art Institute's predecessor, the old Chicago Academy of Fine Arts, French did not merely share the sentiments behind the student protest of the show. To a large extent, he was responsible for them. When he was appointed director of the newly formed Art Institute in 1882, French also retained his role as head of the School. As the School's first dean, he hired faculty members like Vanderpoel and Charles Francis Browne in the 1880s. Like them, he felt that the human figure was the core of academic art study because it was the embodiment of perfection.[18] These sentiments were given voice during the Armory Show by Browne, who was invited as president of the Society of Western Artists to lecture about the show. Browne had registered his moral outrage about modern art earlier by stating that "the body is the temple of God, and the cubists have profaned the temple."[19] The Armory Show itself he called a "toss-up between madness and humbug."[20]

When French died the year after the Armory Show, his nineteenth-century views about art continued but the favored status enjoyed by the School under his administration did not. As one of the last administrators who had been affiliated with the School before it evolved into the Art Institute, French had placed equal emphasis on the school and the museum. By World War I, however, other museum priorities were clearly emerging. As the museum field began to professionalize in the first decade of this century,[21] the broad educational function of the Art Institute began to shift from the art school and art training to the museum and art appreciation. The prime mover in this regard was Charles Hutchinson, the powerful president of the Art Institute Board of Trustees from 1882 until 1924. In 1909, Hutchinson had been instrumental in the establishment of the American Federation of Arts, an association which pioneered the practice of sending traveling exhibitions to cities around the country. "No longer are permanent, unchanging exhibits interesting to the wide-awake public—the cry is perpetually for something new," proclaimed the prospectus of the Federation's magazine *Art and Progress* in 1909.[22] Such sentiments probably lay behind Hutchinson's willingness to support the Armory Show tour in Chicago, though he loathed modern art and called "art for art's sake a selfish and erroneous doctrine."[23] In general, he distrusted contemporary artists, particularly those who "fill our galleries with ugly creations and claim approval solely on the ground of newness and originality—forgetting or ignoring the fundamental traditions of all great Art."[24] His models were, as they had been for French, the artists of the Italian Renaissance, those who "did not set their Art upon a pedestal where few could see it. . . . They placed their Art upon the ground where children could look and gaze at it, and by it be inspired."[25] Among such artists, by 1916, Hutchinson also placed the art collector, because he felt that amassing art collections had become an equally important art of its own. Art collectors were simply, in his view, "artists who can not paint or carve or build, [those] with artistic sense and taste who cannot create."[26]

Hutchinson's views ushered in two decades, the 1920s and 1930s, of vigorous and extremely successful courting of the city's art patrons by the Art Institute, but they put the School into a precarious position. From French's death in 1914 until 1921, both the administration of the School and its artistic direction were held in limbo while the Board decided exactly what to do with the School. In 1916, when George Eggers was named director of the museum, the Board appointed a School subcommittee to address the future of the School. Charged with naming both a new dean and the faculty, the four-person School Committee was headed until the early 1920s by Frank G. Logan, a prominent Chicago businessman and one of the arch-conservatives on the Art Institute Board, whose wife Josephine founded the Sanity in Art movement in 1937.[27] While Logan is not remembered as being particularly unfriendly toward the School, it is unlikely that this highly opinionated man would have entertained any unconventional educational notions. In 1916 the Committee decided to name as dean Theodore Keane, the School registrar who had been acting dean since French's death. A seemingly uncontroversial appointee, Keane raised serious questions about the running of the School when he angrily resigned in 1918. Charging the Board with irresponsibility in the maintenance of school facilities, Keane concluded that "the policy of those in final authority in matters pertaining to the school appears to be that anything will suffice as long as it answers the purpose of a temporary expedient."[28]

There were other signs of the museum's lack of concern about the School. Long hours at low pay were, and are, standard for people teaching at art schools, but conditions at the School were perhaps worse than elsewhere. Howard K. Morse, an instructor of design and art history, almost doubled his teaching hours when he came to the Art Institute from the University of Chicago in 1925—from sixteen hours to thirty hours per week—without a pay increase. This load "leaves too little time for creative work," he told the School subcommittee, and it gave teachers little opportunity to advance.[29] Similarly, Ralph Clarkson had explained that many Chicago artists had to sacrifice their artistic careers to devote themselves to teaching.[30] Annual faculty salaries were low, ranging in 1918 from $2,500 for head of the design department, to a part-time salary of less than $600.[31]

Moreover, the best-paid faculty members were generally those whose artistic values matched the needs of the conservative museum board. For instance, Albin Polasek, a sculptor whose portrait busts were popular among the city's elite, was paid $1,800 in 1918, while the part-time salary for progressive artist John Norton was only $600.[32] Such low salaries and heavy workloads apparently were responsible for the School's inability to attract to its permanent faculty outstanding and innovative artists from outside Chicago, a fact which contributed to serious inbreeding at the School. Indeed, there were several nepotistic faculty families, among them the Vanderpoels and the Buehrs.[33]

Visiting artists were another matter, since they were paid for out of a special museum fund. When George Bellows taught for two months at the School in 1919, he was paid the enormous sum of $2,000.[34] Two years later, Leon Kroll was paid $5,000 to teach two days a week at the School for seven months.[35] Both these artists apparently were invited by the museum director with the blessing of the Board while the School played little, if any, role in the matter.[36] The Bellows visit, for instance, came at the end of a major Bellows show at the museum organized by Director George Eggers, who later wrote a book about the artist. In 1922, when Kroll got into a row with the Dean of the School, Raymond Ensign, Board support for the artist overruled the Dean.[37]

Together, Bellows, Kroll, and Randall Davey, the third Ashcan School artist to teach at the School in the early 1920s, put into motion a minor revolution in Chicago art. It was their espousal of the Ashcan School's non-genteel style of social realist painting that caused the change. For instance, Bellows, an Ohio-born artist whose Republican values and illustrative art appealed enormously to Chicago, had trained with New York artist Robert Henri. Henri, an ardent individualist, worked under the motto, "Anything that strikes you as real is worthy to be painted."[38]

Bellows bridged the radical and conservative forces at odds in American art after the Armory Show. Considered a progressive artist, he was one of the organizers of the Armory Show and a staunch defender of modern art. In his own work, however, he retained an illustrational style and, during World War I, produced a popular series of war images. The Art Institute itself, and particularly the School, had been deeply caught up in the war effort, producing and exhibiting designs for war-related posters.[39] Bellows was embraced in Chicago after the War as a native son, a midwesterner compared to authors Booth Tarkington and Edgar Lee Masters because his work demonstrated that "rich unadulterated strain of good sound middle-western Americanism."[40] Though remembered now largely for his boxing pictures, Bellows was a sensitive chronicler of American life, a talented lithographer, and a teacher whose philosophy of painting differed from the standard fare at the School of the Art Institute.

"Try everything that can be done. Try it in every possible way," he told his students. "Be deliberate and spontaneous. Be thoughtful and painstaking. Be abandoned and impulsive. Learn your own possibilities. . . . The work of art should be a document of the wholeness of man, not of one single part" (fig. 11.3).[41] Bellows was also interested in art theory. As a devotee of the principles of dynamic symmetry espoused by Jay Hambidge, Bellows was most likely responsible, at least indirectly, for the selection of Hambidge as the 1920–21 Scammon lecturer at the Art Institute.

Bellows' philosophy, and those of his friends Randall Davey and Leon Kroll who followed him at the School, had a profound effect on Chicago's art students. Emil Armin, who became a prominent modern artist in the 1920s, cited Davey as an important inspiration for creating expressionistic art: "At every opportunity, Davey stressed the need for personal expression. He admonished the students to learn to draw and paint while at the Institute and then to go out and pour their individual personalities into the molds they had mastered the technique of making."[42] The permanent faculty member whose views were most closely aligned with Bellows's, Davey's, and Kroll's philosophies

11.3 George Bellows with his students at the School of the Art Institute of Chicago, photograph, 1920. Photograph taken from the *Catalogue of the School of the Art Institute of Chicago*, 1920–21, p. 43. © 1989 The Art Institute of Chicago. All Rights Reserved.

was John Norton. By the late 1920s, a handful of people who had studied with Norton and the Ashcan artists, particularly Laura Van Pappelendam and Francis Chapin, were teaching at the School, and they, in turn, encouraged their own students to explore expressive techniques in an illustrational style. At this time, Ivan LeLorrain Albright also taught briefly at the School, and Boris Anisfeld, a Russian painter with expressionist leanings, joined the faculty.

From 1918–21, when views of the museum Board toward the School had clarified considerably and Eggers temporarily took it over after Keane's resignation, yet another direction announced itself, that of training in the industrial arts. For more than a decade, there had been a national effort to establish schools of industrial arts, a movement enthusiastically supported by the American Federation of Arts during Hutchinson's tenure as president and vice president.[43] The feeling was that America was falling behind its European counterparts in industrial design and that it was in the national interest for the country to upgrade its industrial arts. In 1918, when the School embarked on a curriculum reorganization to "meet the demands made on trained artists," it was alluding to industrial applications. "The Art Institute recognizes the responsibility the art school owes to American industry, and the responsibility of the school to the individual whose vocation must render a livelihood," its catalog read.[44] Indeed, after World War I, industrial arts courses were in great demand; eighty-four percent of the student body claimed a desire to enter the art professions by 1921.[45] Enrollment soared at the School in the early twenties, reaching three thousand students in 1922 and causing the museum to boast that one-fifth of the country's painters, sculptors, craftsmen, and art teachers had been trained at the School of the Art Institute.[46]

Such high enrollment turned the School into a major source of revenue for the museum at a time when its curatorial program was rapidly expanding. During these years, School surplus often went toward paying museum expenses rather than going back into the School program; more than half of the School surplus in 1924, for instance, was used to pay off the museum's deficit that had been accumulating since the 1880s.[47] That same year, the museum began charging the School rent for its space at a rate of thirty cents per square foot.[48] Thus when Hutchinson began to promote the development of an industrial arts program, his purposes appeared twofold: to meet the nation's need for industrial designers and to generate revenue for the museum's curatorial program (fig. 11.4).

In the early 1920s, two developments designed to launch the School on its industrial arts program took place. First, major figures trained in industrial arts were hired: a new dean, Raymond Ensign, who came in 1921 from the Cleveland Museum of Art where he had headed the Applied Arts program, and several

11.4 Students in an industrial design course at the School of the Art Institute, photograph, early 1930s. Photograph taken from an undated brochure in a catalog of the School of the Art Institute of Chicago. © 1989 The Art Institute of Chicago. All Rights Reserved.

new design faculty members, among them Alfonso Iannelli, a designer and sculptor brought from California to Chicago by Frank Lloyd Wright to work on his Midway Gardens. Then, in 1922, the museum Board began discussing an expanded industrial arts curriculum to be subsidized by a new Chicago business group called the Association of Arts and Industries.[49] The willingness of the Board in 1922 even to consider collaborating with an outside industrial arts group is significant. Less than ten years earlier, in 1914, the Board had unanimously rejected a similar proposal from the Chicago School of Applied and Normal Art to create an industrial arts program at the school.[50] The feeling then was that such a vocational program would detract from higher aesthetic goals.

From the start, there was resistance to the Board's effort to forge a relationship between the School and the Association of Arts and Industries. Robert Harshe, who followed Eggers as director in 1921, was initially in favor of the idea, but after Hutchinson's death in 1924, his enthusiasm markedly cooled.[51] Students and faculty were also critical of the Board's effort to change the School's direction. At least one student, Louis G. Ferstadt, complained about the "mercenary and commercial" forces at work at the School in 1922, trying to teach "art like business colleges teach stenography (fig. 11.5)."[52] In a letter solicited from alumni in 1923, Ferstadt wrote that "the Art Institute may lose its value as a cultural institution" because of its "lack of interest in the real serious instructors." New design faculty added during the mid-1920s apparently were made to feel unwelcome. Iannelli, who was chairman of the Department of Design and seemed destined to head the new industrial arts school under discussion, resigned in 1929 after what seemed to be lack of School support for his program. Iannelli met resistance from the School because it was felt that the subsidized industrial arts program should be headed by someone more a part of the Art Institute family.[53] He was replaced by Emil Zettler, a designer and a graduate of the School, who married one of the School's assistant deans and was eventually commissioned to design the medal for the museum's Frank G. Logan Award.

By the 1930s, the spirit of educational reform at the School had almost entirely abated, taking with it the embryonic move toward modernism that lay within the international industrial design movement of the time. Declining School enrollment during the Depression decreased the demand to offer industrial arts courses, which no doubt must have been a relief to the faction arguing for a more subtle application of art.[54] In 1935, the relationship with the Association of Arts and Industries was officially terminated. Two years later the Association hired Laszlo Moholy-Nagy, formerly a faculty member of the Weimar Bauhaus, to establish a Chicago industrial arts school. Moholy-Nagy and his school, known originally as the New Bauhaus and later as the Institute of Design, became a major force for international modernism in Chicago in the 1940s.[55] In the meantime, the School of the Art Institute slipped back into its old familiar identity as a bastion of gentility and aesthetic uplift. Museum Director Robert Harshe, a painter who studied with School faculty member Louis Ritman and favored impressionism, reinstated the casual gentlemanly relationship between the museum and the School. When Raymond Ensign resigned in 1929, Harshe appointed the Institute's assistant director, Charles Fabens Kelly, as the new School dean.

Nevertheless, the years of reappraisal left a permanent mark on the School and its program. In 1920, art history from antiquity to the Renaissance was taught for the first time, initially by Helen Gardner and later by her protégé Kathleen Blackshear, among others. The introduction of art history had far-reaching implications at the School, bringing "art philosophy" to the curriculum, a subject which Charles Francis Browne had felt students in 1916 were not advanced enough to understand.[56] At the same time, the old adherence to neo-classical and Renaissance

11.5 Student work produced in industrial design classes at the School of the Art Institute, 1930s. Photograph taken from *Catalogue of Courses, School of the Art Institute of Chicago,* 1933–34, pp. 50–51. © 1989 The Art Institute of Chicago. All Rights Reserved.

models was also gradually being undermined during this period. More attuned to stylistic innovation, students in the thirties would more frequently either pursue the streamlined, geometric stylization of Art Deco or adopt a style of expressionist realism freed from the restrictions of traditional illusionism. Because of the Ashcan School painters who visited the School in the 1920s, the latter style of painting was considered daring and progressive in Chicago for its narrative focus on contemporary urban life. While today often considered conservative or provincial, this so-called regionalist pictorial idiom offered certain progressive artists of the time a means of portraying the complex sociopolitical changes that were occurring in American life between World War I and World War II. As such in Chicago, it often offended entrenched nineteenth-century assumptions about the social function of art as much as abstraction offended ideas in the city about what art should look like. Indeed in 1936, when regionalist artist Doris Lee won the Logan Prize for her painting *Thanksgiving* in the Art Institute's annual American exhibition, Sanity in Art founder Josephine Logan railed against it and other paintings of its expressionist ilk as being "out of focus" and disturbing in their depiction of everyday life.[57]

While the prominence of this painting style at the end of the thirties illustrates the inability of the School of the Art Institute and its community to sustain a hold on modernist innovation, it also demonstrates an ironic continuity with the institution's original purpose. From the earliest years of the century, when Charles Hutchinson declared "art for art's sake" to be a "selfish and errroneous doctrine," emphasis at the School had been placed on the social function of art. Hutchinson espoused a nineteenth-century idealism about art, envisioning a new Renaissance art to uplift the masses to a higher plane of existence. The legacy of that vision persisted at the School in updated incarnations until the 1940s.

If his plans for an industrial arts school had materialized in the 1920s and 1930s, Hutchinson would have found a way to translate artistic concerns into social benefit. The realistic painting of the Depression years permitted art to empathetically portray social conditions. Under the prevailing cultural equation at the School, for art to have done otherwise—for it to have focused totally on psychological perception or intellectual growth— would have been false, if not immoral, and unworthy of a progressive consciousness. Clinging to such notions, the School of the Art Institute moved into the modern era on unsure footing, disoriented by contradictory definitions of modernity to the extent that no clear understanding of it managed to take root in its art.

Charlotte Moser

From the Armory Show to the Century of Progress: The Art Institute Assimilates Modernism

RICHARD R. BRETTELL AND SUE ANN PRINCE

William M. R. French (fig. 12.1), the first director of the Art Institute of Chicago, wrote a letter to Sara Hallowell just prior to the opening of the Armory Show in Chicago. In it he discussed the upcoming exhibition: "We are about to bring the best part, meaning the worst part, of the Post-Impressionist show here. . . . As for me, I expect to go to California in about three days, to be gone a month. I shall no doubt save myself a great deal of mental wear and tear."[1] His words reveal the beginning of an ambivalence that would, for the next thirty years, reveal itself again and again at the Art Institute as it collectively pondered whether modernism was the best part or the worst part of modern and contemporary art production. Whatever the museum decided at any one moment, it was not spared the wear and tear that French apparently saved himself.

French's letter to Hallowell is well known, and historians have frequently taken his absence during the show as an indication of his inability to understand the modernists, his blatant uninterest, or his desire to escape confrontation. However, there is a considerable amount of French correspondence that indicates he not only was very positive about the Armory Show, at least early on, but also was the primary force behind its coming to Chicago. In November 1912, he queried James B. Townsend of *American Art News* about "an exhibition of the most modern foreign pictures in New York this season."[2] In early January 1913 he went to New York for a week to meet with Arthur B. Davies and Walt Kuhn, two of the exhibition's organizers.[3]

The letters French wrote upon his return express great enthusiasm. They reveal his struggle to clear as much space as pos-

The authors wish to thank John Smith for his research work.

sible for the show—even when it meant eliminating or diminishing space designated for previously scheduled exhibitions by local artist Pauline Palmer and others. They also announce his second trip to New York to conclude arrangements for the Chicago venue.[4] French went to New York again in mid-February for about a week. It appears that he wrote down his impressions of the exhibition on the train back to Chicago, enclosing them in a letter sent a few days later to Charles Hutchinson, Art Institute board president, who was traveling in Europe at the time.[5]

The first paragraphs of his impressions reveal that he was caught up in the excitement of the exhibition. He described and summarized the arrangement of the works of art and gave a favorable account of the modernist display:

> The fraction of the exhibition comprising the real modernists, the post impressionists, cubists, pointillists, futurists—six or seven galleries—is eminently satisfactory. Anything more fantastic it would be hard to conceive. Some of the works are mere unmeaning assemblages of form with gay colors, conveying no idea whatever, but bearing such titles as *Dance* or *Souvenir*. A few, more logical, have no titles but merely numbers. As an appeal to curiosity, this part of the show is a decided success.

French went on to relate that he had visited and discussed the show with Walt Kuhn and Arthur B. Davies, and that he had seen other American artists in New York. As he began to discuss the possibility of bringing the show to the Art Institute, however, he became more cautious:

> With regard to the desirability of bringing the exhibition to Chicago, my opinion has changed. I at first thought it would be a good thing to satisfy the curiosity of the public, and as I visited the exhibition for the first time I felt a sort of exhilaration at the absurdity of it all. I still think it would be reasonable and right for us to exhibit a single gallery, perhaps fifty examples, of the most extreme works, so that our public may know what they are. But when it comes to bringing a large part of the exhibit here, to incurring great expense, to turning the Art Institute upside down, as was scarcely done except in honor of Saint-Gaudens or the Société Nouvelle, I hesitate. We cannot make a joke of our guests. It becomes a serious matter. As I visited the exhibition repeatedly, I became depressed to think that people would be found to approve methods so subversive of taste, good sense, and education, of everything that is simple, pure, and of good report.

12.1 William M. R. French, first director of the Art Institute of Chicago, photograph, n.d. Archives of the Art Institute of Chicago. © 1989 The Art Institute of Chicago. All Rights Reserved.

French nonetheless wrote Davies a few days later that he especially wanted the "more novel" part of the exhibition, "the works of Matisse, Gauguin, Redon, Duchamp, Cézanne, Picasso, Van Gogh, Rousseau, and the rest of the well-known and extraordinary foreigners." He was not interested in many of the American works nor did he want, in his words, "the old paintings by the radicals or reformers of other days. Our public is well acquainted with these . . ."[6] While the Art Institute had available only about half the hanging space of the Armory in New York, he suggested hanging more than half of the original exhibition in that space, clearly indicating that he wanted to extend the show beyond the fifty pieces he had suggested earlier.

Indeed, French seems to have tailored his attitude to whomever he was writing or talking. He was positive and enthusiastic when communicating with Davies or Kuhn in New York, for instance, but was cautious with his associates at the Art Institute, especially Hutchinson. For instance, he wrote Sara Hallowell in the aforementioned letter, "I not only do not appreciate most of the Post-Impressionists' work, but a good deal of the Impressionists' work . . ." Notes included with his impressions during the train ride between Chicago and New York reveal his difficulty in understanding the work of the modernist masters:

> Matisse's work: If this work were submitted to me without explanation, I should regard it as a joke. It is asserted that he is an accomplished painter. I have never seen anything to show it, and I am of the opinion that if he ever did anything it really is without merit. It has no subtlety of line, no sweetness of color, no refinement of sentiment, no beauty of any kind.
> Van Gogh's work: Not so good as I expected for some prints I have seen. Other people have done the same things better. It is well known he was violently insane.
> Duchamp and Picabia: The wildest of the cubists. Humbugs—not incapable.
> Gauguin: Heavy and ugly.

As the exhibition drew near, negative reactions from both New York and Chicago increased,[7] and French began to dodge responsibility for bringing the exhibition to Chicago. His California trip, planned as a combined vacation and lecture tour long before he even knew the dates of the exhibition, became a convenient escape. He could say to opposers or potential opposers, be they staff, students, or the general public, that the exhibition was "in the hands of Mr. Carpenter, supported by Mr. Aldis and Mr. Arthur Eddy (fig. 12.2), and other radicals."[8]

Yet it was French who implemented an efficient procedure for the show's installation prior to his departure, leaving the details to Newton H. Carpenter, secretary of the museum. Plans of the Art Institute's galleries were sent to New York so that placement

Richard R. Brettell and Sue Ann Prince

12.2 James McNeill Whistler, *An Arrangement in Flesh Color and Brown (Arthur Jerome Eddy),* oil on canvas, 1894. Arthur Jerome Eddy Memorial Collection, 1931.501. © 1989 The Art Institute of Chicago. All Rights Reserved.

could be determined in advance and expedited quickly upon arrival in Chicago. The 650 works left New York on March 20, and the show opened in Chicago only four days later, on March 24. Even some of the New York organizers apparently acknowledged that the exhibition was installed more beautifully in Chicago than it had been in New York (figs. 12.3 and 12.4; see also fig. 1.8).[9] It may never be known whether French secured the exhibition for Chicago because he was intrigued by the modernists even though he did not understand them, or whether he brought it because he felt it would be a curiosity, an enlightenment, or an object of ridicule. Whatever the case, his engineering of the show is as significant as his absence during its run, which foisted upon the museum an angered public whose outrage has become legendary.[10]

During the teens, after the uproar over the Armory Show had calmed, the museum concerned itself only rarely with modern art, thereby creating little or no controversy. An exception was a 1915 exhibition of twenty-five paintings by Albert Bloch, one of the artists of the Blue Rider group in Germany. Arthur Jerome Eddy, who had convinced the museum to hold the exhibition, wrote enthusiastically in the catalog that "in opening its doors to exhibitions such as . . . the present one of Bloch's, the Trustees of the Art Institute do so on the theory that its members and the public have the right to see and judge for themselves every-

12.3 Gallery 53, Cubist Room, the International Exhibition of Modern Art, photograph, 1913. Archives of the Art Institute of Chicago. © 1989 The Art Institute of Chicago. All Rights Reserved.

Richard R. Brettell and Sue Ann Prince

thing that is new and interesting in art."[11] The museum, however, was less enthusiastic: The only other contemporary works shown during the teens were those of the Taos School of New Mexico and the Ashcan School of New York. Both shows promulgated a relatively safe and naturalistic if not academic depiction of reality.

During the twenties, the museum's activities revealed contradictory impulses in regard to modernism, reflecting an uneven and uneasy process of accommodation that was determined by leaders who appear to have vacillated in their own opinions. In 1920 there were exhibitions of works by Arthur B. Davies, Edgar Degas, and Auguste Renoir, and a show of etchings and lithographs by Odilon Redon; none of the works in these exhibitions were considered avant-garde, some were not even modernist. The only other contemporary exhibition was of works by Alphonse Mucha, a visiting teacher at the School of the Art Institute, who during his month-long stay displayed five of eleven murals comprising his grand history painting titled *Historical Paintings of the Slavic Nations*. Shown on the balcony overlooking the Grand Staircase, the murals were executed in a kind of decorative naturalism that derived more from art nouveau than from the new, modernist abstraction.

From 1921 through 1927, avant-garde exhibitions included works from the collection of the late Arthur Jerome Eddy in 1922, works by Alfonso Iannelli in the winters of 1921–22 and 1925–26, and sculpture by Aristide Maillol in 1926. Exhibitions

12.4 East Gallery, the International Exhibition of Modern Art, photograph, 1913. Archives of the Art Institute of Chicago. © 1989 The Art Institute of Chicago. All Rights Reserved.

that could be called modern but not avant-garde or contemporary included the 1923 showing of the Birch Bartlett loan collection of European impressionism and post impressionism. And George Bellows, Leon Kroll, Eugene Savage, Walter Ufer, Edgar Cameron, and Mary Cassatt were each exhibited once. The Carnegie International and the two annual exhibitions, the Chicago and Vicinity show and the American Painting and Sculpture show—the largest efforts of the Institute to show contemporary art production—were extremely conservative. Their jury system, which supported the academic art of the beaux-arts tradition, provoked rebellion among many local contemporary artists.

This cautious stance with regard to modernism was not unlike that of other major U.S. museums in the twenties. The Metropolitan Museum of Art in New York and the Pennsylvania Academy of Fine Arts in Philadelphia, for instance, each held only three exhibitions during the entire decade that could be considered modernist. It was only at The Brooklyn Museum, under the leadership of William Henry Fox, that a greater commitment to modern art was made, most spectacularly in the 1926 International Exhibition of Modern Art, initiated and implemented largely by the Société Anonyme.[12]

Of all these cities, Chicago was unique in an unusual arrangement that allowed for a regular showing of avant-garde art at the Art Institute even though the museum did not sponsor it. Late in 1920, the Arts Club of Chicago, a group founded in 1916 "to encourage, develop and foster a higher standard of craftsmanship, to maintain permanent galleries and exhibition rooms for works of art, and to promote the mutual acquaintance of art lovers and art workers,"[13] requested that it be allowed to use one of the Art Institute's galleries as an exhibition space. As Charles Hutchinson and Martin Ryerson were founding members of the Club as well as highly influential trustees of the museum, the idea was found to be mutually beneficial and was put into effect immediately.[14] The terms of agreement set forth that the Arts Club committee selecting the exhibitions would contain one representative from the Art Institute and that the Club would install all works of art and pay all expenses. The Institute offered the Club one of its best skylit spaces in the suite of permanent exhibition galleries on the second floor. Although the museum would not agree to call the space the "Arts Club Room," it did agree that each exhibition would be designated with a sign that read "Arts Club Exhibition."[15]

Although no official agreement between the museum and the Arts Club existed as to the kind of art that would be shown in the Arts Club space, the Club's propensity to support avant-garde work had been clear ever since Rue Winterbotham Carpenter had assumed its leadership in 1918 and hired Alice Roullier as chairman of her exhibition committee (fig. 12.5). Car-

12.5 B. J. O. Nordfeldt, *Double Portrait, Rue Winterbotham Carpenter and Alice Roullier,* oil on canvas, ca. 1913. Collection of Emily A. Nordfeldt. Photo courtesy, Paul Kruty.

penter was the independent and energetic daughter of Joseph Humphrey Winterbotham—an arts patron who in 1921 bequeathed a fund to the museum for the ongoing purchase of art—and Roullier was a well-connected, sophisticated connoisseur. Together they engineered a wide variety of avant-garde exhibitions until Carpenter's death in 1931. From 1922 through 1927, many of those exhibitions were held at the Art Institute.[16]

The Arts Club shows were the most progressive in the city. In 1923 the first Chicago showing of Picasso drawings was held in its exhibition room—fifty-three drawings and four sculptures—with a catalog introduction by the distinguished English critic Clive Bell. That exhibition was followed in 1924 by a show of eighteen paintings by Picasso. The drawings from the 1923 show were not from the most radical, cubist period of Picasso's art, between 1906 and 1917, but rather from his more contemporary figurative works, often termed his classical period.

Carpenter also brought Rodin's sculptures and drawings to the museum in 1923 (fig. 12.6). It was the first showing of Rodin's work west of New York. Much of it would likely have been considered obscene in Chicago during the teens or later during the thirties when the Sanity in Art movement was in full bloom.[17] In 1924, in addition to the second Picasso show, Carpenter arranged for an exhibition of paintings by Georges Braque—the first in Chicago—and a show of works by Marie Laurencin. In 1925 Arts Club exhibitions included paintings by Henri de Toulouse-Lautrec and Berthe Morisot and sculpture by Elie Nadelman. Gaston Lachaise, Maurice Vlaminck, and Maurice Utrillo were exhibited in 1926. Also held in that year was a show of modern masters loaned by Arthur B. Davies, which included Picasso, Braque, and modern American artists, as well as modern decorative and industrial arts from the 1925 Exposition Internationale des Arts Décoratifs et Industriels Modernes in Paris.

For the Art Institute, the arrangement with the Arts Club was convenient; it allowed progressive work to be exhibited in, but not necessarily endorsed by, the museum. It was similar to

12.6 Installation of a Rodin exhibition in the Arts Club exhibition room at the Art Institute of Chicago, photograph, 1923. The Arts Club of Chicago Archives, Newberry Library, Chicago.

French's decision to bring the Armory Show to Chicago and then to repudiate it when negative pressure was applied, especially by powerful people. By 1927 the Arts Club arrangement was evidently causing the museum trustees difficulty. Displeased with some of the exhibition choices, the Board passed a motion to create "a committee to confer with the officers of the Arts Club in order to secure better cooperation with the Club so that the Art Institute may have supervision and authority in the selection of exhibits to be held."[18] The Board also asked to appropriate the Arts Club space for that year's Artists of Chicago and Vicinity show. Unwilling to have its exhibitions monitored, the Arts Club responded by withdrawing from the Art Institute later that year. From then on, it mounted all of its exhibitions in its own gallery, which had moved from 610 South Michigan to 410 North Michigan in 1924. Modernist exhibitions at the museum all but disappeared—there were none in 1928 or 1929.

During the twenties the Arts Club had held shows in its own gallery as well as at the Art Institute. Carpenter's vision, which was behind the founding of the Club in 1916, went beyond the visual arts to include dance, theater, music, poetry; the Club invited such innovative artists as Sergei Prokofiev, Igor Stravinsky, Martha Graham, Harold Kreutzberg, and Leonid Massine to perform. Nadia Boulanger gave a lecture, and Edna St. Vincent Millay gave a reading of her poems. Carpenter and Roullier's promotion of the avant-garde in the twenties was among the most influential in the city;[19] it was certainly their leadership, and not that of the museum, that was behind the avant-garde art one saw at the Art Institute.

As in New York in the twenties, when museum leadership chose not to exhibit avant-garde works of art, it fell to progressive, well-to-do women to bring the new art to the city. Carpenter and Roullier's Arts Club was Chicago's counterpart to Katherine Dreier's Société Anonyme in New York. Carpenter and Roullier lacked Dreier's zealous belief in modernism as a means of spiritual enrichment, and their vision of modernism focused almost solely on modern French art to the exclusion of constructivism, dadaism, and expressionism, movements which were championed by Dreier and Marcel Duchamp.[20] But their impetus to bring modernism to the public was similar.

Until 1921 there had been only two works of twentieth-century European art in the Art Institute's holdings, and both were Salon pieces in the nineteenth-century academic tradition. It was in the twenties and early thirties that two patrons donated impressive collections of impressionism and post impressionism and thereby provided the basis for bringing the museum's holdings into the twentieth century. Other patrons began assembling modern art collections and providing for the purchase of recent modernist works. Thus, while the museum was hesitant to endorse modernism in its exhibitions, it began to acquire late-nineteenth-century French works for its collection, a move which in hindsight can be seen as the first step toward a real acceptance and integration of twentieth-century modern art.

One of the first patrons whose modern collection would become important to the museum was Frederick Clay Bartlett, who joined the Institute Board of Trustees in 1923. His collection, exhibited on loan that same year, included mostly nineteenth-century examples of impressionism and post impressionism. It did not yet include some of the major works Bartlett would soon buy, such as Seurat's *Sunday Afternoon on the Island of the Grande Jatte*, Toulouse-Lautrec's *At the Moulin Rouge*, and Picasso's *The Old Guitarist*. These works were installed with the rest of the collection in 1926, when they were given to the museum.[21] In 1932, another collection of impressionism and post impressionism, that of Annie Swan Coburn, was donated to the museum.

A major event of the early twenties for the Art Institute was the creation of the Winterbotham Fund in 1921. It was an endowment established "for the purchase of oil paintings painted by European artists and of foreign subjects"[22] for the permanent collection. There was no stipulation ruling that the works had to be contemporary or modern; in fact Winterbotham once wrote to the Board of Trustees in the postscript of a 1922 letter, "I might add to this that I am *not* partial to the extreme modern art."[23] Nonetheless, the fund was usually directed toward improving the modern collection.

In 1921 the museum used the Fund to purchase Jean Forain's *Sentenced for Life* of 1910 from the Arts Club exhibit of his work, and, in 1923, Gauguin's *Te Burao* of 1892. In 1925 two more significant modern paintings were bought for the Winterbotham Collection: a portrait by Gauguin, then considered a likeness of his wife but now known simply as *Portrait of a Woman* (1890); and Toulouse-Lautrec's *In the Cirque Fernande: The Ring-Master* (1888), one of his greatest early paintings. In 1935 the Winterbotham family changed the purchasing guidelines for its fund, stipulating that no purchases would be made of works by artists who had been dead more than ten years.[24]

The museum was less adventuresome when it came to contemporary avant-garde art. A rare exception was the exhibition in 1922 of a portion of Arthur Jerome Eddy's collection—without question the most advanced in the city—including pioneering works by such artists as Kandinsky, Duchamp, Picabia, Villon, and Bloch, some of which had been purchased as early as 1913 at the Armory Show. While such local artists as Raymond Jonson were apparently impressed by the exhibition, it was considered incomplete and, according to artist Albert Bloch, disappointing: "The exhibition is a fizzle from any artistic point of view. It bears all the hallmarks of haste and casualness. The selections are haphazard and slovenly . . . not one of a whole series of Klees is shown."[25]

Following the exhibition, the museum showed no interest in acquiring Eddy's collection, which had been available since his death two years earlier. An inquiry from Eddy's widow as late as March 1928 about the museum's interest evidently elicited no response from the Board.[26] Meanwhile, Walter Arensberg, a Philadelphia collector whose comprehensive collection of avant-garde twentieth-century work the museum would actively pursue but fail to acquire in the 1940s, purchased many of Eddy's cubist paintings, thereby removing them from the city. In 1931, the museum accepted twenty paintings and three sculptures from Eddy's wife and son, including Constantin Brancusi's *Sleeping Muse*, Franz Marc's *The Bewitched Mill*, Albert Bloch's *Three Pierrots and a Harlequin*, and four paintings by Kandinsky. The rest of the collection was scattered and sold.[27] At the time there seems to have been no regret on the part of the Art Institute or Chicagoans in general that these landmark works were leaving the city.

During the twenties the Institute arranged its collections according to donors—each room or group of rooms celebrated a patron, not the art he or she bought. In 1926 and early 1927, for instance, Frederick Clay Bartlett spent considerable time helping to install his collection in the Nickerson Room, which was

12.7 Installation view of the Helen Birch Bartlett Memorial Collection at the Art Institute of Chicago, photograph, early 1930s. Archives of the Art Institute of Chicago. © 1989 The Art Institute of Chicago. All Rights Reserved.

renamed the Helen Birch Bartlett Memorial Gallery following the death of his wife. He insisted on having the gallery painted white and stripped of all ornament (fig. 12.7), a striking contrast to the Henry Field Memorial Gallery designed by Louis Comfort Tiffany, where nineteenth-century academic French paintings were displayed. Of the room Bartlett later wrote, "I had always had a theory that modern pictures looked more at home and hung better together when framed in simple well-proportioned mouldings in a tone of white than in the ornate mouldings of the various Loui's (sic)."[28] Thus the paintings in Bartlett's Collection were hung in uniform, white frames regardless of scale. Perhaps the first paintings ever presented in any general art museum as "modern," they attracted the attention of Europeans such as Samuel Courtauld of the Courtauld Institute and J. B. Manson of the Tate Gallery.

Bartlett not only participated in the hanging of his collection, he made a financial contribution for the upkeep of the memorial gallery and continued to select pieces especially for the space. In retrospect, when his concept was threatened, he would write, "My sole purpose was to make the Helen Birch Bartlett room as perfect a UNIT as possible and to frame and hang it in such a way as to make it entirely harmonious."[29]

By the early thirties the separation of the museum's holdings into donors' galleries was an arrangement no longer favored by Robert Harshe, director since 1921, and Daniel Catton Rich, then associate curator of painting and sculpture and special assistant to the director for the Century of Progress exhibition. For that exhibition in 1933, Rich and Harshe dismantled the museum's series of donor rooms in order to display all the works of art in a single chronological sequence. Rather than emphasizing the difference between the modernism of Bartlett's collection and the traditionalism of other works, their presentation stressed the collection's continuity with the past. The installation alienated Bartlett, who wrote:

> I am much in favor of continuing the historical and educational exhibit now in progress until Chicago has had a reasonable chance to see it. I will be frank and say that I thought the present so-called historical hanging was harmful in spots, as it could not help being, to the artistic aspect and I doubt if the historical side of the hanging is strong enough to educate offhand the average intelligent visitor nor does he go primarily to an art museum for a lesson in history. Too much dryness adds to the tomb quality of museums, well exemplified by the historical hanging in the Metropolitan.
>
> In my opinion the education of taste is a higher and more legitament [sic] function for an art museum than history. One generally agrees that the function of art

Richard R. Brettell and Sue Ann Prince

is to please the eye and the intelectual [*sic*] sense and not to encroach too much on the literary, historical or scientific fields of the pen.[30]

Bartlett's decision to hang his paintings in simple frames against a background of white had indeed been a modern concept for the museum. But his preference for connoisseurship over history and for the separation of his own collection was not.

More innovative by contemporary museum standards was an installation organized according to contemporary art historical notions, one that presented the history of art as a related, evolutionary sequence of formal artistic developments. Harshe wrote: "I think it is obvious that when you have two collections of Barbizon pictures in the same institution a block apart, it is unfortunate, and when you have three groupings of impressionist paintings widely separated and a gallery which contains English 18th century, Dutch 16th century and Barbizon paintings, you have a hodge-podge which cannot be reconciled."[31] The historical arrangement of the art exhibition at the Century of Progress fair effected the institutionalization of modernism in Chicago, integrating all paintings and sculptures from the thirteenth century through the early twentieth century into one chronological sequence. Every period of art was granted the same consideration. Paintings were hung at eye level, surrounded by large expanses, garlanded where appropriate, and heroicized (fig. 12.8).[32]

12.8 Century of Progress exhibition at the Art Institute of Chicago, 1933–34, *Sunday Afternoon on the Island of the Grande Jatte* by Seurat, flanked by two works of Henri Rousseau, photograph, 1933. Archives of the Art Institute of Chicago. © 1989 The Art Institute of Chicago. All Rights Reserved.

12.9 Century of Progress exhibition at the Art Institute of Chicago, 1933–34, Grand Staircase with works by Miró, Duchamp, and others, photograph, 1933. Archives of the Art Institute of Chicago. © 1989 The Art Institute of Chicago. All Rights Reserved.

The installation of modern art, though it was not referred to as "modern" in the catalog, occupied twenty-seven galleries and included an impressive display of modern French painting. In contrast to the European section, the "Contemporary American Painting" gallery was old-fashioned. It included one work each by 178 contemporary artists, many of whom worked in a traditional figurative mode and are forgotten today.

The last space in the exhibition was the most dramatic—the staircase at the end of the east wing between the first and second floors by which one left the modern art installation. Included in this space were Miró's *Dog Barking at the Moon* and Duchamp's *Nude Descending a Staircase,* which had had not been in Chicago since the 1913 Armory Show (fig. 12.9). There were major works by De Chirico and a Picasso of 1927, flanked by two major Kandinskys. Descending the stairs, one came to more paintings by many of the artists whose work had caused public outrage twenty years earlier at the Armory Show (fig. 12.10).

The presentation of the Century of Progress art exhibition, representing the continuity of modernism with the past, marked the acceptance of modernism by the Art Institute, an institution that had vacillated for twenty years in its response to modern twentieth-century art. And while it was donors that

224 *Richard R. Brettell and Sue Ann Prince*

12.10 Century of Progress exhibition at the Art Institute of Chicago, 1933–34, Grand Staircase with works by Kandinsky, Picasso, and others, photograph, 1933. Archives of the Art Institute of Chicago. © 1989 The Art Institute of Chicago. All Rights Reserved.

first collected late-nineteenth-century modernist works and small outside organizations that first exhibited contemporary avant-garde work in Chicago, it was the Art Institute that first brought together, in 1933 and 1934, an exhibition that finally and permanently integrated modernism into Chicago's conception of art history. Commonly considered a bastion of conservatism in the early part of the century, the museum nonetheless became the first in the country to amalgamate modernism into the historical mainstream of world art in a major exhibition. It was a triumph for Chicago and a watershed in the history of museum exhibitions.[33]

CHRONOLOGY

This timeline is not comprehensive. It includes events specifically addressed in the essays in this book, other key modernist-related events and activities between 1910 and 1940, and selected earlier milestones in the city's art scene. Exhibitions at the Katharine Kuh Gallery are not listed here; see appendix to chapter 9.

1855	O'Brien's Art Emporium founded
1868	Chicago Academy of Design opens
1871	The Chicago Fire
1880	W. Scott Thurber's gallery founded
	The Union League Club of Chicago founded
1882	The Chicago Academy of Fine Arts reorganized as the Art Institute of Chicago (hereafter AIC)
	Charles Hutchinson becomes president of AIC
1887	Chicago Society of Artists founded
	First exhibition held at AIC
1890s	Central Art Association founded
1893	The World's Columbian Exposition
1895	Palette and Chisel Club founded
1897	Chicago Arts and Crafts Society founded
1898	Eagle's Nest summer art colony founded in Oregon, Illinois
1898–99	Award system for contemporary artists begun
1899	The Industrial Art League founded
1901	Frank Lloyd Wright essay "The Art and Craft of the Machine" published
1903	B. J. O. Nordfeldt arrives in Chicago; lives in 57th Street artists' colony
1905	Ferguson fund for public monuments established

1906	Ferguson Foundation organized
	Midway Studios, University of Chicago, founded; Lorado Taft moves his studio there
1907	Browne's Bookstore founded in Fine Arts Building
	Cliff Dwellers Club founded
1908	Margaret Anderson arrives in Chicago
1908–9	*Friday Literary Review* of the *Chicago Evening Post* founded by Francis Hackett
1909	D. H. Burnham and E. H. Bennett Plan of Chicago ("The Burnham Plan") presented
	Frank Lloyd Wright gives up full-time residency in the city
1910	Friends of American Art established at the AIC
	Raymond Jonson arrives in Chicago
1911	Jerome Blum show at Thurber's gallery
	John Vanderpoel, SAIC instructor, dies
	Floyd Dell appointed associate editor of *Friday Literary Review*
1911–12	The Little Theatre founded in Fine Arts Building by Maurice and Ellen Browne
1912	B. J. O. Nordfeldt show at Thurber's gallery
	Arthur Dove show at Thurber's gallery
	Poetry: A Magazine of Verse founded by Harriet Monroe
	John Norton begins teaching at the School of the Art Institute of Chicago (hereafter SAIC)
1913	Lorado Taft's "Fountain of the Great Lakes," the first Ferguson Fund monument, installed
	Suit initiated against art store displaying Paul Chabas' *September Morn*
	International Exhibition of Modern Art (Armory Show, known in Chicago as "Post-Impressionist Exhibition") at AIC
	W. Scott Thurber dies
	Ezra Pound and Imagism presented in *Poetry* magazine
	Margaret Anderson announces her intention to found *The Little Review*
	Rudolph Weisenborn and Sherwood Anderson both return to Chicago
	Stanislaus Szukalski arrives in Chicago
	B. J. O. Nordfeldt leaves Chicago
	Floyd Dell and Margery Currey join the 57th Street artists' colony; Dell leaves Chicago
1913–14	Manierre Dawson paints full time and exhibits several times in Chicago; leaves the city permanently in 1914
1914	William M. R. French, AIC director, dies
	Newton H. Carpenter becomes interim director of AIC
	Theodore Keane becomes dean of SAIC
	First issue of *The Little Review,* founded by Margaret Anderson, appears in March
	City of Chicago $5,000 fund established for purchase of

	sculpture and paintings by local artists for public buildings Arthur Jerome Eddy's *Cubists and Post-Impressionism* published Committee for the Encouragement of Local Art established Midway Gardens designed by Frank Lloyd Wright
1915	Exhibition of paintings by Albert Bloch at AIC Renaissance Society of University of Chicago founded *Spoon River Anthology* by Edgar Lee Masters published
1916	First and only Independent Society of Artists exhibition The Arts Club of Chicago founded Jane Heap joins *The Little Review* staff George Eggers becomes acting director of AIC Frank Lloyd Wright closes his Chicago office
1916–17	Two one-man shows of works by Stanislaus Szukalski at AIC
1917	Lorado Taft gives Scammon Lectures at AIC Logan Prize established at AIC Eleanor Jewett joins the *Chicago Tribune* staff George Eggers becomes director of AIC
1917–18	*The Little Review* moves to New York
1918	Claude Buck show at J. W. Young Gallery The Arts Club of Chicago comes under the leadership of Rue Carpenter and Alice Roullier George Eggers becomes dean of SAIC; reorganization of SAIC
1919	George Bellows is visiting professor at SAIC, followed by Leon Kroll and Randall Davey in the early 1920s Claude Buck moves to Chicago Ox Bow Summer School and Alumni Association of SAIC partnership formed for Ox Bow School in Saugatuck, Michigan George Eggers becomes director of AIC
1919–21	Arts Club exhibitions of American modernists such as Charles Sheeler, John Marin, Charles Demuth, Joseph Stella, Randall Davey, Maurice Prendergast, and William Glackens; sculpture by Gaston Lachaise, Alfeo Faggi, Auguste Rodin, Hunt Diederich, and Auguste Renoir; and painting by post impressionists such as Vincent Van Gogh, Paul Cézanne, Henri Matisse, André Derain, Georges Seurat, and Paul Signac
1920	Art history offered as a course for first time at SAIC Arthur Jerome Eddy dies Claude Buck show at Thurber's gallery Business Men's Art Club founded
1921	Arts Club exhibits the Introspectives and a loan exhibition of American and French paintings assembled by Forbes Watson (Van Gogh, Toulouse-Lautrec, Cézanne, Seurat, Redon, Vuillard, and Picasso)

	Cor Ardens group is founded
	Salon des Refusés exhibition held at Rothschild's
	Robert Harshe becomes director of AIC
	Raymond Ensign becomes dean of SAIC
	Winterbotham Fund for purchases of art work initiated at AIC
1922	Exhibition of a portion of Arthur J. Eddy Collection at AIC
	Chicago No-Jury Society of Artists founded with Rudolph Weisenborn as president
	First annual No-Jury exhibition held (annual exhibitions thereafter)
	Association of Arts and Industries founded
	Albert Bloch joins faculty of Chicago Academy of Fine Arts
	Potter Palmer Collection donated to AIC
1922–27	Arts Club holds exhibitions at AIC
1923	Frederick Clay Bartlett joins AIC Board of Trustees; Birch Bartlett Collection exhibited at AIC
	Stanislaus Szukalski's *The Work of Szukalski* published
	Association of Chicago Painters and Sculptors founded
1923–25	Alfonso Iannelli begins teaching at SAIC
1924	Charles Hutchinson, AIC Board of Trustees president, dies
	The Magazine of the Art World of the *Chicago Evening Post* founded
	Clarence J. Bulliet joins staff of the *Post* as director and art critic of *The Magazine of the Art World*
	Raymond Jonson leaves Chicago permanently
	Boris Anisfeld becomes head of painting and drawing at SAIC
1925	South Side Art Association founded
	Chicago Galleries Association founded
	Igor Stravinsky gives program, Nadia Boulanger lectures, and Edna St. Vincent Millay gives reading at Arts Club
1926	Bartlett Collection donated to AIC
	Exhibition of works by Aristide Maillol at AIC
	Neo-Arlimusc group founded by Rudolph Weisenborn
1927	Society of Typographic Artists founded
	Clarence J. Bulliet's *Apples and Madonnas* published
	First large U.S. exhibition of Constantin Brancusi at Arts Club, installed by Marcel Duchamp
	Alfonso Iannelli rejoins AIC staff
	Exhibition of modern French painting and sculpture at Renaissance Society
	Charles Faben Kelley becomes dean of SAIC
1928	Julius Meier-Graefe visits Chicago
	"Examples of Modern French Painting and Sculpture" exhibited at Renaissance Society
1929	Douglas McMurtrie's *Modern Typography and Layout* published

Stanislaus Szukalski's *Projects in Design* published
Second exhibition of "Modern French Paintings and
    Sculpture" at Renaissance Society (annual exhibitions
    of modern French painting through 1933)
Industrial Art School established as a separate branch
    of SAIC
The Increase Robinson Gallery opens

1929–31	One-person shows of Henri Rousseau, Georges Rouault, Pablo Picasso, Jacques Villon, Foujita, Joan Miró, and Auguste Renoir at Arts Club
	Aaron Copland, Archibald MacLeish, Buckminster Fuller, Marsden Hartley, Fernand Léger, Andres Segovia, Arthur Honegger, Serge Prokofiev, Harold Kreutzberg, Martha Graham, Escudero, and Massine give program or exhibit work at Arts Club
1930–40	Increasing number of modernist exhibitions at Renaissance Society, including Matisse (1930), Storrs (1931), Noguchi and the Blue Four (1932), group show of Picasso, Gris, Braque, and Léger (1934), Léger and modern German graphics (1936), Moholy-Nagy and modern sculpture (1939)
1931	Designer's League founded
	A portion of Arthur J. Eddy's collection donated to AIC
	The Little Gallery, run by Raymond Katz and Samuel Greenburg, opens in Louis Sullivan's Auditorium Building
1932	J. Z. Jacobson's *Art of Today: Chicago 1933* published
	Annie Swan Coburn Collection donated to AIC
	C. J. Bulliet becomes art critic at the *Chicago Daily News* following the demise of the *Chicago Evening Post*
1932–35	Schonberg, Stravinsky, Gertrude Stein, Le Corbusier, Madame Galka E. Scheyer at Arts Club
	Exhibitions of Soutine, Gris, Monet, Sir Francis Rose, Jacques Villon, *The Blue Four,* Calder, Picabia, Masson, Matisse, Cocteau, Tchelitchew, Picasso, Rouault, Hopper, and Le Corbusier at Arts Club
1933	Exhibition of modern sculpture and drawings at Arts Club (Maillol, Lehmbruck, Matisse, Modigliani, Picasso, Zadkine, Daumier, Degas, Duchamp-Villon, Lachaise, Laurent, Noguchi, Rodin, and Zorach)
	Public Works of Art Project, the first of the New Deal art projects, established, with Increase Robinson as regional director
	Martin A. Ryerson Collection donated to AIC
1933–34	Century of Progress exhibition at AIC
1935	Attempts to establish Industrial Art School at AIC fail conclusively
	The Federal Art Project of the WPA established, with Increase Robinson as first director
	The Katharine Kuh Gallery opens, taking over the Increase Robinson Gallery space

1935–39	C. J. Bulliet's series, "Artists of Chicago Past and Present," appears in *Chicago Daily News*
1936	Martin A. Ryerson dies
	Katharine Kuh begins offering art classes at her gallery
	C. J. Bulliet's *The Significant Moderns* published
1937	Laszlo Moholy-Nagy and Gyorgy Kepes arrive in Chicago
	The New Bauhaus established with Moholy-Nagy as director
	Sanity in Art movement founded by Josephine Hancock Logan; her handbook of the same title is published
	Remaining works in the Arthur J. Eddy collection sold at auction
	Exhibitions of Gris, Picasso (including *Guernica*), Glackens, Lehmbruck, Braque, Duchamp (first one-man show in Chicago), Sickert, and "Origins of Modern Art" at Arts Club
	Paul Hindemith and Béla Bartok give programs at Arts Club
1938	Mies van der Rohe arrives in Chicago
	Potter Palmer becomes interim director of AIC
	Norman L. Rice becomes dean of SAIC
1939	Daniel Catton Rich becomes director of AIC
1940	Exhibitions of Paul Klee, Max Beckmann, Salvador Dali, and Oskar Kokoschka (first one-man shows for Dali and Kokoschka in Chicago), and "Contemporary British Art" at Arts Club
	Society for Contemporary American Art formed at AIC

NOTES

1. The Chicago Setting

1. Major scholarly works on Chicago's art history include Ethel Joyce Hammer, "Attitudes Toward Art In the Nineteen Twenties In Chicago" (Ph.D. diss., University of Chicago 1975); Kenneth R. Hey, "Five Artists And The Chicago Modernist Movement 1909–1928" (Ph.D. diss., Emory University, 1973); Esther Sparks, "A Biographical Dictionary Of Painters and Sculptors in Illinois, 1808–1945" (Ph.D diss., Northwestern University, 1971); Eugenia Remelin Whitridge, "Art In Chicago: The Structure Of The Art World In A Metropolitan Community" (Ph.D diss., University of Chicago, 1946).

2. There is a large body of literature on Chicago writing. For references to these commentaries and for the best extended discussion see Carl S. Smith, *Chicago and the American Literary Imagination, 1880–1920* (Chicago: University of Chicago Press, 1984).

3. Peter Conrad, *The Art of the City: Views and Versions of New York* (New York: Oxford University Press, 1984).

4. For an example of the elaborate art portfolios containing renditions of the fairgrounds see William Walton, *Columbian Exposition 1893. Art And Architecture* (Philadelphia: George Barrie, 1893).

5. The process of gathering the art works is summarized in Rossiter Johnson, ed., *A History Of The World's Columbian Exposition* (New York: Appleton, 1897), 2, chapter 15. The Art Palace and its contents are described, among many other places, in John J. Flinn, comp., *Official Guide To The World's Columbian Exposition* (Chicago: Columbian Guide, 1893).

6. For more on Denslow, Chicago, and Baum see Douglas G. Greene and Michael Patrick Hearn, *W. W. Denslow* (Clarke Historical Library, Central Michigan University, 1978), n.p.

7. Robert Bruegmann, "Burnham, Guérin, and the City as Image," in John Zukowsky, ed., *The Plan of Chicago: 1909–1979* (Chicago: Art Institue of Chicago, 1979), 16–28, assesses the impact of the graphic art that was part of the Plan.

8. *Inland Printer* 19 (April 1897): 56–57. The letter writer signed him-

self "C. H.," and was replying to a letter from O. G. Formhals, an advertising specialist, which had appeared in another journal.

9. *Chicago Tribune* June 17, 1905, quoted in Eugenia Whitridge, "Art in Chicago," 115.

10. Ralph Clarkson, "Chicago Painters, Past And Present," *Art and Archaeology* 12 (September/October 1929): 135.

11. *Chicagoan* 15 (January 1935): 5.

12. H. L. Mencken, "The Literary Capital of the United States," *Nation* 28 (April 17, 1920): 92. The article is summarized and characterized in "Mr. Mencken's Chicagoiad," *Literary Digest* 66 (July 24, 1920): 29.

13. Samuel Putnam, "Chicago: An Obituary," *American Mercury* 8 (August 1926): 417–25.

14. "Blasts From Literary Chicago," *Literary Digest* 79 (October 20, 1923): 21.

15. Robert Morss Lovett, "Chicago: 'Gigantic, Wilful, Young,'" *New Republic* 50 (April 20, 1927): 243–46.

16. Walter James Sherwood, "Chicago's Place In The Fine Arts," *Chicago: The World's Youngest Great City* (Chicago: American Publishers, 1929), 35. Actually, Sherwood claimed the situation was changing, and his remark applied to "a few years ago."

17. Lovett, "Chicago," 246.

18. See the review of Chatfield-Taylor's book by James Weber Linn, "Chicago," *New Republic* 17 (January 4, 1919): 278–80.

19. J. H. Oppenheim, "Autopsy On Chicago," *American Mercury* 40 (December 1937): 454–61.

20. Edgar Lee Masters, *The Tale Of Chicago* (New York: Putnam's, 1933), 342.

21. *Art Institute of Chicago. Thirty-Fourth Annual Report For The Year 1912–13*, 37.

22. Ibid., 37.

23. For Kauffer's reaction see Mark Haworth-Booth, *E. McKnight Kauffer: A Designer and His Public* (London: Gordon Fraser, 1979), 13–14. As more is learned about local artists it may well be necessary to emphasize far more the impact of the Chicago venue of the Armory Show.

24. Kuhn to Elmer MacRae, Chicago, March 25, 1913, reproduced in Milton W. Brown, *The Story Of The Armory Show* (New York: The Joseph A. Hirschhorn Foundation, 1963), in a group of photographs after p. 22.

25. Brown, *The Story Of The Armory Show*, chapter 11.

26. Ibid, 170, 149, 182.

27. Quoted ibid., 174.

28. This story is recounted in Ethel Joyce Hammer, "Attitudes Toward Art In The Nineteen Twenties," 25. For the Pattison quote see James William Pattison, "Public Censorship of Art," *Fine Arts Journal* 28 (April 1913): 244.

29. For police interventions see C. J. Bulliet, "How Modern Art Came To Town: The War Years and The Advent of No-Jury Shows," *Chicagoan* 12 (September 1932): 31–32, 70–74; and Bulliet, "What'll We Do With It? An Inquiry Into the Future of Modern Art," *Chicagoan* 12 (February 1932): 43–44.

30. Samuel Putnam, "Chicago and Me. An Expatriate Returns and Reviews," *Chicagoan* 12 (October 1931): 23.

31. Price Collier, *America And The Americans From A French Point Of View* (New York: Scribner's, 1897), 263.

32. Lewis Mumford, "Reflections on Chicago," *New Republic* 68 (February 27, 1929): 45.

33. Lloyd Lewis and Henry Justin Smith, *Chicago: The History Of Its Reputation* (New York: Harcourt, Brace, 1929), 491.

34. Mauritz A. Hallgren, "Help Wanted—for Chicago," *Nation* 134 (May 11, 1932): 534–36.

35. Margaret Marshall, "Chicago: Two Exhibits," *Nation* 136 (June 28, 1933): 715-17.

36. Ben Hecht, *A Child of the Century* (New York: Simon and Schuster, 1954), 330. This is part of some excerpts from *The Chicago Literary Times* republished by Hecht in his autobiography.

37. For an example of this disparagement see Douglas Haskell, "Frank L. Wright and the Chicago Fair," *Nation* 131 (December 3, 1930): 605.

38. For a brief description see "Another Great Art Exhibit for World's Fair," *Literary Digest* 118 (August 4, 1934): 24; and F. A. Gutheim, "Another Year of Progress," *American Magazine of Art* 27 (July 1934): 414–22.

39. Dudley Crafts Watson, "What Chicago Learned. The Art Institute of Chicago Appraises the World's Art Exhibition," *American Magazine of Art* 27 (February 1934): 77.

40. Ibid., p. 79.

41. "Another Great Art Exhibit," p. 24.

42. C. J. Bulliet, "How Modern Art Came to Town. VI. The Part the Institute Played," *Chicagoan* 12 (January 1932): 43–44, 72–74.

43. J. Z. Jacobson, *Art of Today: Chicago 1933* (Chicago: L. M. Stein, 1932), xix.

44. Ibid., xviii.

45. Ibid., xx.

46. Ibid.

2. Arthur Dove in Chicago, 1912

1. James Spencer Dickerson, quoted in Gardner Teall, "Our Western Painters: What Chicago Is Doing Toward the Development of a Vital National Spirit in American Art," *Craftsman* 15, no. 2 (November 1908): 139.

2. Quoted in Alson J. Smith, *Chicago's Left Bank* (Chicago: Henry Regnery, 1953), 3.

3. "Friend of Art and Artists Lost When Veteran Passes," *Chicago Evening Post*, September 26, 1913; James William Pattison, "The Loss of W. Scott Thurber," *Fine Arts Journal* 29 (November 1913): 683–84.

4. "Art Gallery Designed by Frank Lloyd Wright, Architect," *International Studio* 39 (February 1910): 95–96; Evelyn Marie Stuart, "Development of Art in the West—Thurber Galleries," *Fine Arts Journal* 21 (December 1909): 284–90.

5. Grant Carpenter Manson, *Frank Lloyd Wright to 1910: The First Golden Age* (New York: Reinhold, 1958).

6. *Frank Lloyd Wright: The Early Work*, with an introduction by Edgar Kaufmann, Jr. (New York: Horizon, 1968), 101–3; "The Japanese Print Exhibition," *Bulletin of the Art Institue of Chicago* 1 (April 1908): 36–38.

7. Perry Duis, "'Where Is Athens Now?': The Fine Arts Building 1898 to 1918," *Chicago History* 6, no. 2 (Summer 1977): 66–78; Ralph Fletcher Seymour, *Some Went This Way: A Forty Year Pilgrimage Among Artists, Bookmen and Printers* (Chicago: Ralph Fletcher Seymour, 1945), 49–60.

8. For a fuller account of Dove's career, see Ann Lee Morgan, *Arthur Dove: Life and Work, With a Catalogue Raisonné* (Newark, Del.: University of Delaware Press; London and Toronto: Associated University Presses, 1984).

9. For a more extended description of their early relationship, see Ann Lee Morgan, "An Encounter and Its Consequences: Arthur Dove and Alfred Stieglitz, 1910–1925," *Biography* 2, no. 1 (Winter 1979): 33–59.

10. This problem is discussed more fully in Morgan, *Arthur Dove*, 43–46.

11. Paul Kruty, "Arthur Jerome Eddy and His Collection: Prelude and Postscript to the Armory Show," *Arts* 61 (February 1987): 40–47.

12. Arthur Jerome Eddy, *Cubists and Post-Impressionism* (Chicago: A. C. McClurg, 1914), facing p. 48.

13. Morgan, *Arthur Dove*, 44–47.

14. B. L. T. [Bert Leston Taylor], "A Line-O'-Type or Two," *Chicago Tribune*, March 25, 1912, 10.

15. B. L. T. [Bert Leston Taylor], "A Line-O'-Type or Two," *Chicago Tribune*, March 27, March 29, March 30, April 1, and April 8, all 1912.

16. H. Effa Webster, "Artist Dove Paints Rhythms of Color," *Chicago Examiner*, March 15, 1912, 5.

17. [Maude I. G. Oliver], "The Local Galleries," *Record-Herald* (Chicago), March 17, 1912, sec. 7, p. 5.

18. [Maude I. G. Oliver], "The Local Galleries," *Record-Herald* (Chicago), March 24, 1912, sec. 7, p. 5.

19. L. M. McCauley, "Art and Artists," *Chicago Evening Post*, March 16, 1912, 6.

20. Glenn Dillard Gunn, "'Sumurun' and the Futurists in Painting, Music, and Drama," *Chicago Tribune*, March 17, 1912, sec. 10, p. 3.

21. Harriet Monroe, "'One-Man Shows' Allow Wide Choice," *Chicago Tribune*, March 17, 1912, sec. 2, p. 5.

22. Bernard Duffey, *The Chicago Renaissance in American Letters: A Critical History* (East Lansing, Mich.: Michigan State College Press, 1964), 172–79.

23. Dale Kramer, *Chicago Renaissance: The Literary Life in the Midwest 1900–1930* (New York: Appleton-Century, 1966), 13–23.

24. George Cram Cook, "Causerie; Post Impressionism: After Seeing Mr. Dove's Pictures at Thurber's," *Chicago Evening Post Friday Literary Review*, March 29, 1912, 1–2. By presenting his views in the form of a dialogue, which produced some ambiguity about which voice was his, Cook muffled his own radicalism. From this column alone it is not clear that Cook wholeheartedly endorsed the views cited here; nevertheless, from the larger context of his life and writing, one may assume he held such opinions. The *Friday Literary Review*'s attention to Dove continued in C. T. Hallinan, "Causerie; Post Impressionism Again: After Reading the Article in This Space Last Week," April 5, 1912, 1. Although Hallinan concluded that he was not prepared to follow such "'New Thought' cults in Art" as Dove's, he nevertheless gave a serious appraisal of Dove's intentions.

25. "Dove's Form and Color," *American Art News* 10 (March 2, 1912): 2; [Elizabeth Luther Cary], "News and Notes of the Art World: Plain Pictures," *The New York Times*, March 3, 1912, sec. 5, p. 15; Henry Tyrrell, "Up and Down Picture Lane," *The World* (New York), March 9,

1912; "Things Seen in the World of Art," *The Sun* (New York), March 3, 1912, sec. 2, p. 10; "Notes of the Art World," *New York Herald*, March 6, 1912, 8; [Joseph Edgar Chamberlain], "Pattern Paintings by A. G. Dove," *Evening Mail* (New York), March 2, 1912, 8 (reprinted in *Camera Work* 38 [April 1912]: 44); [Arthur Hoeber], *Globe* (New York), February 1912 (reprinted in *Camera Work* 38 [April 1912]: 44–45.); Paul Haviland, "Photo Secession Notes: Exhibition of Pastels by Arthur G. Dove," *Camera Work* 38 (April 1912): 36.

26. Harriet Monroe, *A Poet's Life: Seventy Years in a Changing World*, (1938; reprint, New York: AMS Press, 1969). She does not mention Dove and has little to say about her work as an art critic.

27. Stefan Germer, "Pictures at an Exhibition," *Chicago History* 16, no. 1 (Spring 1987): 4–21; Leslie Goldstein, "Art in Chicago and the World's Columbian Exposition of 1893," master's thesis, University of Iowa, 1970.

28. Hobart Chatfield-Taylor, "Memories of Chicago: II. The Age of Gentility," *Century Magazine*, n.s. 128 (August 1925): 465. He cites Mayor Joseph Kirkland, "Chicago's pioneer man of letters as well as her historian."

29. "The Inness Collection," *Bulletin of the Art Institute of Chicago* 4, no. 4 (April 1911): 53–55. Nearly all of the Inness paintings were acquired in March 1911, when trustee Edward B. Butler purchased a private collection of eighteen paintings dating from the 1860s through the 1890s and gave them directly to the museum.

30. Birge Harrison, "The 'Mood' in Modern Painting," *Art and Progress* 4, no. 9 (July 1913): 1015–20.

31. Mabel Tuek Priestman, "History of the Arts and Crafts Movement in America," *House Beautiful* 20 (November 1906): 14.

32. See, especially, Oscar Lovell Triggs, *Chapters in the History of the Arts and Crafts Movement* (Chicago: Bohemia Guild of the Industrial Art League, 1902).

33. Helen Lefkowitz Horowitz, *Culture and the City: Cultural Philanthropy in Chicago from the 1880s to 1917* (Lexington, Ky.: University Press of Kentucky, 1976), 131–40. For a brief but broadly perceptive account of Addams's relation to culture in general, see the chapter on her in Christopher Lasch, *The New Radicalism in America (1889–1963): The Intellectual as a Social Type* (New York: Random House [Vintage], 1965), 3–37.

34. Sharon Darling, "Arts and Crafts Shops in the Fine Arts Building," *Chicago History* 6, no. 2 (Summer 1977): 79–85.

35. For example, Denman W. Ross, *A Theory of Pure Design* (Boston: Houghton, Mifflin, 1907); Wooliscroft Rhead, *Modern Practical Design* (New York: Charles Scribner's Sons, 1912).

36. Visual correspondences between Dove's art and Arts and Crafts objects are suggestively noted in Susan Fillin Yeh, "Innovative Moderns: Arthur G. Dove and Georgia O'Keeffe," *Arts* 56 (June 1982): 70–71.

37. T. J. Jackson Lears, *No Place of Grace: Antimodernism and the Transformation of American Culture 1880–1920* (New York: Pantheon, 1981), 74–75.

38. H. Allen Brooks, "Chicago Adventure: Its Debt to the Arts and Crafts," *Journal of the Society of Architectural Historians* 30, no. 4 (December 1971): 312–17. Monroe's particular sensitivity to architecture was undoubtedly colored by the fact that the architect John Wellborn Root

was her brother-in-law. After his untimely early death in 1891, she wrote his biography: *John Wellborn Root: A Study of His Life and Work* (Boston: Houghton Mifflin, 1896).

39. B. L. T. [Bert Leston Taylor], "A Line-O'-Type or Two," *Chicago Tribune,* March 30, 1912, 10.

40. B. L. T. [Bert Leston Taylor], "A Line-O'-Type or Two," *Chicago Tribune.* The publication date of this literary effort remains a minor mystery, despite my best efforts to locate it in the *Tribune.* An undated clipping is included on microfilm ND70 at the Archives of American Art, Smithsonian Institution.

41. Letter from Dove to Stieglitz, January 11, 1943, cited in Ann Lee Morgan, ed., *Dear Stieglitz, Dear Dove* (Newark, Del.: University of Delaware Press; London and Toronto: Associated University Presses, 1988), 480.

3. Lorado Taft, the Ferguson Fund, and Modernism

1. Lorado Taft, "Man vs. Clothes in Art," *Chicago Record,* May 20, 1899.

2. Daniel H. Burnham and Edward H. Bennett, *Plan of Chicago,* (Chicago: The Commercial Club, 1909; reprint, New York: Da Capo Press, 1970).

3. "Gives $1,000,000 for Chicago Art," *Chicago Daily Tribune,* April 15, 1905. Lorado Taft, "A Million Dollars for Sculpture," *The World Today* 8 (June 1905): 628–30; "Chicago and the Ferguson Fund," *The City Club Bulletin* 6 (February 17, 1914): 61–68.

4. *Chicago Daily News,* October 26, 1910.

5. *Catalogue of the Exhibition of the National Scupture Society Under the Auspices of the Municipal Art Society* (Baltimore: Fifth Regiment Armory, 1908), 18.

6. I am indebted to Harold Haydon for information and documents. "High Winds in Chicago," *Time* 65 (June 13, 1955): 82; Harold Haydon, "Art Institute vs. Latham Castle," *The Art News League* 3 (November 1955): n. p.; "Irate Sculptors Opposed to 'Statuary' Fund Buildings," *Architectural Forum* 106 (February 1957): 10–12; Elinor Rickey, "Accused: The Chicago Art Institute," *Focus/Midwest* 1 (September 1960): 8–9; Luis Kutner, "The Desecration of the Ferguson Fund: The Need for Watchdog Legislation," *De Paul Law Review* 12 (Spring/Summer 1963): 217–39.

7. *Armory Show: 50th Anniversary Exhibition, 1913–1963* (Utica, N.Y.: Munson Williams Proctor Institute, 1963); Milton W. Brown, *The Story of the Armory Show* (New York: The Joseph A. Hirshhorn Foundation, 1963).

8. Lorado Taft, *Modern Tendencies in Sculpture* (Chicago: University of Chicago Press, 1921), 27, 28, 29, 63, 118, 131, 145, 146.

9. *The Official Pictures of a Century of Progress Exposition* (Chicago: Century of Progress International Exposition, 1933).

10. Jewett E. Ricker, ed., *Sculpture at A Century of Progress Chicago, 1933, 1934* (Chicago: Ricker, 1933); S. L. Tesone, "Symbolism in Fair Sculpture," *World's Fair Weekly* 25 (October 21, 1933): 33.

11. Charles Harris Whitaker and Hartley Burr Alexander, *The Architectural Sculpture of the State Capitol at Lincoln, Nebraska* (New York: American Institute of Architects, 1926); Walter Raymond Agard, *The New Architectural Sculpture* (New York: Oxford University Press, 1935).

12. I am indebted to Dorothy B. Crombie of Joliet for her helpful information.

13. The work was presented to the church by Mr. and Mr. James Lewis Kraft.

14. *Social Action*, November 15, 1937, front and back covers; Emily Taft Douglas, "Lorado Taft's Peace Medal," *Survey Graphic* 17 (August 1938): 494.

4. Modernism and Chicago Art

1. J. Z. Jacobson, ed., *Art of Today: Chicago, 1933* (Chicago: L. M. Stein, 1932), ix. All of the works mentioned in this paragraph are reproduced in Jacobson's book.

2. Ibid, xviii.

3. Wassily Kandinsky, "On the Question of Form" in Wassily Kandinsky and Franz Marc, eds., *Der Blaue Reiter Almanach* (Munich: Piper Verlag, 1912), Eng. trans. ed. Klaus Lankheit (New York: Viking Press, 1974), 153.

4. Ibid., 252. Franz Marc's subscription prospectus is reprinted in the English translation of the *Blue Rider Almanac*. It was written in mid-January 1912.

5. Jacobson, ix.

6. There is only one abstract artist, Paul Kelpe, represented in Jacobson's book. The vast majority of Chicago artists have chosen to work in a representational mode. The predominance of figurative art in Chicago persisted into the 1970s. There is still a healthy figurative tradition in the city. Because of time constraints at the symposium, this discussion was limited to a few artists, all painters, who worked primarily in the 1920s and 1930s; this does not mean that these are the only artists of interest or significance living and working in this period. Most of the modernist artists shared the attitudes of the artists discussed in this paper.

7. Manierre Dawson, unpublished journal, December 26, 1908, as quoted in Mary Mathews Gedo, *Manierre Dawson (1887–1969): A Retrospective Exhibition of Painting*, November 13, 1976–January 2, 1977 (Chicago: Museum of Contemporary Art, 1976), 7. For illustrations and discussion of Dawson's work see also Kenneth R. Hey, "Five Artists and the Chicago Modernist Movement, 1909–1928." Ph.D. diss., Emory University, 1973, 128–66; Kenneth R. Hey, "Manierre Dawson: Fix on the Phantoms of the Imagination," *Archives of American Art Journal* 14 (1974): 7–12; Abraham A. Davidson, "Two from the Second Decade: Manierre Dawson and John Covert," *Art in America* 63, no. 5 (September–October 1975): 50–55; Earl A. Powell III, "Manierre Dawson's 'Woman in Brown,'" *Arts Magazine* 51, no. 1 (September 1976): 76–77; and catalogs published by the Schoelkopf Gallery, New York, in 1969 and 1981, and the Ringling Museum, Sarasota, Florida, in 1967.

8. Mary Matthews Gedo, "Modernizing the Masters; Manierre Dawson's Cubist Transformations," *Arts* 55, no. 8 (April 1981): 137–40.

9. Gedo, *Manierre Dawson Retrospective*, 15.

10. *Exhibition of Painting and Sculpture in "The Modern Spirit"* (Milwaukee: Milwaukee Art Society, 1914), n.p., as quoted in Hey, "Five Artists," 148–49.

11. Arthur Jerome Eddy, *Cubists and Post-Impressionism* (Chicago: A. C. McClurg, 1914), 112.

12. Alson J. Smith, *Chicago's Left Bank* (Chicago: Henry Regnery, 1953), 32–33.

13. Ibid., 23–31; see also, Margaret Anderson, *My Thirty Years War* (New York: Covici, Friede, 1930).

14. Louis H. Sullivan, *Kindergarten Chats and Other Writings* (New York: Wittenborn, Schultz, 1947), 240.

15. As cited in Ethel Joyce Hammer, "Attitudes Toward Art in the Nineteen Twenties in Chicago" (Ph.D. diss., University of Chicago, 1975), 104.

16. Harriet Monroe, "International Art Show to Open at the Institute on March 24," *Chicago Daily Tribune*, March 16, 1913.

17. Hey, "Five Artists," 165.

18. Paul Kruty, "Mirrors of a 'Post-Impressionist' Era: B. J. O. Nordfeldt's Chicago Portraits," *Arts* 61, no. 5 (January 1987): 27–33.

19. For a discussion of the Little Theatre, Nordfeldt, and Jonson, see Kruty, "Mirrors of a Post-Impressionist Era," 31, 33n.44. A number of Jonson's studies for stage designs are in the Jonson Gallery, University of New Mexico, Albuquerque, New Mexico. Reproductions and discussion of Jonson's work before he left Chicago can be found in Ed Garman, *The Art of Raymond Jonson, Painter* (Albuquerque: University of New Mexico Press, 1976); Nicolai Cikovsky, Jr., intro., *Raymond Jonson: (1891–1982): Pioneer Modernist of New Mexico* (New York: Berry-Hill Galleries, 1986); and Elizabeth Ann McCauley, intro., *Raymond Jonson: The Early Years* (Albuquerque, New Mexico: Art Museum, University of New Mexico, 1980).

20. Jonson diary, November 11, 1918, Jonson Gallery Archives, Albuquerque, New Mexico. I am grateful to Tiska Blankenship, assistant curator, Jonson Gallery, for sending me excerpts from the Jonson diaries. All of the paintings by Jonson discussed in this paper are in the collection of the Jonson Gallery.

21. Jonson diary, August 5, 1921, as quoted in Garman, *Art of Raymond Jonson*, 56.

22. Jonson diary, June 25, 1921, Jonson Gallery Archives.

23. Ibid., August 16, 1921.

24. Blanche Gambon, "Stanislaw Szukalski: Painter, Sculptor, Architect, Philosopher," *The New American* (September 1935): n.p.

25. Stanislaus Szukalski, *The Work of Szukalski* (Chicago: Covici-McGee, 1923). In addition to the words of Szukalski, this book contains reproductions of many of his works, almost all of which were lost in a bombing of Warsaw during World War II. When Szukalski returned to Warsaw before the outbreak of the war, bringing much of his oeuvre with him, he was honored with the creation of the Szukalski National Museum, which was later completely destroyed. For an anecdotal treatment of Szukalski's Chicago period, see Ben Hecht, *A Child of the Century* (New York: Simon and Schuster, 1954), especially 239–43.

26. Smith, *Chicago's Left Bank*, 167.

27. Checklists of these exhibitions exist in Ryerson and Burnham Libraries, the Art Institute of Chicago.

28. "Wrecks Drawings to Spite the British," *Chicago Herald*, May 22, 1917.

29. "Artist Tears Pictures from Institute Wall," *Chicago Tribune*, May 22, 1917; Ben Hecht reported that Szukalski forced the critic Albrecht Montgelas (which Hecht repeatedly misspells as Monteglas) from his

studio for attempting to touch one of his sculptures with his cane. He did not allow critics to touch his work (Hecht, *Child of the Century*, 240–41).

30. Szukalski, "Autobiographical Note," in *Work of Szukalski*, n.p.

31. "Artist Tears Pictures from Institute Wall," *Chicago Tribune*, May 22, 1917.

32. Stanislaus Szukalski, *Projects in Design* (Chicago: University of Chicago Press, 1931), 26–27.

33. See Kandinsky, "On the Question of Form," 174, for example.

34. Szukalski, "Autobiographical Note," *Work of Szukalski*.

35. "Szukalski Speaks," *The Art Student* 1 (April–May 1916): 181, quoted in Hammer, "Attitudes toward Art in Chicago," 64.

36. Szukalski, *Projects in Design*, 33.

37. Szukalski, *Work of Szukalski*, n.p.

38. This drawing is reproduced in Szukalski, *Work of Szukalski*. Since Szukalski refused to sell his works because they were ". . . part of himself . . ." (Albrecht Montgelas, "Szukalski Work is Held to be too Personal," *Chicago Examiner*, April 27, 1916), this drawing, in Weisenborn's possession when Szukalski left Chicago, may be the only surviving work from this period. The portrait of Clarence Darrow is reproduced in the *Catalog of the 2nd Annual Exhibition: Chicago No-Jury Society of Artists*, October 1–13, 1923 (Chicago, 1923).

39. Hey, "Five Artists," 201.

40. *Catalog of the Salon des Refusés* quoted in Hey, 210–11.

41. My knowledge of many of these works is dependent on the following sources: reproductions in the No-Jury Society of Artists' Catalogs; a series of photographs from the Bulliet papers, Archives of American Art; and Mack Gilman of Gilman/Gruen Galleries, Chicago, dealer for the estate of Gordon Weisenborn, who generously shared his large collection of slides of Weisenborn's work with me.

42. Fritzi Weisenborn, "Chicago to Be Theme of Neo-Arlimusc Show," manuscript for a newspaper article (August 1927), Weisenborn papers, Archives of American Art; quoted in Hey, "Five Artists," 229.

43. Samuel Putnam, "Neo-Arlimusc Idea," *Magazine of the Art World, The Chicago Evening Post*, December 26, 1926, quoted in Hey, "Five Artists," 229–30.

44. Rudolph Weisenborn, notes for an autobiographical sketch, Weisenborn papers, quoted in Hey, "Five Artists," 239.

45. *Catalog of the 2nd Annual Show*, n.p.

46. Unlike the other artists discussed in this paper, Emil Armin is discussed in a number of sources; see, for example, J. Z. Jacobson, *Thirty-five Saints and Emil Armin* (Chicago: L. M. Stein, 1929); Hammer, "Attitudes toward Art in Chicago"; and Maureen A. McKenna, *Emil Armin: 1883–1971* (Springfield, Ill.: Illinois State Museum, 1980).

47. Jacobson, *Thirty-five Saints and Emil Armin*, 40.

48. Sam Putnam, "Ramon Shiva," *The Palette and Chisel* (April 1925): 2. Very little is known about Ramon Shiva. In addition to this short article by Putnam, he is discussed in Esther Sparks, *A Biographical Dictionary of Painters and Sculptors in Illinois 1808–1945* (Ph.D. diss., Northwestern University, 1971) and in a pamphlet for an exhibition at Knoedler and Company in 1930 (artist's file, Ryerson and Burnham Libraries, the Art Institute of Chicago).

49. He served on the Board of Directors of the Chicago No-Jury Society of Artists in 1923, for example.

50. Putnam, "Shiva," 2.

51. C. J. Bulliet, "Artists in Chicago," *Chicago Daily News*, September 26, 1936; unless otherwise noted, all of the information about Angarola is based upon material in the Angarola Papers, Archives of American Art, Smithsonian Institution. I am also grateful to Richard Angarola, Anthony Angarola's son, for his generous help. Angarola's work was exhibited for the first time since the 1930s at ACA Galleries, New York, in May 1988. The exhibition was accompanied by an illustrated catalog with an introduction by Matthew Baigell. I wish to thank Jeff Bergen of ACA Galleries for providing me with slides of many of the paintings in the exhibition.

52. "Art Notes," *Chicago Journal*, May 5, 1916.

53. C. J. Bulliet, "Artless Comment," *Chicago Evening Post*, August 20, 1929.

54. "Anthony Angarola, American, Modern, Painter is Teaching," n.d. or newspaper name, clipping in Angarola Papers, Archives of American Art, Smithsonian Institution.

55. "Angarola to Open Art School Here," *Chicago Evening Post*, September 22, 1925, Angarola Papers.

56. Alexander Kostellow to Anthony Angarola, postmarked September 20, 1927, Angarola Papers.

57. Eleanor Jewett, "Children's Exhibit Feature this Week at Art Institute," *Chicago Tribune*, March 2, 1924, Angarola Papers.

58. Kandinsky, "On the Question of Form," 174.

59. Angarola did a portrait of Jonson, which is now in the Jonson Gallery, University of New Mexico, Albuquerque, New Mexico.

60. Works like *Backyard Paradise, Taylor Falls, Evening*, and *Dog Pound* exemplify this attitude.

61. Some of these qualities persist in the present. I am referring to the so-called Chicago Imagists, whose work is dependent on sincerity and freedom of expression rooted in visual imagery outside the Western post-Renaissance tradition. In his preface to the catalog for the 1974 exhibition *Made in Chicago* (Washington, D.C.: Smithsonian Institution Press, 1974), Don Baum writes that in Chicago "there are obvious and logical differences of style and technique, but the ironic humor, pleasure in the vision of the lower-middle class, and disregard for the 'grand tradition' bind this group together." In the catalog essay, Whitney Halstead describes the personal, even idiosyncratic, nonprogrammatic quality of Chicago art, relating these qualities to the isolation of the artist in the city. To a large extent, these descriptions are applicable to the artists of the period 1910–40 as well.

62. Ed Paschke, "A conversation" in the catalog for the exhibition, *Some Recent Art From Chicago* (Chapel Hill, N.C.: The Ackland Art Museum, 1980), 37.

63. Wassily Kandinsky, *Concerning the Spiritual in Art* (1912; reprint ed., New York: George Wittenborn, 1963).

5. Chicago's Alternative Art Groups of the 1920s

1. Albert Boime, "The Salon des Refusés and the Evolution of Modern Art," *Art Quarterly* 32 (Winter 1969): 411. For a contemporary review

of the exhibition, see Linda Nochlin, *Realism and Tradition in Art, 1848–1900, Sources and Documents* (Englewood Cliffs, N.J.: Prentice-Hall, 1966), 60–63.

2. As Boime put it, "the Impressionist exhibition was a privately organized Salon des Refuses," p. 423. Paul Tucker expands on these precedents in "The First Impressionist Exhibition in Context," in *The New Painting: Impressionism 1874–1886* (San Francisco: Fine Arts Museum of San Francisco, 1986), 93–117.

3. Limited in number to twenty artists who were elected to the society by present members, Les XX had a constitution and a secretary, and held annual exhibitions. See Jane Block, *Les XX and Belgian Avant-Gardism* (Ann Arbor: UMI Research Press, 1985).

4. For an account of the founding of the Paris Independents, see Pierre Angrand, *Naissance des Artistes Indépendants 1884* (Paris: Nouvelle Editions Debresse, 1965).

5. Of the 1908 show of The Eight (the Ashcan School), Homer has written, "It proved conclusively, and for the first time in America, that a group of artists who were strongly anti-academic could attract wide public notice and financial returns"; in William Innes Homer, *Robert Henri and his Circle* (Ithaca, N.Y.: Cornell University Press, 1969), 145.

6. Five hundred works by over one hundred artists were shown on three floors of a vacant building on West 35th Street. See Homer, op. cit.: 151–55; and *The Fiftieth Anniversary of the Exhibition of Independent Artists in 1910* (Wilmington, Del.: Delaware Art Center, 1960).

7. Robert Henri, "The New York Exhibition of Independent Artists," *Craftsman* 18 (May 1910): 170–71.

8. This "monster" show included over 2,500 works of art by 120 artists. For an analysis of the exhibition, see Francis Naumann, "The Big Show: The First Exhibition of the Society of Independent Artists," *Art Forum* 17 (February 1979): 34–39. A complete history of the society may be found in Clark S. Marlor, *The Society of Independent Artists; the Exhibition Record 1917–1944* (Park Ridge, N.J.: Noyes Press, 1984). Henri published his criticisms of this show in "The 'Big Exhibition,' the Artist and the Public," *Touchstone* 1 (June 1917): 174–77, 216. In the same issue, Glackens explained, "My own remedy for a great crowd of pictures which is more or less bewildering to the public, is that every city and village in the country should have their own Independent Shows." "The Biggest Art Exhibition in America and, Incidently, War," *Touchstone* 1 (June 1917): 173.

9. See Paul Kruty, "Mirrors of a 'Post-Impressionist' Era: The Chicago Portraits of B. J. O. Nordfeldt," *Arts* 61 (January 1987): esp. 29–30.

10. Little is known about this fascinating group. The *Chicago Tribune* reported, "The exhibit of the Independent Society of Artists . . . is being well attended. This exhibition is practically jury free in that each member is entitled to show two works of art jury free. . . . The annual dues are $2." *Chicago Sunday Tribune,* April 9, 1916, sec. 8, p. 11.

11. For the Arts Club, see C. J. Bulliet, "How Modern Art Came to Chicago: III. The Rise and Reign of the Arts Club of Chicago," *Chicagoan* 12 (October 31, 1931): 35–37, 62, 64; and the catalog *Portrait of an Era: Rue Winterbotham Carpenter and the Arts Club of Chicago, 1916–1931* (Chicago: The Arts Club, 1986).

12. The best account of the Introspectives may be found in Charles C. Eldredge, "Claude Buck and the Introspectives," in *The Shape of the Past*

(Los Angeles: University of California, [1984]), 307–21. For more information on Buck (1890–1974) and Tofel (1891–1959), see Paul J. Karlstrom, *Claude Buck: American Symbolist* (San Francisco: Glastonbury Gallery, 1983); and Jeffrey R. Hayes, *Jennings Tofel* (Mahwah, N.J.: Ramapo College Art Gallery, 1983). No study of Felix Russmann (1888–1962) has ever been published.

13. The most complete review of the exhibition, which was open from May 6 to June 1, was Katherine E. Roberts, "The Introspectives Challenge Chicago Critics," *Fashion Art* 6 (June 1921): 32. *Art News* 79 (May 14, 1921): 10 reported, "This is said to be the first exhibition of the Arts Club at which interest in the pictures surpassed the interest in the social side and the tea." See also "Introspective Artists," *Chicago Evening Post*, May 10, 1921, unpaged clipping in the Emil Armin Papers, Archives of American Art, Smithsonian Institution.

14. Indeed, the New York origins of the movement soon faded, and it was remembered locally as a purely Chicago phenomenon. In his 1929 biography of Emil Armin, J. Z. Jacobsen claimed that Armin and his friends began calling themselves "Introspectives" in 1920 and explained the Chicago show as if the local artists were entirely responsible for it. See J. Z. Jacobsen, *Thirty-Five Saints and Emil Armin* (Chicago: L. M. Stein, 1929): 94–96.

15. Emil Armin (1883–1971) was the only one of these artists to be the subject of a biography early in his career—Jacobsen's *Thirty-Five Saints . . .*, issued in 1929. See also Maureen McKenna, *Emil Armin* (Springfield, Ill.: Illinois State Museum, 1980). Raymond Jonson (1891–1982) has been the subject of a book, Ed Garman's *The Art of Raymond Jonson, Painter* (Albuquerque: University of New Mexico Press, 1976), and of an exhibition of his early work, Elizabeth McCauley's *Raymond Jonson, the Early Years* (Albuquerque: University of New Mexico Art Museum, 1980). The fullest coverage of Rudolph Weisenborn (1881–1974) may be found in Kenneth Hey's "Five Artists and the Chicago Modern Movement, 1909–1928" (Ph.D. diss., Emory University, 1973). Fred Biesel (1893–1954) and his wife Frances Strain (1898–1967) await the coverage due them.

16. The *Chicago Evening Post* (August 30, 1921) reported that "'The Cor Ardens' is the new organization crystallized in the heat of summer, which is to make a sensation in the winter to come."

17. Born in Munich, Carl Hoeckner (1883–1972) only came to Chicago in 1910. See the exhibition catalog *Not a Pretty Picture, Carl Hoeckner, Social Realist* (San Francisco: Atelier Dore, 1984). In the yearly editions of the *American Art Annual*, the Cor Ardens continued to be listed through 1926. The last three years (1924–1926), Agnes Squire Potter is listed as president and the Chicago address of the group given is 5515 S. Woodlawn Avenue. However, there is no indication that the group continued as a viable organization.

18. Introduction to the "Tentative Constitution of Cor Ardens," copy of typescript in the possession of Thomas Yanul, Chicago. I wish to thank Mr. Yanul for sharing with me his knowledge of Chicago art of the 1920s. The membership list is dated March 11, 1922. Emil Armin's induction into the Cor Ardens is recorded in Jacobsen's biography (pp. 101–3): "Rudolph Weisenborn, in those days the stormy petrel among Chicago artists, came over one evening with his inseparable ten gallon hat and bulldog pipe and said in his characteristically casual way,

'Come and meet the people. . . .' Emil went and was introduced to a number of artists, among them Carl Hoeckner, president of the Cor Ardens, and Raymond Jonson. Someone explained the aims and purposes of the society to him, and President Hoeckner in the manner of a municipal court judge questioned him: 'Do you join this organization of your own free will? Do you know what this organization stands for? Are you in for pure art and not commercial art?' Emil answered 'Yes' to all these queries and was forthwith taken into the organization."

19. Yanul Collection. The letter is dated August 22, 1922, and signed by Agnes Squire Potter, chairman of the exhibition committee. It clearly states that "We wish to show that the no jury system is preferable to the partialities and inhibitory aspects of the jury system." Reviewing the exhibition, the *Chicago Evening Post* (November 28, 1922) complained, "Under the conditions of 'No Particular School' there can be no standards for judgement." Participants included Fred Biesel, Claude Buck, Carl Hoeckner, Raymond Jonson, Ramon Shiva, Walter Ufer, Rudolph Weisenborn, and sculptor Alfeo Faggi. In her letter, Agnes Potter also reported that the exhibit was to travel to three other cities after its run at the Arts Club, but there is no evidence that this happened.

20. "'Salon des Refuses,'" *Chicago Evening Post,* November 15, 1921. In the same issue of the *Post,* Lena McCauley explained that "they are not quarreling with the conservatives or with the Art Institute; they only ask the public to look at what they have done."

21. C. J. Bulliet, "How Modern Art Came to Town: IV. No-Jury: Its Rise, Rage and Decline," *Chicagoan* 12 (November 1931): 49.

22. See Paul Kruty, "Arthur Jerome Eddy and his Collection: Prelude and Postscript to the Armory Show," *Arts* 61 (February 1987): esp. 45.

23. The *Chicago Evening Post,* after noting the connection between Bloch's arrival and the Eddy show, quoted the critic Hi Simon: "The Academy becomes, thus, the first school in the west to afford its students the advantages of contact with a great modern." *Magazine of the Art World, Chicago Evening Post,* September 12, 1922, 11.

24. "The No-Jury Society," *Chicago Evening Post,* August 29, 1922, 7.

25. Except for Weisenborn, the board members of the No-Jury society had studios in the 57th Street artists' colony on Chicago's south side. Charles Biesel (1865–1945) was a founding member of the New York Independents and a close friend of John Sloan's. Prior to his arrival in Chicago in the teens, Biesel had painted in Newport, Rhode Island, where he was patronized by Gertrude Vanderbilt Whitney. See C. J. Bulliet, "Artists of Chicago, Past & Present, No. 20," *Chicago Daily News,* July 6, 1935. According to Bulliet, Biesel's friendship with the director of Marshall Field's art gallery resulted in the No-Jury society exhibiting at Field's during the 1920s. Biesel's son, Fred Biesel (1893–1954) and Fred's wife, Frances Strain (1898–1967), had studied with Sloan in New York, had even lived in his apartment, and had shown with the New York group several times.

26. Foreword by "The Committee," *First Annual Exhibition of the Chicago No-Jury Society of Artists* (Chicago, 1922).

27. Lena McCauley, "No-Jury Exhibit is Nation-Wide," *Chicago Evening Post,* October 3, 1922, 9. On October 10, p. 22, that paper reported that "the crowds thronging the galleries have advertised the event."

28. *Catalogue of the 27th Annual Exhibition, Chicago and Vicinity,* February 1 to March 11, 1923.

29. For an account of Clarence J. Bulliet (1883–1952), see Sue Ann Kendall, "C. J. Bulliet, Chicago's Lonely Champion of Modernism," *Archives of American Art Journal* 26, nos. 2/3 (1986): 21–32. No comparable article has appeared on Sam Putnam (1892–1950). In 1934 Putnam said of his former associate at the *Chicago Evening Post*, "Came then to Chicago, out of the nowhere, one C. J. Bulliet, whose fanatic devotion to the painter's art made mine seem Laodician." In "Painting Is Dead; Painting Go Red," *The New Hope* 2 (August 1934): 5. In his autobiography, Putnam elaborated, "Bulliet was the most impassioned lover of modern painting that I have ever known, and for a year or two I had the time of my life with him, assaulting the battlements of the local academicians as represented by the Art Institute and defending the cause of the No Jury painters." Samuel Putnam, *Paris Was Our Mistress* (New York: Viking Press, 1947), 42.

30. "Pleads at No-Jury Rally for Genuinely Independent Art," *Magazine of the Art World, Chicago Evening Post*, December 27, 1925, 1.

31. Bulliet, *Chicagoan* (November 1931): 49. Bulliet noted that "John Sloan . . . , a friend of Biesel's, had suggested some such Chicago organization." But, Bulliet continued, the name had been suggested by Chicago artist Helen West Heller.

32. The events scheduled for the first ball included a "Kubist Kostume Kontest" and a "Selection by Silhouette of the Most Beautiful Model in Chicago." The second and third balls were held in October 1924 and January 1926 on the eve of the third and fourth No-Jury exhibitions. For an illustration of the announcement for the second artists balls, designed by Weisenborn, as well as an account of Midway Gardens, see Paul Kruty, "Pleasure Garden on the Midway," *Chicago History* 16 (Fall/Winter 1987–88): 4–27.

33. The list of the first eight exhibitions of the No-Jury Society of Artists is as follows:

1st	Oct. 2–16	1922	365 works
2nd	Oct. 1–13	1923	315 works
3rd	Oct. 6–18	1924	378 works
4th	Jan. 25–Feb. 4	1926	487 works
5th	Jan. 10–22	1927	393 works
6th	Feb. 27–Mar. 10	1928	472 works
7th	Nov. 25–Dec. 10	1928	382 works
8th	Jan. 11–25	1930	224 works

The first six shows were held at Marshall Field's. After that, the site varied, often from year to year.

34. C. J. Bulliet, "No-Jury Show a Glowing Surprise After So Much Placid Mediocrity," *Magazine of the Art World, Chicago Evening Post*, January 26, 1926, 1. He further characterized the exhibition as "the most vivid and the most interesting show of local art in many moons."

35. Ibid. Bulliet noted that Anderson's sculpture, including her portrait of Samuel Putnam and a mask of a woman, "are examples of her vivid sculpture that is bringing her rapidly into fame."

36. Archibald Motley's single entry in 1926, *Syncopation*, was given the unusual price of $1,000, although this was considerably less than the price of $2,500 for John Sloan's *Picnic on the Ridge*. Motley (1891–1981) also exhibited at No-Jury in 1927, showing a landscape and a portrait of his brother-in-law. In 1926, in addition to *Cabaret*, Frances Strain showed a landscape of New Mexico, as did Fred Biesel.

37. In France, Putnam turned his attention to translating French literature and eventually expanded into Italian, Spanish and Portuguese. He became an expert on Brazilian literature. See C. H. Gardiner, *Samuel Putnam, Latin Americanist* (Carbondale, Ill.: Southern Illinois University, 1970). In the late 1920s, Putnam wrote a column in *Chicagoan* called "Chicago Art Letter—From Paris." In the issue of April 21, 1928, he wrote "I believe the No-Jury to be as dead in Chicago as the Independents are in Paris and in New York. . . . As for Chicago, the No-Jury died the day Rudolph Weisenborn resigned," p. 14. Nevertheless, he asserted that "among the Chicago artists of today who will then be hung in the Institute, my offspring will encounter Ramon Shiva and Emil Armin."

38. Artist Edgar Miller has left a choice, if exaggerated, account of the first ball. In a letter to his friend Albert Bloch, Miller complained, "In their scrambling for grandeur, the people putting on the Ball hired the most expensive ballroom and made a frantic effort to get society interested—and no one came—the 'house was papered' with free tickets at the last minute—with one in ten in costume—an artists ball with artists and no costumes"; undated letter [ca. October 1923] in the possession of Mrs. Albert Bloch, Lawrence, Kansas.

39. A clipping in the Weisenborn papers, ca. early December 1926 but unfortunately undated, explains, "Rudolph Weisenborn, who resigned the presidency of the Chicago No-Jury Society of Artists a few days ago, due to a disagreement over management of the society's ball and annual exhibit, last night announced a new society of so-called radical artists." Weisenborn Papers, roll 865, frame 1274.

40. Weisenborn papers, roll 865, frame 1276.

41. Weisenborn papers, roll 865, frame 1285. Weisenborn explained that "Neo-Arlimusc is the only gallery which does not charge artists for exhibiting and [where] the full amount of each sale is turned over to the artist."

42. Samuel Putnam, "Neo-Arlimusc Idea," *Magazine of the Art World, Chicago Evening Post*, December 21, 1926. Putnam hoped that at Neo-Arlimusc "we might learn the difference between paint and painting, between literature and the Saturday Evening Post." For an account of the first Neo-Arlimusc meeting, see J. Z. Jacobson, "Our Little Group of Serious Talkers," *Chicago Evening Post*, January 18, 1927, 8, 12. Jacobson, who attended the event with Emil Armin, summarized the orations of Ramon Shiva, Sam Putnam, and Helen West Heller.

43. "Discord Enters City's Newest Club of Artists," undated clipping [ca. November 25, 1927], Weisenborn Papers, roll 865, frame 1291.

44. Participating artists included Weisenborn, Hoeckner, Shiva, Russman, Tennessee Anderson, Kathryn Dudley and Helen West Heller. For Sam Putnam's critical review, see "Nudes Too Tame—Devoid of 'Kick'—Must Go," *Magazine of the Art World, Chicago Evening Post*, April 19, 1927, 1.

45. See undated clippings, Weisenborn papers, roll 865, frames 1289 and 1299. For the former, Weisenborn enlisted a professor from the Sorbonne and a Chicago lawyer to debate the topic "My Lady—Should She Wear Clothes?" For the latter, he organized a symposium with the same title as the exhibition.

46. In a telephone interview of March 7, 1988, Blair recalled that at the time he was writing a dissertation at the University of Chicago and was approached by Weisenborn about speaking to the Neo-Arlimusc.

He recalled that the gallery was filled with a capacity crowd. His talk on old jokes was much appreciated by Bulliet and the publisher Covici, but the connection with Weisenborn struck him as odd, for, according to Blair, "Weisenborn was very intense but had no sense of humor."

47. Weisenborn papers, roll 865, frame 1285.

48. "Modernists to Offer Midnight 'Alley Oop,'" *Chicago Daily News*, November 22, 1927.

49. Blanche Matthias, "Neo-Arlimusc and its Moment of Now," *Magazine of the Art World, Chicago Evening Post*, November 22, 1927, 3. The text noted that "already the saws are buzzing" in "the new gallery, which is to supplant the upstairs one now in use."

50. "Meier-Graefe, German Art Critic, to Visit U. S.," *Magazine of the Art World, Chicago Evening Post*, January 17, 1928, 1. By February 3, Meier-Graefe's Chicago itinerary had been arranged. For information on the critic, see Kenworth Moffett, *Meier-Graefe as Art Critic* (Munich: Prestel Verlag, 1973).

51. Undated clipping, Weisenborn papers, frame 1308. The Albright work was entitled *It*. Other painters included Todros Geller, Heller, Thomas and Tud Kempf, Karl Mattern, Gregory Prusheck, Torry Ross, Russmann, and Shiva, and sculpture was by Armin. The catalog, a copy of which is in the possession of Thomas Yanul, Chicago, lists a total of eighty works.

52. Jewett's statement was part of a review of an Arts Club exhibition two months later. *Chicago Tribune*, April 22, 1928, sec. 8, p. 6.

53. The visit was well documented by Chicago newspapers. Several articles reported Meier-Graefe's criticism of Eddy's large Kandinsky collection and his praise for the Art Institute's El Grecos. See "'Ohos!' 'Ahs!' Tumble as Critic Scans City," unidentified clipping dated February 20, 1928, Weisenborn Papers, frame 1295; C. J. Bulliett, "Artless Comment," *Magazine of the Art World, Chicago Evening Post*, February 14, 1928, 8; Bulliet, "Meier-Graefe Begins His Tour of Inspection," *Magazine of the Art World, Chicago Evening Post*, February 21, 1928, 4.

54. C. J. Bulliet, "Artless Comment," *Magazine of the Art World, Chicago Evening Post*, February 28, 1928.

55. Information gathered mostly from the list of organizations published annually in Florence N. Levy, ed., *American Art Annual*, Washington, D.C.: American Federation of Arts.

6. Chicago Critics Take On Modernism

1. Helen Lefkowitz Horowitz, "Culture and the City: Cultural Philanthropy in Chicago, 1890–1917" (Ph.D. diss., Harvard University, 1969), 43. For another discussion of the cultural milieu see Kenneth Robert Hey, "Five Artists and the Chicago Modernist Movement, 1909–1928" (Ph.D. diss., Emory University, 1973), 6.

2. "When is Art Art? When Wicked?," *Chicago Tribune*, March 14, 1913. The incident was also reported in the *Chicago Examiner*, March 13, 1913. Fred D. Jackson and Eleanor Semelmeyer were the proprietors of the 44 S. Wabash gallery which displayed the copy.

3. Since the present location of the painting is unknown, we can only surmise what the chickens were up to. "Cast out Picture; Stir Norwegians," *Chicago Tribune*, March 11, 1913.

4. See, for example, Lena May McCauley, *Chicago Evening Post*, Octo-

ber 31, 1912, and Harriet Monroe, *Chicago Tribune*, March 17, 1912, and November 9, 1912.

5. "Mysteries of Cubist and Radical Art Dissolved by Understanding," *Chicago Inter-Ocean*, March 14, 1913. The Exhibition of Contemporary Scandinavian Society.

6. George Zug, *Chicago Inter-Ocean*, March 14, 1913. An unsigned *Inter-Ocean* article of March 10, 1913, said, "There may be good art without stupidity, and if there is a revolt against the dull methods of academies gone to seed, it need not exhibit itself in a structureless craftsmanship which is a libel on harmony, simplicity and beauty, which is a caricature on the national integrity." See also "Mysteries of Cubism and Radical Art Dissolved by Understanding," *Chicago Inter-Ocean*, March 14, 1913, and Zug, *Chicago Inter-Ocean*, March 10 and March 14, 1913.

7. See *Chicago Tribune*, February 17, 1913, and *Chicago Inter-Ocean*, March 9, 1913, among many others. Articles which were moderate in tone were sometimes given misleading headlines; see, for example, Harriet Monroe, "Art Show Open to Freaks," *Chicago Tribune*, February 17, 1913, in which the headline belies the writer's enthusiasm for the show.

8. The newspapers ran numerous articles flippantly or, in some cases, viciously attacking the exhibition or incidents related to it. See, for example, "Director French Flees Deluge of Cubist Art," *Chicago Record Herald*, March 21, 1913, and "Futurist Pain Puzzles Arrive; Look Like State of Mind," *Chicago Examiner*, March 19, 1913; "Cubist Critic Sees It, Raves," *Chicago American*, March 20, 1913.

9. Several reporters covered the Gertrude Stein story. See especially "Cubist Art Is Explained Clearly by a Post-Impressionist Writer," *Chicago Inter-Ocean*, March 21, 1913.

10. "Students Wreak Vengeance Upon Cubist Designs," *Chicago Evening Post*, April 17, 1913

11. "The Cubist Art," *Chicago Tribune* (editorial), April 2, 1913.

12. H. Effa Webster, "Moderns Here on Exhibition Called Art Desecration," *Chicago Examiner*, April 1, 1913.

13. "May Bar Youngsters from Cubists' Show," *Chicago Record-Herald*, March 27, 1913.

14. George Zug, *Chicago Inter-Ocean*, March 16, 1913.

15. Zug, *Chicago Inter-Ocean*, April 6, 1913.

16. Ibid.

17. McCauley, *Chicago Evening Post*, March 20, 1913.

18. McCauley, *Chicago Evening Post*, April 6, 1910.

19. "Fair Play for Insurgent Art," *Chicago Evening Post*, March 24, 1913. This article was unsigned, but the writing reflects McCauley's stance on the show.

20. McCauley, *Chicago Evening Post*, March 27, 1913: "Taking 'Art' as a science of drawing, composition and color for the interpretation of an ideal principle, these men are outside the pale. They make no claim to any of the tenets of art . . . and message they have none."

21. Harriet Monroe, *Chicago Tribune*, November 9, 1912.

22. Monroe, "Art Show Open to Freaks," *Chicago Tribune*, February 16, 1913.

23. Monroe, "International Art Show to Open on March 24," *Chicago Tribune*, March 16, 1913.

24. Monroe, "Art Exhibition Opens in Chicago," *Chicago Tribune*, March 25, 1913.

25. Monroe, "Live Exhibit at the Art Institute: Visitors' Opinions Strong," *Chicago Tribune*, March 30, 1913.

26. Monroe, "Cubist Works Protest Against Narrow Conservatives," *Chicago Tribune*, April 6, 1913.

27. Monroe, "Record Breaking Crowds See the Cubist Exhibit," *Chicago Tribune*, April 13, 1913.

28. Monroe, "Live Exhibit at the Art Institute: Visitors Opinions Strong," *Chicago Tribune*, March 30, 1913. Monroe was inconsistent in this article, stating first that Picabia, Picasso, and Sousa Cardoza were probably not of much permanent value; but then she wrote that they were interesting as experiments, the first "dim gropings toward an art of pure color which may delight the 21st century as much as symphonic music delights us."

29. Manierre Dawson journal, January 10, 1914, Dawson Collection, Ringling Museum of Art, Sarasota Florida, quoted in Hey, p. 165.

30. The *Chicago Daily News* reported statistics on attendance at the show on April 22, 1913.

31. "Said Bad Housing Causes Cubist Art," *Chicago Tribune*, April 10, 1913. A landscape architect, Jens Jensen, made the accusation in a lecture given April 9.

32. "Literature and Art," *Current Opinion* 54 (April 1913): 316.

33. Milton Brown, *American Painting from the Armory Show to the Depression* (Princeton: Princeton University Press, 1955), 55.

34. "Eleanor Jewett Has Been Trib Art Critic Since 1917," *Chicago Tribune*, November 1930, and telephone interview with Jewett's son, William Lundberg, September 23, 1987. Jewett was the daughter of Samuel R. Jewett and Luch McCormick, the niece of Colonel Cyrus McCormick. All biographical information on Jewett derives from these two sources.

35. For this and further information on Bulliet's life, see Sue Ann Kendall, "Clarence J. Bulliet: Chicago's Lonely Champion of Modernism," *Archives of American Art Journal*, 26, nos. 2 and 3 (1986): 21–32.

36. Eleanor Jewett, *Chicago Tribune*, June 19, 1921.

37. Jewett, *Chicago Tribune*, November 13, 1918, and October 2, 1927.

38. Jewett used the term equally for George Luks, John Sloan (April 21, 1918), Arthur B. Davies (May 4, 1918), and Stanislaus Szukalski, whom she liked even though he is now considered one of Chicago's earliest radical modernists. She praised his symbolic use of the human form.

39. Jewett, "November Holds First Promise of Art Activities," *Chicago Tribune*, October 21, 1923.

40. Jewett, *Chicago Tribune*, September 28, 1924.

41. Jewett, "Illinois Products Exposition Gives Floor to Artists," *Chicago Tribune*, October 12, 1924. For one of her assessments of the Birch Bartlett Collection, see Jewett, "See This Exhibit, If You Like Noise," *Chicago Tribune*, October 4, 1925. As late as 1930 she attacked the pieces in that collection; see her *Tribune* review of Bartlett's lecture explaining modern art, March 23, 1930.

42. Bulliet's belief in individualism and artistic freedom relates to the notions of honesty, inner necessity, and personal liberation espoused by Chicago writers such as Sherwood Anderson and Carl Sandburg and by Chicago artists such as Stanislaus Szukalski and Emil Armin. See

Ethel Joyce Hammer, "Atittudes Towards Art in the 1920s in Chicago" (Ph.D. diss., University of Chicago, 1975), esp. 115–98.

43. Clarence J. Bulliet, *Magazine of the Art World, Chicago Evening Post,* October 7, 1924.

44. For Bulliet's own retrospective account of his becoming a critic, see Bulliet, "How Modern Art Came to Town; A Bit of Autobiography," *The Chicagoan,* December 1931, 51.

45. Bulliet, *Apples and Madonnas* (New York: Covici, Friede, 1927), 3.

46. Bulliet, "Artless Comment," *Magazine of the Art World, Chicago Evening Post,* May 19, 1925, and "Mestrovic's Giant Sculpture Now on Display Here," *Magazine of the Art World, Chicago Evening Post,* May 5, 1925.

47. Jewett, "What Price Genius in the Guise That is Mestrovic's?" May 24, 1925. See also "Stark Realism is Pervading Note of Mestrovic Exhibit," *Chicago Tribune,* May 10, 1925.

48. Letter from Jewett to Covici of Covici, Freide, no date (Covici sent it to Bulliet November 8, 1928), Bulliet Papers, Archives of American Art, Smithsonian Institution.

49. After *Apples and Madonnas,* Bulliet wrote the following books: *Art Masterpieces in a Century of Progress: Fine Arts Exhibition at the Art Institute of Chicago* (Chicago: North Mariano Press, 1933); *Venus Castina: Famous Female Impersonators, Celestial and Human* (New York: Covici, Friede, 1933); *Paintings: An Introduction to Art* (Chicago: Integrated Knowledge, 1934); and *The Significant Moderns and Their Pictures* (New York: Covici, Friede, 1936). After 1938 Bulliet wrote *Masterpieces of Italian Art* (1939); *How Grand Opera Came to Chicago* (1940–41); *French Art from David to Matisse: As Set Forth in 20 Masterpieces of the French Exhibit at the Art Institute of Chicago* (1941); *Art Treasures from Vienna* (1949); and *The Story of Lent in Art* (1951). Prior to becoming an art critic, Bulliet had written *Robert Mantell's Romance* (Boston: J. W. Luce, 1918), a biography of the Shakespearean actor.

50. Jewett reviewed the exhibition in several articles but had little to say about the post-impressionist and modernist works, focusing instead on the old masters. See, for example, her *Chicago Tribune* articles of May 21, July 16, and July 23, 1933, other articles throughout the summer, and "Building for the World's Fair: Strong Modernistic Influence Seen in the Structures Now Under Construction," n.d., Jewett Papers, Archives of American Art, Smithsonian Institution.

51. Telephone interview with Katharine Kuh, February 3, 1987.

52. Jewett, undated clipping in Jewett Collection, Archives of American Art, Smithsonian Institution. Jewett also reported at length on research that "proved" that mentally abnormal persons painted as well as the modernists; see "Frenchman Investigates Modern Art," *Chicago Tribune,* March 9, 1930.

53. Jewett, "Current Exhibits in East," *Chicago Tribune,* undated clipping in scrapbook, Jewett Papers, Archives of American Art, Smithsonian Institution. The article is from the spring of 1930.

54. Josephine Hancock Logan, *Sanity in Art* (Chicago: A. Kroch, 1937), 10–11.

55. Bulliet, "Bulliet's Artless Comment," *Chicago Daily News,* August 27, 1938.

56. The painting was submitted for exhibition in 1937, but rejected by the Chicago No-Jury Society of Artists, which supposedly did not jury exhibition entries.

57. Bulliet's series of articles began on February 23, 1935, appearing consecutively at first, then intermittently. No indication was given that the September 30, 1939, article was the end of the series, but no further articles seem to have appeared.

58. Bulliet used these phrases repeatedly in his writing, especially in the thirties. A typical example is Bulliet, "Bulliet's Artless Comment," *Chicago Daily News*, January 26, 1935.

59. Bulliet, *The Significant Moderns and Their Pictures* (New York: Covici, Friede, 1936), vi.

7. Modernism and Design

1. Paul E. Sprague pinpointed the location of the first balloon frame structure in his "The Origin of Balloon Framing," *Journal of the Society of Archictectural Historians* 40, no. 4 (December 1981): 311–19; see also idem, "Chicago Balloon Frame: The Evolution During the 19th Century of George W. Snow's System for Erecting Light Frame Buildings from Dimension Lumber and Machine-made Nails" in: H. Ward Jandl, ed., *The Technology of Historic American Buildings: Studies of the Materials, Craft Processes, and the Mechanization of Building Construction* (Washington, D.C.: The Foundation for Preservation Technology, 1983), 35–61.

2. Sigfried Giedion, *Space, Time and Architecture: The Growth of a New Tradition* (Cambridge: Harvard University Press, 1941), 269, 271.

3. Sigfried Giedion, *Mechanization Takes Command: A Contribution to Anonymous History* (New York: W. W. Norton, 1948), 211–28.

4. Giedion, *Mechanization*, 219.

5. Giedion, *Mechanization*, 153.

6. Quoted in: Giedion, *Mechanization*, 153.

7. Lloyd C. Engelbrecht, "The Association of Arts and Industries: Background and Origins of the Bauhaus Movement in Chicago" (Ph.D. diss., University of Chicago, 1973), 217–20, 297, 317–21, 325.

8. Sidney Lens, *The Labor Wars, from the Molly Maguires to the Sitdowns* (Garden City, N.Y.: Doubleday, 1973). See also Paul Avrich, *The Haymarket Tragedy* (Princeton: Princeton University Press, 1984); and Nick Salvatore, *Eugene V. Debs, Citizen and Socialist* (Urbana, Ill.: University of Illinois Press, 1982). The "Memorial Day Massacre" of 1937 during a strike at Republic Steel resulted in the deaths of ten striking steel workers who were killed by police; it showed that labor unrest, followed by harsh repression, continued into the modern era. See: Daniel Leab, "The Memorial Day Massacre," *Midcontinent American Studies Journal* 8, no. 1 (Fall 1967): 3–17.

9. John Ruskin, "The Nature of Gothic," chapter VI, *The Stones of Venice*, vol. II, "The Sea Stories," in: *The Complete Works of John Ruskin*, vol. X (London: George Allen, 1904), 192. This portion of *The Stones of Venice* was first published in 1853.

10. William Morris, "The Lesser Arts, Delivered before the Trades' Guild of Learning, December 4, 1877," in *The Collected Works of William Morris*, vol. XXII, "Hopes and Fears for Art; Lectures on Art and Industry," (London: Longmans Green, 1914), 5.

11. The constitution of the Chicago Arts and Crafts Society was published in Chicago Architectural Club, *Catalogue of the Eleventh Annual Exhibition by the Chicago Architectural Club at the Art Institute of Chicago, March 23 to April 10, 1898* (Chicago: Chicago Architectural Club, 1898), 118.

12. [Thorstein] V[eblen], "Arts and Crafts," review of *Chapters in the History of the Arts and Crafts Movement*, by Oscar Lovell Triggs, in *The Journal of Political Economy* 9 (December 1902): 108.

13. Rosenwald contributed $50,000 of the $260,000 raised by the Association in its fund-raising campaign to support design education in Chicago; see Engelbrecht, "The Association of Arts and Industries," 77.

14. M. R. Werner, *Julius Rosenwald, the Life of a Practical Humanitarian* (New York: Harper and Brothers, 1939), 90–94.

15. Wright's recollections were delivered in a lecture at Hull House, Chicago, November 8, 1939; a mimeographed text is in the Esther Kohn Papers, Jane Addams Memorial Collection, Library of the University of Illinois, Chicago. The concerns of the Arts and Crafts movement were not unknown to a later generation of modernists, as is demonstrated by the fact that in attendance at Wright's 1939 lecture were Laszlo Moholy-Nagy and Ludwig Mies van der Rohe; see: "An Interview with Katharine Kuh," conducted by Avis Berman, ed. by William McNaught, *Archives of American Art Journal*, 27, no. 3 (1987): 23–24.

16. Frank Lloyd Wright, "The Art and Craft of the Machine," in *Writings and Buildings*, ed. by Edgar Kaufmann and Ben Raeburn (Cleveland: The World Publishing Co., 1960), 55, 68 *et passim*. "The Art and Craft of the Machine" prefigured Wright's role as a design critic in Chicago in the 1930s.

17. Engelbrecht, "Association of Arts and Industries," 29–30, 332.

18. Ibid., 307–8. From 1884 to 1892 Pelouze served as sales manager for the Tobey Furniture Company, one of Chicago's chief furniture makers influenced by the English Arts and Crafts movement. No stranger to the contradictions inherent in the movement, Pelouze served in 1894 as a major with a National Guard unit constituting part of the Federal forces which suppressed the Pullman strike, over the protest of Illinois Governor John Peter Altgeld. See Engelbrecht, "Association of Arts and Industries," 309–10, 325; and "Pelouze, William Nelson," *The National Cyclopaedia of American Biography*, vol. 33 (New York: James T. White, 1947), 284–85.

19. Engelbrecht, "Association of Arts and Industries," 125–27.

20. Quoted in Laszlo Moholy-Nagy to Walter Gropius, TLS, May 28, 1937, copy in the Bauhaus-Archiv, West Berlin; see also Engelbrecht, "Association of Arts and Industries," 226–27.

21. Norma K. Stahle to Frank Lloyd Wright, TLS, February 2, February 9, February 18, March 23, April 17, June 2, June 9, July 2, all 1931; April 21, April 29, May 6, May 17, and June 1, all 1932; Frank Lloyd Wright Archives, Frank Lloyd Wright Foundation, Scottsdale, Arizona.

22. Norma K. Stahle to Frank Lloyd Wright, TLS June 9, 1931, Frank Lloyd Wright Archives, Frank Lloyd Wright Foundation, Scottsdale, Arizona. The letter reads, in part, "I was very much interested in your letter to Rudolph Schindler and in the Schindler-Neutra circular. Sometime I have some interesting side-lights to give you in this connection."

23. Engelbrecht, "Association of Arts and Industries," 62–64. Richards began with the effects on art of the Industrial Revolution, continued with the Great Exhibition in London in 1851, William Morris and his work, the Arts and Crafts movement in England, the Glasgow School, Baillie Scott, French applied art from the Empire to art nouveau, Jugendstil and other German developments, the Viennese School, and

the modern movement in Scandinavia and Switzerland, and concluded with recent developments in France.

24. *Chicago Daily News,* November 5, 1927, 4; *Magazine of the Art World, Chicago Evening Post,* October 23, 1927, (1); summarized in Engelbrecht, "Associations of Arts and Industries," 83–85.

25. The first occasion was a speech Wright gave on February 13, 1931. Norma K. Stahle to Frank Lloyd Wright, TLS, February 2, 1931, with a handwritten, unsigned reply by Frank Lloyd Wright on bottom and reverse of letter. The topic was "Glass Houses" and Iannelli was present, but little is known about what was said. The only known comments on Wright's talk are enthusiastic but unrevealing of the content. They are in a letter, Norma K. Stahle to Frank Lloyd Wright, TLS, February 18, 1931, Frank Lloyd Wright Archives, Frank Lloyd Wright Foundation, Scottsdale, Arizona.

26. Iannelli, who surveyed design schools in Europe, including the Bauhaus, was deeply impressed by the fact that Wright was regarded as a crucial influence on the formal vocabulary and creative outlook of European modernists. Iannelli had been one of Wright's collaborators on the 1914 Midway Gardens commission in Chicago, but only after his talks with European architects and designers did he fully understand Wright's significance, a point which is clearly evident from a speech given by Iannelli at the Art Institute on November 25, 1924, shortly after his return. See "Art Institute of Chicago News Letter" (mimeographed), November 29, 1924.

27. Norma K. Stahle to Frank Lloyd Wright, TLS, April 29, 1932; Wright had written to Stahle, "I don't see that my show in the proposed debate would be worth much. So please ask somebody on the ground [i.e., in Chicago, since Wright was living in Wisconsin]," Frank Lloyd Wright to Norma K. Stahle, unsigned carbon copy of a letter, April 27, 1932. Both letters are in the Frank Lloyd Wright Archives, Frank Lloyd Wright Foundation, Scottsdale, Arizona.

28. *Chicago Tribune,* May 1, 1932, sect. 2, p. 6, and May 6, 1932, sect. 1, p. 5; portions quoted in: Engelbrecht, "Association of Arts and Industries," 114–15.

29. *Magazine of the Art World, Chicago Evening Post,* March 24, 1931, 12.

30. Engelbrecht, "Association of Arts and Industries," 134–35.

31. Oscar Lovell Triggs, "A School of Industrial Art," *The Craftsman* 3, no. 2 (January 1903): 216, 221–23; idem, *The Changing Order; a Study of Democracy* (Chicago: Oscar L. Triggs, 1905), 250, 258–60. On Triggs, see Engelbrecht, "The Association of Arts and Industries," 6, 13–21; and Eileen Boris, "'Dreams of Brotherhood and Beauty': the Social Ideas of the Arts and Crafts Movement," in Wendy Kaplan, *"The Art that is Life": The Arts & Crafts Movement in America, 1875–1920* (Boston: Museum of Fine Arts, 1987), 212–15. In view of Triggs's disagreement with Wright, noted above, it should be added that nothing in the available documents clarifies why Wright and Triggs were at odds with each other. Certainly much of what each wrote during the Arts and Crafts era would seem to indicate that there were wide areas of agreement.

32. Engelbrecht, "Association of Arts and Industries," 144.

33. See chapter 11 for more information on the joint effort by the Association and the School of the Art Institute.

34. Sheldon Cheney and Martha Candler Cheney, *Art and the Machine: An Account of Industrial Design in 20th-Century America* (New York: Whittlesey House, 1936), 269.

35. Wright's attempt to use some of the Association's funds for his projected school, Taliesin Fellowship, at Spring Green in Wisconsin, was rejected. See Norma [K.] Stahl[e] to Frank Lloyd Wright, telegram, December 1, 1931, Frank Lloyd Wright Archives, Frank Lloyd Wright Foundation, Scottsdale, Arizona. Wright's initial plans for Taliesin emphasized design to an extent which did not materialize in the actual operation of the school. See Engelbrecht, "Association of Arts and Industries," 10–13; and Cheney, *Art and the Machine*, 279–80.

Shortly after Laszlo Moholy-Nagy was appointed to head the Association's new school, he tried to hire Wright for his faculty. Needless to add, teaching in someone else's school was not a high priority for Wright, and nothing came of Moholy-Nagy's attempt. See: Laszlo Moholy-Nagy to Walter Gropius, TLS, October 8, 1937, Bauhaus-Archiv, West Berlin; William A. Kittredge to Frank Lloyd Wright, TLS, October 11, 1937, Frank Lloyd Wright Archives, Frank Lloyd Wright Foundation, Scottsdale, Arizona; Frank Lloyd Wright to William A. Kittredge, TL with AL passage added, October 12, 1937, and Frank Lloyd Wright to William A. Kittredge, carbon copy of TL, October 19, 1937, Frank Lloyd Wright Archives, Frank Lloyd Wright Foundation, Scottsdale, Arizona. Kittredge was a member of the Association's Board.

36. See below, and Engelbrecht, "The Association of Arts and Industries," 228–30 et passim.

37. Laszlo Moholy-Nagy, *Von Material zu Architektur* Bauhausbücher 14 (Munich: Albert Langen Verlag, 1929). The most important U.S. editions are idem, *The New Vision, from Material to Architecture* (New York: Brewer, Warren, and Putnam, [1932]); and idem, *The New Vision: Fundamentals of Design, Painting, Sculpture, Architecture*, revised and enlarged edition (New York: W. W. Norton, 1938).

38. Lloyd C. Engelbrecht, "Foundation Course (*Grundkurs*)," in Peter Hahn and Lloyd C. Engelbrecht, eds., *50 Jahre New Bauhaus: Bauhausnachfolge in Chicago*, (Berlin: Argon Verlag, 1987), 121–35 and 246–47; and idem, "*Bauhäusler*: A Case Study of Two-Way Traffic Across the Atlantic," *Yearbook of German-American Studies* 22 (1987): 158, 163–64. The open-endedness of foundation course work is often far removed from the simplistic view of the Bauhaus recently promoted by some apologists for postmodernism.

39. Lloyd C. Engelbrecht, "Foundation Course (*Grundkurs*)," 121.

40. George McVicker, "European Influence on Chicago Designers," *Print, Magazine of the Graphic Arts*, "Special STA Chicago issue," 7, no. 5 (March 1953): 27–28.

41. Douglas C. McMurtrie, *Modern Typography & Layout*, (Chicago: Eyncourt Press, 1929; London: The Library Press, 1930), 33.

42. Engelbrecht, "Association of Arts and Industries," 137–43.

43. McMurtrie, *Modern Typography*, 48.

44. Ibid., 116.

45. The printing industry in Chicago during the first third of this century is described in: Ernest T. Grundlach, "Chicago's Growing Leadership in Printing, Publishing and Advertising" in Glen A. Bishop, ed., *Chicago's Accomplishments and Leaders* (Chicago: Bishop, 1932), 76–80.

46. Douglas C. McMurtrie, *Modern Typography*, 26.

47. *James Marston Fitch, American Building: The Forces That Shape It* (Boston: Houghton Mifflin, 1947), 141.

48. From the introduction by Henry Russell Hitchcock, in Skidmore,

Owings, and Merrill, *Architecture of Skidmore, Owings & Merrill 1950–1962*, text by Ernest Danz (New York: Frederick A. Praeger, 1963), 9.

49. Engelbrecht, "Association of Arts and Industries," 167; Sharon Darling, *Chicago Furniture; Art, Craft, & Industry, 1833–1983* (New York: The Chicago Historical Society, in association with W. W. Norton, 1984), 281–83.

50. Engelbrecht, "Association of Arts and Industries," 167–69; Thomas M. Slade, "'The Crystal House' of 1934," *Journal of the Society of Architectural Historians* 29, no. 4 (December 1970): 350–53.

51. Emily Genauer, *Modern Interiors Today and Tomorrow: A Critical Analysis of Trends in Contemporary Decoration as Seen at the Paris Exposition of Arts and Techniques and Reflected at the New York World's Fair* (New York: Illustrated Editions, 1939) 11–12; quoted in Engelbrecht, "Association of Arts and Industries," 166–67.

52. Concerning this exhibition, see Henry Russell Hitchcock and Philip Johnson, *The International Style: Architecture Since 1922* (New York: Museum of Modern Art, 1932); on the Chicago showing, see Engelbrecht, "Association of Arts and Industries," 121–22.

53. Quoted in: *The Architectural Forum* 59, no. 1 (July 1933): 25.

54. Cheney, *Art and the Machine*, 250, 270.

55. Boris Emmet and John E. Jueck, *Catalogues and Counters: a History of Sears, Roebuck and Company* (Chicago: University of Chicago Press, 1950), 391–92; Cheney, *Art and the Machine*, 90, 252; Sears, Roebuck and Co., *Spring and Summer, 1935, Catalog*, no. 170 (Chicago: Sears, Roebuck Co., 1935), 576–77.

56. Laszlo Moholy-Nagy to Walter Gropius, TLS, June 8, 1938, Bauhaus-Archiv, West Berlin; portions quoted in Peter Hahn, "Vom Bauhaus Zum New Bauhaus," Hahn and Engelbrecht, eds., *50 Jahre New Bauhaus*, 14. The letter reads, in part: "Ich selbst fuhle mich in erster Linie als Maler. . . ."

57. Certainly this statement is true if one uses as a measure the amount of Moholy's work in permanent collections of major European and American museums. The best summary of Moholy's work in Chicago, including his work as an artist and photographer, is in Terry Suhre, ed., *Moholy-Nagy: A New Vision for Chicago* (Springfield, Ill.: Illinois State Museum, 1990).

8. The Little Review

1. The best general overview of little magazines is still Frederick J. Hoffman, Charles Allen, and Carolyn F. Ulrich, *The Little Magazine: A History and a Bibliography* (Princeton: Princeton University Press, 1946). On *The Little Review*, see chapter IV.

2. Mrs. Herbert Adams to Mr. W. M. R. French, March 13, 1913, Archives of the Art Institute of Chicago.

3. Floyd Dell, *Homecoming: An Autobiography* (Port Washington, N.Y.: Kennikat Press, 1933 (1961, 1969 reissue), 238.

4. Ibid.

5. Harriet Monroe, "Live Exhibit at the Art Institute, Visitors' Opinions Strong," March 30, 1913; "Cubist Art a Protest Against Narrow Conservatism," April 6, 1913; "Record Breaking Crowds See the Cubist Exhibit," April 13, 1913, incompletely identified clippings, Archives of the Art Institute of Chicago. Several publications discuss Monroe's important role in the history of Chicago culture, including Bernard Duffey,

The Chicago Renaissance in American Letters: A Critical History (Ann Arbor: Michigan State University Press, 1954), chapter 4, and Ellen Williams *Harriet Monroe and the Poetry Renaissance: The First Ten Years of Poetry, 1912–1933* (Urbana, Ill.: University of Illinois Press, 1977). See also Harriet Monroe, *A Poet's Life* (New York: MacMillan, 1938).

6. "At the Institute," *Friday Literary Review,* April 4, 1913.

7. Floyd Dell, untitled, *Friday Literary Review,* November 15, 1912.

8. Floyd Dell, *Homecoming,* 234.

9. Floyd Dell, "At the Institute." For more information on Nordfeldt see Paul Kruty, "Mirrors of a 'Post Impressionist' Era; B. J. O. Nordfeldt's Chicago Portraits," *Arts* (January 1987): 27–33.

10. Floyd Dell, *Women as World Builders: Studies in Modern Feminism* (Chicago: Forbes, 1913). The book includes such people as Charlotte Perkins Gilman, Emmeline Pankhurst, Jane Addams, and Margaret Dreier Robins.

11. Van Deren Coke, *Nordfeldt the Painter* (Albuquerque: University of New Mexico, 1972), 81.

12. Letter from Floyd Dell to Arthur Davison Ficke, May 26, 1913, Floyd Dell Papers, Newberry Library, Chicago.

13. On the early performances of the Little Theatre in Chicago see Constance D'Arcy Mackay, *The Little Theatre in the United States* (New York: Henry Holt, 1917), 103–9. Of Browne's initial contact with Dell see Dale Kramer, *The Chicago Renaissance* (New York: Appleton-Century, 1966), 121–22.

14. Floyd Dell, *Homecoming,* 233, mentions Ernestine Evans and Mary Randolph as two other artists who lived at the 57th Street studios. Among the academics were George Burman Foster, professor of philosophy at the University of Chicago; and among the political figures were Susan Glaspell and George Cram Cook, both friends of Dell's from Davenport, Iowa; Jackson R. Bryer, "'A Trial-Track for Racers': Margaret Anderson and the 'Little Review,'" (Ph.D. diss., University of Wisconsin, 1965), 23.

15. Duffey, part 1, discusses this earlier phase of Chicago culture.

16. Bryer, 8, discusses possible starting dates for Anderson's work for Dell.

17. Margaret Anderson, *My Thirty Years' War* (New York: Covici, Friede, 1930), 37. The first part of the book describes her early rebelliousness and first adventures in Chicago.

18. Dell, *Homecoming,* 228.

19. Anderson, *My Thirty Years' War,* 35.

20. Bryer, 22, 23 and note.

21. Ray Lewis White, ed., *Sherwood Anderson's Memoirs: A Critical Edition* (Chapel Hill, N.C.: University of North Carolina Press, 1969), 338.

22. Kramer, 232–36. Sherwood Anderson's memoirs as edited by Paul Rosenfeld contain a lengthy reference to the so-called "Post-Impressionist Exhibition," Sherwood Anderson, *Sherwood Anderson's Memoirs* (New York: Harcourt, Brace, 1942), Paul Rosenfeld, ed., p. 234. This reference was edited out of the later edition of the memoirs; White, *Sherwood Anderson's Memoirs.* Sherwood Anderson first came to Chicago in 1896; he left shortly afterwards to fight in the Spanish American War (ibid., 145).

23. Sherwood Anderson, "Real-Unreal," *The New Republic* (June 11, 1930): 104.

24. For more information on the Little Room see Duffey, chapter 4.

25. Mark Turbyfill, "Whistling in the Windy City: Memoirs of a Poet-Dancer," 15. Typescript at the Newberry Library, Chicago.

26. Ibid., 22.

27. Anderson, *My Thirty Years' War*, 68.

28. [Margaret C. Anderson] "Announcement," *The Little Review* 1, no. 1 (March 1914): 2.

29. Sherwood Anderson, "The New Note," *The Little Review* 1, no. 1 (March 1914): 23.

30. For a brief account of Jonson's early career see Elizabeth Anne McCauley, *Raymond Jonson, The Early Years* (Albuquerque: University of New Mexico Art Museum, 1980).

31. William Saphier, "The Old Spirit and the New Ways in Art," *The Little Review* 1, no. 8: 55–56. The illustrations appeared on pp. 33 (Blum), 32 (Szukalski), and 49 (Jonson).

32. Marinetti, "War, the Only Hygiene of the World," *The Little Review* 1, no. 7 (November 1914): 30–31.

33. Margaret Anderson, "To the Innermost," *The Little Review* 1, no. 7 (October 1914): 3, 5.

34. Margaret Anderson, "Art and Anarchism," *The Little Review* March 1916: 3.

35. See for example the announcement, vol. 3, no. 2 (April 1916), facing p. 1.

36. Margaret Anderson, "Announcement" (see n. 28), 1.

37. *The Little Review* 2, no. 4 (June 1915): 59.

38. "Editorial," *The Little Review* 3, no. 5 (August 1916): 1.

39. Kramer, 315–16.

40. *The Little Review* 3, no. 6 (September 1916): n.p.

41. The reasons for this move have been widely discussed from different perspectives. See Williams, 74–82, 208–9; see also Noel Stock, *The Life of Ezra Pound* (San Francisco: Northpoint Press, 1982): 203–4.

42. The Pound phase and the Ulysses incident have been thoroughly discussed by Bryer, chapters 5, 7.

43. For a discussion of this later phase of the magazine, as well as more information on Jane Heap, see my article, "Mysticism in the Machine Age: Jane Heap and *The Little Review*," *Twenty One/Art and Culture* 1, no. 1, 18–44.

9. The Katharine Kuh Gallery

1. All quotations from Katharine Kuh are composite excerpts drawn from three sources: Katharine Kuh, oral history with Avis Berman, March 18, 1982–March 23, 1983, Archives of American Art, Smithsonian Institution; Katharine Kuh, interview with Avis Berman, February 22, 1988; and Katharine Kuh, interview with Avis Berman, March 15, 1988. To avoid needless repetition, direct quotations are not footnoted hereafter.

2. For the names of these artists, as well as all others shown in the gallery, see the chapter appendix.

3. Eleanor Jewett, "New Gallery Has Moderns That Please," *Chicago Daily Tribune*, November 9, 1935.

4. Eleanor Jewett, partial clipping, *Chicago Tribune*, February 1936, Roll 267, Katharine Kuh Papers, Archives of American Art.

5. Paul T. Gilbert, "Two Artists' Abstractions Exhibited at Kuh Galleries," *Chicago Herald and Examiner*, October 3, 1937.

6. Ibid.

7. Jewett, "This Month to Give Us Many Art Exhibits," *Chicago Tribune*, December 10, 1939; "City Abounds in Interesting Art Exhibits," *Chicago Tribune*, December 17, 1939.

8. Gilbert, "Landscapes and Flowers in Exhibit," *Chicago Herald and Examiner*, December 13, 1936.

9. John and Molly Thwaites were later posted to Poland, and the painting was destroyed during World War II when the Germans shelled Katowice.

10. One of the Jawlenskys went into the Morton May Collection, another recently entered the collection of the Vassar College Art Gallery, and *Five Figures*, the painting by Man Ray, is now owned by the Whitney Museum of American Art.

11. Gilbert, "'Dreams' Become Nightmare," *Chicago Herald and Examiner*, clipping, November 1938, Roll 267, Katharine Kuh Papers, Archives of American Art.

12. Jewett, "An Old Blotter Becomes Art in Miro Exhibition," *Chicago Daily Tribune*, November 9, 1938.

13. In 1943 Katharine Kuh joined the Art Institute of Chicago. After working in the public relations department, she was made curator of modern painting and sculpture and then curator of paintings. She left the museum in 1959 and moved to New York to become the art editor of *Saturday Review*, a position she held until 1977. Still active as an art consultant and writer, Katharine Kuh lives and works in New York City.

10. Patterns in Chicago Collecting

1. Clarence J. Bulliet, *The Significant Moderns and Their Pictures* (New York: Covici, Friede, 1936), v.

2. The "feeling of closure" characteristic among the spokesmen writing for many publications on the arts in the late 1920s and the early 1930s did not indicate that the production of modern art had itself abruptly ended. On the contrary, for example, the Katharine Kuh Gallery and the New Bauhaus in Chicago continued to be important places for modern art. What had changed, however, since the heroic days of the avant-garde were the conditions of production of modern art. Not only had political and economic developments fundamentally altered the social position of the artist, but by the early 1930s the avant-garde itself had been made into a historical phenomenon; writers such as Carl Einstein (*Die Kunst des 20. Jahrhunderts*, 1926), Philip Johnson and Henry Russell Hitchcock (*The International Style*, 1932), Nikolaus Pevsner (*Pioneers of the Modern Movement*, 1936), and Alfred Barr (*Cubism and Abstract Art*, 1936) attempted to formulate a "modern tradition." The current production thus was placed within a historical continuum. Producing modern art in the 1930s meant to choose a stylistic option; modern art was thereby transformed into a self-consciously "modernist" art.

3. Alfred Barr, *Cubism and Abstract Art* (New York: The Museum of Modern Art, 1936), 11.

4. Cf. Ethel Joyce Hammer, *Attitudes Towards Art in the 1920's in Chicago* (Ph.D. diss., University of Chicago, 1975).

5. Letter from Julius Meier-Graefe to Robert B. Harshe (January 23, 1928), Archives of the Art Institute of Chicago.

6. Cf. my "Pictures at an Exhibition," *Chicago History* 16, no. 1 (Spring 1987): 4–21.

7. Frances Weitzenhoffer, *The Havemeyers, Impressionism Comes to America* (New York: Harry N. Abrams, 1986), 88.

8. Arthur Jerome Eddy, "The Apotheosis of the Commonplace," *Contributors Magazine* (1893): 33.

9. Arthur Jerome Eddy, *Cubists and Post-Impressionism* (Chicago: McClurg, 1914), 122.

10. Roger Fry, "An Essay in Aesthetics," in *Vision and Design* (Cleveland: World Publishing Co., 1956), 29.

11. Alan Bowness, "Introduction," in catalog of the exhibition *Post-Impressionism, Cross-Currents in European Painting* (London: Weidenfeld and Nicolson, 1979–80), 9–12.

12. Roger Fry, "Art and Life," in *Vision and Design,* 12.

13. Cf. the listings in the Ryerson and Burnham Libraries accession books.

14. The notebook is kept in the Archives of the Art Institute of Chicago.

15. Cf. Roger Fry, "El Greco," in *Vision and Design,* 213.

16. Clive Bell, "The Aesthetic Hypothesis," in *Modern Art and Modernism, A Critical Anthology,* ed. Francis Frascina and Charles Harrison (New York: Harper and Row, 1982), 72.

17. *Description of the Martin A. Ryerson Collection,* in August F. Jaccaci Papers, Archives of American Art, Microfilm D 126, 2.

18. Cf. Paul Kruty, "Arthur Jerome Eddy and His Collection: Prelude and Postscript to the Armory Show," *Arts* (February 1987): 40–47.

19. Eddy, *Cubists and Post-Impressionism,* 18.

20. Cf. Judith Zilczer, *The Noble Buyer John Quinn, Patron of the Avant-garde* (Washington, D.C.: Smithsonian Institution Press, 1978).

21. Eddy, *Cubists and Post-Impressionism,* 104.

22. Cf. Kruty, "Arthur Jerome Eddy . . . ," 44.

23. Eddy, *Cubists and Post-Impressionism,* 3.

24. Ibid., 101.

25. Milton Brown, *American Painting from the Armory Show to the Depression* (Princeton: Princeton University Press, n.d.), 93–99.

26. Malcolm Gee, *Dealers, Critics and Collectors of Modern Painting: Aspects of the Parisian Art Market Between 1910 and 1930* (Ph.D. diss., Courtauld Institute, London, 1977), 37 ff.

27. Ibid., 72.

28. Cf. the bills conserved in the Coburn Papers, Archives of the Art Institute of Chicago.

29. Letter from Robert B. Harshe to Martin A. Ryerson, July 22, 1925, Ryerson and Burnham Libraries, the Art Institute of Chicago.

30. Letter to author from Mary McKenna, research assistant at the Wildenstein Gallery, New York, April 22, 1987.

31. Cf. Coburn Files, Archives of the Art Institute of Chicago.

32. Letter from Joseph Durand-Ruel of March 7, 1925, Archives of the Art Institute of Chicago.

33. Cf. Bertha Fenberg, "Mrs. Lewis Coburn Plans to Give City Famous Collection," *Chicago Daily News,* June 11, 1931.

34. Letter from F. C. Bartlett to Robert B. Harshe, July 12, 1933, Archives of the Art Institute of Chicago.

35. Letter from F. C. Bartlett to Robert B. Harshe, October 27, 1924, Archives of the Art Institute of Chicago.

36. Offer from Fischer of February 12, 1926, Archives of the Art Institute of Chicago. On Bartlett as a collector in general see Richard R. Brettell, "The Bartletts and the Grande Jatte: Collecting Modern Painting in the 1920's," *Museum Studies* 12, no. 2 (Spring 1986): 103–13.

37. Gee, *Dealers*, 245.

38. Ibid., 245–47.

39. Paul Signac, *D'Eugène Delacroix au Neo-Impressionisme* (Paris, 1911), 20. "Les neo-impressionistes ont repudié le cadre doré, dont le brillant criard modifie ou détruit l'accord du tableau. Ils usent généralement de cadres blancs, qui offrent un excellent passage entre la peinture et le fond, et qui exaltent la saturation des teintes sans en troubler l'harmonie."

40. Letter from Robert B. Harshe to Frederic C. Bartlett, July 14, 1933, Archives of the Art Institute of Chicago.

11. The School of the Art Institute of Chicago

1. Quoted in *The American Renaissance: 1876–1917* (Brooklyn: Brooklyn Museum of Art), 1979, 188–89.

2. Minutes of the School Committee, May 11, 1916, 72.

3. Adam Emory Albright, *For Art's Sake* (published privately, 1953), 167.

4. For background, see Helen Horwitz, *Culture in the City* (Lexington, Ky.: University Press of Kentucky), 1979.

5. Catalog, School of the Art Institute of Chicago, 1913, 1.

6. Nancy Hale and Fredson Bowers, *Leon Kroll: A Spoken Memoir.* (Charlottesville: University Press of Virginia, 1983), 59.

7. Catalog, School of the Art Institute of Chicago, 1918–19, 23.

8. Minutes of the School Committee, May 3, 1916, 28.

9. Minutes of the School Committee, May 11, 1916, 71.

10. Ed Garman, *The Art of Raymond Jonson, Painter* (Albuquerque: University of New Mexico Press, 1976), 14.

11. Roger Gilmore, ed., *Over a Century: A History of the School of the Art Institute of Chicago, 1866–1981* (Chicago: School of the Art Institute of Chicago, 1982), 71.

12. Milton W. Brown, *The Story of the Armory Show* (New York: The Joseph A. Hirshhorn Foundation, 1963), 175.

13. "Growth of Chicago's Practical Art School," *Monumental News* (June 1912): 462.

14. Thomas W. Tallmadge, "John Warner Norton: 1876–1934," typewritten manuscript, January 1935, 11.

15. Minutes of the School Committee, May 8, 1916, 35.

16. Brown, 178.

17. Ibid.

18. In 1896, French was reported in the *Chicago Tribune* to have said that "the study of the human figure is by universal consent the vital stem or basis of academic art study." Quoted in Gilmore, 70.

19. Brown, 174.

20. Ibid., 176.

21. The American Association of Museums was founded in 1904; the Association of Art Museum Directors in 1916. Writing in 1916 in the American Federation of Arts magazine whose name was changed in 1915 from *Art and Progress* to *The American Magazine of Art*, Charles Hutchinson singled out the introduction of the educational function into museum administration as "the most significant fact in the progress of the Fine Arts in recent years." "The Democracy of Art," *The American Magazine of Art* (August 1916): 398.

22. "Prospectus," *Art and Progress* 1, no. 1 (November 1909): 18.

23. Hutchinson, Charles, "The Democracy of Art," *The American Magazine of Art* (August 1916): 398.

24. Ibid., 400.

25. Ibid., 399.

26. Ibid.

27. See Josephine Logan, *Sanity in Art* (Chicago: A. Kroch, 1937). Immediately before the Chicago installation of the Armory Show, Logan was the only board member to vote against including three paintings in question, including Gauguin's *The Spirit of Evil*.

28. Minutes of the School Committee, May 28, 1918, 179. The physical condition of the School provides a good indicator of its changing importance within the museum. In 1912, due to the friendly budget-bending of Newton Carpenter, the School's 800-foot-long skylighted corridor at the rear of the museum, west of the Illinois Central railroad tracks, was modernized. New lighting, heating, and ventilation systems were installed. In addition, studios were added as part of general museum expansion. Four years later, when the museum built Gunsaulus Hall in 1916 across the railroad tracks, the School was moved into basement quarters. Most of the complaints in Keane's resignation letter were directed at problems caused by the gallery construction. He complained that Gunsaulus Hall blocked sunlight into the studios, requiring working completely from artificial light. The new wing over the tracks directed train noise, already a disturbance at the School, even more toward the underground studios. The only windows in his office, placed high enough to reach above street level, were rarely opened because of the street soot and locomotive gases which blew in.

29. Minutes of the School Committee, November 17, 1925, 13.

30. Ralph Clarkson, "Chicago Painters, Past and Present," *Art and Archeology* 12 (November 1921): 142.

31. Minutes of the Board of Trustees, May 28, 1918, 156.

32. Ibid., 157.

33. Matilda Vanderpoel, younger sister of John, taught life drawing and directed the Junior Department at the School. George Buehr, son of Karl, taught landscape painting in the 1930s and 1940s.

34. Charles H. Morgan, *George Bellows: Painter of America* (New York: Reynal, 1965), 228.

35. Hale, 58.

36. Faculty members, however, were asked their feelings about visiting artists. Most agreed that such visitors were a good thing if they "fit into" the existing program. Minutes of the School Committee, May 8, 1916.

37. Hale, 59.

38. Morgan, 39.

39. See Bulletin, Art Institute of Chicago, March 1918.

40. "Bellows in Chicago," *Arts and Decoration* 12 (November 1919): 10.

41. Morgan, 230.

42. Maureen A. McKenna, *Emil Armin: 1883–1971* (Springfield, Ill.: Illinois State Museum, 1980), 2.

43. The American Federation of Arts devoted its sixth annual convention in 1915 to the topic of art education. One of its main sessions dealt with industrial art education.

44. Catalog, School of the Art Institute of Chicago, 1918–19, 10.

45. Annual Report, Art Institute of Chicago, 1921, 12.

46. Ibid.

47. Minutes, Board of Trustees, January 10, 1924, 123.

48. Ibid.

49. For background, see Lloyd Englebrecht, "The Association of Arts and Industries: Background and Origin of the Bauhaus Movement in Chicago" (Ph.D. diss., University of Chicago, June 1973).

50. Minutes of the School Committee, September 24, 1914, 1.

51. Englebrecht, 46.

52. Alumni letter, May 22, 1922.

53. Englebrecht, 93.

54. Annual Report, Art Institute of Chicago, 1933, 90. Enrollment for the academic year 1932–33 was 2,796, a loss of more than 750 students from the previous year's enrollment of 3,551.

55. For background, see Englebrecht and James Sloan Allen, *The Romance of Commerce and Culture* (Chicago: University of Chicago Press, 1983).

56. Minutes of the School Committee, May 8, 1916, 76.

57. Virginia Gardner, *Chicago Tribune*, November 7, 1935, "Society Donors Join Fiery Art Show Disputes: 'Atrocious!' Seems to be Majority Idea," Art Institute of Chicago scrapbooks, vol. 63–67, roll 11.

12. The Art Institute Assimilates Modernism

1. Letter from W. M. R. French to Sara Hallowell, March 18, 1913. Art Institute of Chicago Archives (hereafter AIC Archives).

2. James B. Townsend to W. M. R. French, November 23, 1912. AIC Archives.

3. From French's correspondence it is possible to ascertain that he left for New York on about January 6 and returned to the office by January 14. William M. R. French correspondence, AIC Archives.

4. On January 14 French wrote a letter to Arthur B. Davies in which he said, "I immediately held a conference with our President, Mr. Hutchinson, and we have called a meeting of the Art Committee for Thursday afternoon." French went on to apologize for having made definite arrangements for other exhibitions that would fill the temporary galleries, but wrote, "I hope however I can compress these, and secure a hanging space of somewhere from five hundred to one thousand linear feet . . . this is small, indeed, compared with your great exhibition. If we had been able to fix a date in advance, we could have given much more space to it. Everybody that I talk with expresses great interest in the exhibition." French wrote letters to Pauline Palmer and Alfred Partridge Klots about changing dates for their exhibitions or cutting down on the number of works to be shown. He turned down other

possible exhibitions. William M. R. French correspondence, AIC Archives.

5. He left on about February 19 and was back in the office by February 26. The impressions written on the train exist in a four-page typescript dated February 22, 1913, currently in the Arthur J. Eddy file of the Art Institute of Chicago Archives. There is no indication of authorship, no salutation, and no signature. While it has sometimes been thought that the author of the typescript was Arthur J. Eddy, that assumption is almost certainly incorrect. It seems impossible that Eddy could have returned to Chicago in late February because he was busy buying works in New York at that time. French did return at least by February 26 and could very well have been on the train on February 22. Furthermore, in a letter he wrote on March 5 to Hutchinson, who was in Paris, he said, "I believe Mr. Carpenter has enclosed to you my impressions of the Modern Art Exhibition. . . ." As far as can be ascertained, there was no other official or staff member of the Art Institute who went to New York in February.

6. Letter from French to Arthur Davies, March 8, 1913. AIC Archives.

7. See, for instance, French's March 19 response to Mrs. Abigail Adams, who had sent him an assessment of some of the paintings by a New York psychiatrist who had seen the Armory Show when it was in New York. AIC Archives.

8. Letter from French to Charles Hutchinson, March 20, 1913. AIC Archives.

9. Letter from Newton H. Carpenter to W. M. R. French, March 26, 1913; and letter to Carpenter, March 5, 1913, partially missing (no closing or signature), AIC Archives.

10. See Milton W. Brown, *The Story of the Armory Show* (New York: The Joseph A. Hirshhorn Foundation, 1963), 160–83. See also chapter 6.

11. Arthur Jerome Eddy, *Exhibition of Modern Paintings by Albert Bloch of Munich* (Chicago: The Art Institute of Chicago, 1915), 10.

12. In 1920 the Metropolitan Museum of Art hosted a show of French impressionism called "Modern French Art." In 1921, an exhibition called "Modern French Painting," instigated by avant-garde collector John Quinn, included more recent modernism. A George Bellows show was held in 1925. At the Pennsylvania Academy of Fine Arts, the modern exhibitions were a 1920 loan exhibition of paintings and drawings by representative modern masters, a 1921 exhibition of American drawings and paintings showing the latest tendencies in art, and a 1923 show titled "Contemporary European Paintings and Sculpture" from the Barnes Collection. For more information on contemporary and modernist exhibitions at the Brooklyn Museum during the early twentieth century, see William Henry Fox exhibition files, Records of the Office of the Director, Brooklyn Museum Archives, and Linda Ferber, *Masterpieces of Art in The Brooklyn Museum* (New York, 1988).

13. Minutes of the Arts Club board meeting, 1916, Arts Club of Chicago Papers, Newberry Library, Chicago.

14. Letter from Rue Carpenter to Charles Hutchinson, Nov. 19, 1921, and letter from Robert B. Harshe to the president and directors of the Arts Club, Jan. 27, 1922. AIC Archives.

15. Board of Trustees minutes, January 7, 1921, AIC Archives.

16. This and all following information on Rue Carpenter come from

the following two sources: Art Institute of Chicago, *Joseph Winterbotham Collection: A Living Tradition,* with an essay by Lyn DelliQuadri (Chicago: The Art Institute of Chicago, 1986), 7–14; and James S. Wells, *The Arts Club of Chicago: Portrait of an Era, Rue Winterbotham Carpenter and the Arts Club of Chicago,* Seventieth Anniversary Exhibition Catalog (Chicago: The Arts Club of Chicago, 1986).

17. Sanity in Art was a movement founded in Chicago in 1937 by Josephine Hancock Logan, who was viciously anti-modernist. In 1917 she and her husband had given the museum an endowment for the purpose of awarding prizes to contemporary artists whose work was displayed at the annual American Painting and Sculpture exhibition. She had become disillusioned with the selections made by the Art Institute, believing that the award-winning works were too modern. She formed Sanity in Art as an attempt to bring back the values of nineteenth-century academic art.

18. Board of Trustees minutes of Art Institute of Chicago, March 13, 1927. See also minutes of the Committee on Painting and Sculpture just prior to the trustee meeting. AIC Archives.

19. Carpenter was one of only a handful of cultural leaders in Chicago who championed the avant-garde. Others include Margaret Anderson, C. J. Bulliet, and later, Katharine Kuh. In 1930 the Renaissance Society of the University of Chicago was incorporated. Like the Arts Club, it exhibited avant-garde art during the thirties.

20. See introduction to Susan Noyes Platt, *Modernism in the 1920s: Interpretations of Modern Art in New York from Expressionism to Constructivism* (Ann Arbor: UMI Research Press, 1985). See also John R. Lane and Susan C. Larsen, eds., *Abstract Painting and Sculpture in America 1927–1944* (Pittsburgh: Museum of Art, Carnegie Institute, 1984), 17–19. On the Société Anonyme, see *Société Anonyme: The First Museum of Modern Art,* vol. 1 (1920–44): Documents. Reprint of original catalog of 1926–27 exhibition (New York: Arno Press, 1972).

21. For more information on the Bartletts, see Richard R. Brettell, "The Bartletts and the Grande Jatte: Collecting Modern Painting in the 1920s," *Museum Studies* 12, no. 2 (1986): 103–13.

22. Original agreement with Joseph Winterbotham, April 9, 1921. AIC Archives.

23. Letter from Joseph Winterbotham to Board of Trustees, dated June 8, 1922, read at June 22, 1922, Board of Trustees meeting and recorded in the minutes. AIC Archives.

24. Letter from Joseph Winterbotham to Chauncey McCormick, September 27, 1949, requesting that the museum return to the broader stipulation as established in 1921.

25. Catalog of the exhibition annotated by Albert Bloch. Collection of Mrs. Albert Bloch, quoted from Paul Kruty, "Arthur Jerome Eddy and his Collection: Prelude and Postscript to the Armory Show," *Arts* (February 1987): 47, n. 82.

26. Board of Trustees minutes, March 29, 1928. It was reported that Eddy was "anxious to turn over a number of the pictures." The Board took no action.

27. For more information on Eddy, see Kruty, "Arthur Jerome Eddy and his Collection": 46.

28. Letter from Frederick Clay Bartlett to Robert Harshe, July 12, 1933. AIC Archives.

29. Ibid.

30. Ibid.

31. Letter from Robert B. Harshe to Frederick Clay Bartlett, July 14, 1933. AIC Archives. Bartlett then stipulated that his collection always remain together, a requirement that is still in effect today.

32. See also chapter 10.

33. Alfred Barr had organized the various movements of modernism chronologically at the Museum of Modern Art, and Gertrude Vanderbilt Whitney had revealed the continuity of twentieth-century American art in the Whitney Collection, but both these collections were limited to modernism and explicitly separated it from earlier art.

SELECTED BIBLIOGRAPHY

The following entries have been selected from the footnotes in the preceding chapters. Major sources of information on Chicago's early art scene have been included. Single newspaper article citations have not.

Albright, Adam Emory. *For Art's Sake.* Published privately, 1953.

Allen, James Sloan. *The Romance of Commerce and Culture.* Chicago: University of Chicago Press, 1983.

Anderson, Margaret. *My Thirty Years' War.* New York: Covici, Friede, 1930.

Anderson, Sherwood. "Real-Unreal." *The New Republic,* June 11, 1930, 104.

Angarola, Anthony. Papers. Archives of American Art, Smithsonian Institution.

Archives of the Art Institute of Chicago.

Armory Show: 50th Anniversary Exhibition, 1913–1963. Utica, N.Y.: Munson Williams Proctor Institute, 1963.

"Art Education: A Brief Statistical Survey Made by the American Federation of Arts." *Art and Progress,* May 1915.

"Art Gallery Designed by Frank Lloyd Wright, Architect." *International Studio* 39 (February 1910): 95–96.

Banham, Reyner. *Theory and Design in the First Machine Age,* 2nd ed. New York: Praeger Publishers, 1967.

Bauhaus-Archiv, West Berlin.

Brettell, Richard R. "The Bartletts and the Grande Jatte: Collecting Modern Painting in the 1920's." *Museum Studies* 12, no. 2 (Spring 1986): 103–13.

Brooks, H. Allen. "Chicago Architecture: Its Debt to the Arts and Crafts." *Journal of the Society of Architectural Historians* 30, no. 4 (December 1971): 312–17.

Brown, Milton W. *American Painting from the Armory Show to the Depression.* Princeton: Princeton University Press, 1955.

———. *The Story of the Armory Show.* New York: The Joseph A. Hirshhorn Foundation, 1963.

Bryer, Jackson R. "'A Trial-Track for Racers': Margaret Anderson and the 'Little Review.'" Ph.D. diss., University of Wisconsin, 1965.

Bulliett, C. J. *Apples and Madonnas.* New York: Covici, Friede, 1927.

———. *Art Masterpieces in a Century of Progress: Fine Arts Exhibition at the Art Institute of Chicago.* Chicago: The North Mariano Press, 1933.

———. "Artists of Chicago: Past and Present." *The Chicago Daily News.* Series appeared from February 23, 1935, through September 30, 1939, first consecutively then intermittently.

———. Papers. Archives of American Art, Smithsonian Institution.

———. "How Modern Art Came to Town: III. The Rise and Reign of the Arts Club of Chicago." *Chicagoan* 12 (October 31, 1931): 35–37ff.

———. "How Modern Art Came to Town: IV. No-Jury: Its Rise, Rage and Decline." *Chicagoan* 12 (November 1931): 49.

———. "How Modern Art Came to Town: V. A Bit of Autobiography." *Chicagoan* 13 (December 1931): 51ff.

———. *The Significant Moderns and Their Pictures.* New York: Covici, Friede, 1936.

Burnham, Daniel H., and Edward H. Bennett. *Plan of Chicago.* Chicago: The Commercial Club, 1909. Reprinted, New York: Da Capo Press, 1970.

Carpenter, N. H. "How the Art Institute of Chicago Has Increased Its Usefulness." *The American Magazine of Art* (May 1916): 100–103.

Catalogue of the Exhibition of the National Sculpture Society Under the Aupices of the Municipal Art Society. Baltimore: Fifth Regiment Armory, 1908.

Chatfield-Taylor, Hobart. "Memories of Chicago: II. The Age of Gentility." *Century Magazine,* n.s. 128 (August 1925): 459–65.

"Chicago and the Ferguson Fund." *The City Club Bulletin* 6 (February 17, 1914): 61–68.

Cikovsky, Nicolai, Jr. *Raymond Jonson (1891–1982): Pioneer Modernist of New Mexico.* New York: Berry-Hill Galleries, 1986.

Clarkson, Ralph. "Chicago Painters, Past And Present." *Art and Archaeology* 12 (September/October 1921): 129–43.

Darling, Sharon. "Arts and Crafts Shops in the Fine Arts Building." *Chicago History* 6, no. 2 (Summer 1977): 79–85.

———. *Chicago Furniture: Art, Craft, & Industry, 1833–1983.* New York: The Chicago Historical Society, in association with W. W. Norton, 1984.

Davidson, Abraham A. "Two from the Second Decade: Manierre Dawson and John Covert." *Art in America* 63, no. 5 (September–October 1975): 50–55.

Dell, Floyd. *Homecoming: An Autobiography.* Port Washington, N.Y.: Kennikat Press, 1933.

———. *Women as World Builders: Studies in Modern Feminism.* Chicago: Forbes, 1913.

"Description of the Martin A. Ryerson Collection." August F. Jaccaci Papers, Archives of American Art, Smithsonian Institution, Microfilm D 126, 2.

Duffey, Bernard. *The Chicago Renaissance in American Letters: A Critical History.* East Lansing, Mich.: Michigan State College Press, 1944.

Duis, Perry. "'Where Is Athens Now?': The Fine Arts Building 1898 to 1918." *Chicago History* 6, no. 2 (Summer 1977): 66–78.

Duncan, Hugh D. *Culture and Democracy: The Struggle for Form in Society* and *Architecture in Chicago and the Middle West during the Life and Times of Louis H. Sullivan.* Totowa, N.J.: Bedminster Press, 1965.

Eddy, Arthur Jerome. "The Apotheosis of the Commonplace." *Contributors Magazine* (1893): 33–35.

———. *Cubists and Post-Impressionism.* Chicago: A. C. McClurg, 1914.

Engelbrecht, Lloyd C. "The Association of Arts and Industries: Background and Origins of the Bauhaus Movement in Chicago." Ph.D. diss., University of Chicago, 1973.

Garman, Ed. *The Art of Raymond Jonson, Painter.* Albuquerque: University of New Mexico Press, 1976.

Garvey, Timothy J. *Public Sculptor: Lorado Taft and the Beautification of Chicago.* Urbana, Ill.: University of Illinois Press, 1988.

———. "The Artist is Out: Recreations of the 'Little Room' and 'Eagle's Nest.'" *Transactions of the Illinois State Historical Society:* Selected papers from the Fifth and Sixth Illinois History Symposia of the Illinois State Historical Society (1988): 59–67.

Gedo, Mary Mathews. *Manierre Dawson (1887–1969): A Retrospective Exhibition of Painting.* Chicago: Museum of Contemporary Art, 1976.

———. "Modernizing the Masters: Manierre Dawson's Cubist Transformations." *Arts* 55, no. 8 (April 1981): 135–45.

Germer, Stefan. "Pictures at an Exhibition: The Art Market in Chicago 1870–1890." *Chicago History* 16, no. 1 (Spring 1987): 4–21.

Giedion, Sigfried. *Mechanization Takes Command: A Contribution to Anonymous History.* New York: W. W. Norton, 1948.

———. *Space, Time and Architecture: The Growth of a New Tradition.* Cambridge: Harvard University Press, 1941.

Gilmore, Roger, ed. *Over a Century: A History of the School of the Art Institute of Chicago, 1866–1981.* Chicago: School of the Art Institute of Chicago, 1982.

Goldstein, Leslie. "Art in Chicago and the World's Columbian Exposition of 1893." M.A. thesis, University of Iowa, 1970.

Griggs, Joseph. "Alfonso Iannelli: The Prairie Spirit in Sculpture." *The Prairie School Review* 2, no. 4 (fourth quarter 1965): 20ff.

"Growth of Chicago's Practical Art School." *Monumental News* (June 1912): 459–63.

Hammer, Ethel Joyce. *Attitudes Towards Art in the Nineteen Twenties in Chicago.* Ph.D. diss., University of Chicago, 1975.

Harshe, Robert B. Letter to Martin A. Ryerson, July 22, 1925, Ryerson and Burnham Libraries, the Art Institute of Chicago.

Hecht, Ben. *A Child of the Century.* New York: Simon and Schuster, 1954.

Hey, Kenneth Robert. "Five Artists And The Chicago Modernist Movement, 1909–1928." Ph.D. diss., Emory University, 1973.

Hoffman, Frederick J., Charles Allen, and Carolyn F. Ulrich. *The Little Magazine: A History and a Bibliography.* Princeton: Princeton University Press, 1946.

Horowitz, Helen Lefkowitz. *Culture and the City: Cultural Philanthropy in Chicago from the 1880s to 1917.* Chicago: University of Chicago Press, 1989. Reprint. Originally published: Lexington, Ky.: University Press of Kentucky, 1976.

Hutchinson, Charles. "The Democracy of Art." *The American Magazine of Art* (August 1916) 398ff.

Jacobsen, J. Z. *Art of Today: Chicago, 1933.* Chicago: L. M. Stein, 1932.

———. "Our Little Group of Serious Talkers." *Chicago Evening Post*, January 18, 1927, 8, 12.

———. *Thirty-Five Saints and Emil Armin*. Chicago: L. M. Stein, 1929.

Jewett, Eleanor. Papers, Archives of American Art, Smithsonian Institution.

Joseph Winterbotham Collection: A Living Tradition. Chicago: The Art Institute of Chicago, 1986.

Kendall, Sue Ann. "Clarence J. Bulliet: Chicago's Lonely Champion of Modernism." *Archives of American Art Journal* 26, nos. 2 and 3 (1986): 21–32.

Kohn, Esther. Papers, Jane Addams Memorial Collection, Library of the University of Illinois, Chicago.

Kramer, Dale. *The Chicago Renaissance: The Literary Life in the Midwest, 1900–1930*. New York: Appleton-Century, 1966.

Kruty, Paul. "Arthur Jerome Eddy and His Collection: Prelude and Postscript to the Armory Show." *Arts* 61 (February 1987): 40–47.

———. "Mirrors of a 'Post-Impressionist' Era: The Chicago Portraits of B. J. O. Nordfeldt." *Arts* 61, no. 5 (January 1987): 27–33.

———. "Pleasure Garden on the Midway." *Chicago History* 16 (Fall/Winter 1987/88): 4–27.

Kuh, Katharine. Oral history with Avis Berman, March 18, 1982–March 24, 1983. Archives of American Art, Smithsonian Institution.

———. Papers, Archives of American Art, Smithsonian Institution.

Kutner, Luis. "The Desecration of the Ferguson Fund: The Need for Watchdog Legislation." *De Paul Law Review* 12 (Spring/Summer 1963): 217–39.

Lears, T. J. Jackson. *No Place of Grace: Antimodernism and the Transformation of American Culture 1880–1920*. New York: Pantheon, 1981.

Lewis, Lloyd, and Henry Justin Smith. *Chicago: The History Of Its Reputation*. New York: Harcourt, Brace, 1929.

"Literature and Art." *Current Opinion* 54 (April 1913), 316ff.

Logan, Josephine Hancock. *Sanity in Art*. Chicago: A. Kroch, 1937.

Mackay, Constance D'Arcy. *The Little Theatre in the United States*. New York: Henry Holt, 1917.

Masters, Edgar Lee. *The Tale of Chicago*. New York: Putnam's 1933.

McCauley, Elizabeth Ann. *Raymond Jonson, the Early Years*. Albuquerque: University of New Mexico Art Museum, 1980.

McKenna, Maureen A. *Emil Armin: 1883–1971*. Springfield, Ill.: Illinois State Museum, 1980.

McMurtrie, Douglas C. *Modern Typography and Layout*. Chicago: Eyncourt Press, 1929; London: The Library Press, 1930.

McNaught, William, ed. "An Interview with Katharine Kuh." *Archives of American Art Journal*, 27, no. 3 (1987): 2–36.

Mencken, H. L. "The Literary Capital of the United States." *Nation* 28 (April 17, 1920): 92.

Monroe, Harriet. *A Poet's Life: Seventy Years in a Changing World*. New York: MacMillan, 1938. Reprint: New York: AMS Press, 1969.

Not a Pretty Picture: Carl Hoeckner, Social Realist. San Francisco: Atelier Dore, 1984.

The Official Pictures of a Century of Progress Exposition. Chicago: Century of Progress International Exposition, 1933.

Pattison, James William. "The Loss of W. Scott Thurber." *Fine Arts Journal* 29 (November 1913): 683–84.

Powell, Earl A., III. "Manierre Dawson's 'Woman in Brown.'" *Arts* 51, no. 1 (September 1976): 76–77.

Putnam, Samuel. "Chicago: An Obituary." *American Mercury* 8 (August 1926): 417–25.

———. "Painting Is Dead; Painting Go Red." *The New Hope* 2 (August 1934): 4–5ff.

———. *Paris Was Our Mistress*. New York: Viking Press, 1947.

Ricker, Jewett E., ed. *Sculpture at A Century of Progress Chicago, 1933, 1934*. Chicago: Ricker, 1933.

Roberts, Katherine E. "The Introspectives Challenge Chicago Critics." *Fashion Art* 6 (June 1921): 32.

Rosenfeld, Paul, ed. *Sherwood Anderson's Memoirs*. New York: Harcourt, Brace, 1942.

Seymour, Ralph Fletcher. *Some Went This Way: A Forty Year Pilgrimage Among Artists, Bookmen and Printers*. Chicago: Ralph Fletcher Seymour, 1945.

Slade, Thomas M. "'The Crystal House' of 1934." *Journal of the Society of Architectural Historians* 29, no. 4 (December 1970): 350–53ff.

Smith, Alson Jesse. *Chicago's Left Bank*. Chicago: Henry Regnery, 1953.

Smith, Carl S. *Chicago and the American Literary Imagination, 1880–1920*. Chicago: University of Chicago Press, 1984.

Sparks, Esther. "A Biographical Dictionary of Painters and Sculptors In Illinois, 1808–1945." Ph.D. diss., Northwestern University, 1971.

Stuart, Evelyn Marie. "Development of Art in the West—Thurber Galleries." *Fine Arts Journal* 21 (December 1909): 284–90.

Sullivan, Louis H. *Kindergarten Chats and Other Writings*. New York: Wittenborn, Schultz, 1947.

Szukalski, Stanislaus. *Projects in Design*. Chicago: University of Chicago Press, 1931.

———. *The Work of Szukalski*. Chicago: Covici-McGee, 1923.

Taft, Lorado. "A Million Dollars for Sculpture: How Shall Chicago Use the Ferguson Bequest?" *The World Today* 9 (1905): 628–30.

———. *Modern Tendencies in Sculpture*. University of Chicago Press, 1921.

———. Papers. Urbana, Ill.: University of Illinois Archives.

Tallmadge, Thomas W. "John Warner Norton: 1876–1934." Typewritten manuscript, January 1935.

Teall, Gardner. "Our Western Painters: What Chicago Is Doing Toward the Development of a Vital National Spirit in American Art." *Craftsman* 15, no. 2 (November 1908): 139–53.

Tesone, S. L. "Symbolism in Fair Sculpture." *World's Fair Weekly* 25 (October 21, 1933): 33.

Triggs, Oscar Lovell. *Chapters in the History of the Arts and Crafts Movement*. Chicago: Bohemia Guild of the Industrial Art League, 1902.

———. "A School of Industrial Art." *The Craftsman* 3, no. 2 (January 1903): 216–23.

———. *The Changing Order: A Study of Democracy*. Chicago: Oscar L. Triggs, 1905.

Turbyfill, Mark. "Whistling in the Windy City: Memoirs of a Poet-Dancer-Painter." Typescript, Newberry Library, Chicago.

Weller, Allen. *Lorado Taft: The Blind*. Champaign, Ill.: Krannert Art Museum, 1988.

Wells, James S. *The Arts Club of Chicago: Portrait of an Era, Rue Winter-*

botham Carpenter and the Arts Club of Chicago, Seventieth Anniversary Exhibition Catalog. Chicago: The Arts Club, 1986.

Werner, M. R. *Julius Rosenwald, the Life of a Practical Humanitarian.* New York: Harper and Brothers, 1939.

White, Ray Lewis, ed. *Sherwood Anderson's Memoirs: A Critical Edition.* Chapel Hill, N.C.: University of North Carolina Press, 1969.

Whitredge, Eugenia Remelin. "Art in Chicago: The Structure of the Art World in a Metropolitan Community." Ph.D. diss., University of Chicago, 1946.

Williams, Ellen. *Harriet Monroe and the Poetry Renaissance: The First Ten Years of Poetry, 1912–1933.* Urbana, Ill.: University of Illinois Press, 1977.

INDEX

Boldface pages indicate illustrations, which are listed in addition to textual references.